Buffalo II!

Buffalo II!
More Lessons Learned

by

Craig Boddington

SAFARI PRESS
ESSEX, CONNECTICUT

SAFARI PRESS INC.

An imprint of Globe Pequot, the trade division of
The Rowman & Littlefield Publishing Group, Inc.
4501 Forbes Boulevard, Suite 200
Lanham, Maryland 20706

Distributed by NATIONAL BOOK NETWORK

Boddington, Craig T.

Second edition

ISBN 978-1-57157-531-9

Library of Congress Catalog Card Number: 2019939050

Printed in India

Dedicated to the Memory
of
JOE WILSON BISHOP
December 30, 1936 to January 2, 2019

"Boddington, it's all about shot placement." *Joe Bishop*

Boddington and Joe Bishop above the Ubangi River in Bangui, 1997. The Central African Republic was one of Bishop's favorite places.

Preface

Every couple of weeks—for the past thirty years—the phone would ring and a gruff, cheerful voice would say, "Boddington, what's this I read about XXX?" In truth, my buddy Joe Bishop wasn't a huge reader, but he read enough of my stories to make sure he could give me grief . . . and carefully enough to call me out if I ever goofed, and he was probably one of the finest field marksmen I ever knew. We did a lot of the tough hunts together—for bongo, Derby eland, Kuban tur, Marco Polo argali, mountain nyala, and many more. Joe never complained, and he always came through, usually with a more difficult shot at a larger animal.

Joe and I hunted buffalo together, and he had some exceptional buffalo bulls in his den, but, unlike me, Joe wasn't besotted by the African buffalo, or, for that matter, any other particular species. He rarely repeated hunts, so it's a tribute to the Cape buffalo that he had multiples in his home! So, having climbed most mountains and explored most forests, Joe didn't do a lot of hunting in his last few years. Instead, a major focus became developing his ranch in central Namibia.

A lightning strike there in 2016 burned his house to the ground. So, he and Sara and their Namibian partner, our mutual buddy, Dirk de Bod, turned to and rebuilt it, completing construction in 2018. His Engadin Farm was a showpiece; one of his goals was to return to it all the native species that had originally been present. This included buffalo, which remained a distant plan with his passing because Namibian law doesn't allow movement of buffaloes for disease control below the "red line." But it was still a plan! One of my favorite "Bishopisms" was "Don't waste your time looking back; you're not going that way."

To the end Joe was looking ahead and making plans, but he lost his battle with cancer on the day I finished this manuscript. So, it's more than appropriate that this volume be dedicated to Joe Bishop, my longtime friend and hunting buddy.

However, much credit must also be given to another old friend and mentor who was enthralled by the African buffalo, at least as much as I. Actually, in some measure this book belongs to him: Col.

Charles Askins (1907–1999). We referred to him as "Charlie," but to his face I can assure you he was "Colonel Askins." His father, Maj. Charles Askins, was also a gunwriter, specializing mostly in shotgunning. The son, Charles Askins Jr., was a good all-round hand with anything that shot: twice national handgun champion, lifelong rifleman, and deadly serious shotgunner. No doubt inspired by his dad, he started writing in 1929 and continued throughout his long life, his body of work including a dozen books and many hundreds of magazine articles.

Askins served in the border patrol in the 1930s, recounting that during these years he averaged "a gunfight a week." He was a career officer in the U.S. Army, serving from 1940 until his retirement as a colonel (Ordnance Corps) in 1971. Make no mistake: Askins was the real deal. He suffered fools poorly, and, like most gunwriters of his day—maybe all days—he hated editors, especially young editors.

These youngsters were mostly terrified of him—if they were smart. Oddly, in his later years he was my friend, *but* I was never "his" editor except in the context of a small handful of articles and book chapters. My uncle Art Popham and his younger sister, my mom, met Askins (and George Parker and Jack O'Connor) in Arizona in the midthirties while Art was attending the University of Arizona. I gather my teenage mom had a bit of a crush on the much older and no doubt dashing Border Patrolman Askins.

Fast forward forty years. I was the new kid editor at the old Petersen Publishing Company. In the space of a few years we lost Warren Page, Jack O'Connor, and then Elmer Keith. Colonel Charlie was thus the last man standing, America's senior gunwriter. Unlike most career army officers, Charlie liked Marines . . . perhaps because his son, Maj. Bill Askins, was a Marine. For whatever reason, Charlie befriended me, and I treasured the friendship.

I was still in the infancy of my African hunting in those days, but Askins had done a lot of it, and he was crazy about buffaloes. I have a letter received by our publisher, Ludo Wurfbain of Safari Press, dated 11 March 1986. The letter reads, in part:

. . . I'll be back in Zambia this year. It will be my 31st safari. I have shot 88 buffalo and I must get those other 12 bulls. When people come up to me and say, 'You ever been in Africa?' When I admit that, yes, I have been on the Dark Continent, the very next question: "You ever shoot a buffalo?" I want to be able to reply, "Well, just a hundred."

Cordially yours,
Colonel Charles Askins*

He autographed books the same way, "Cordially yours," but if he liked you, then the inscription might read—as does mine in his autobiography *Unrepentant Sinner*—"Craig, old hoss, if you ever need anybody shot, you know who to call." I never doubted he was serious.

So, Askins wanted very badly to say that he had shot a hundred buffaloes before he was done, and write a book about his buffaloes. We can accept that this is a silly goal, but it's also a bit of fun. Safari Press didn't do an Askins book. To this day Ludo wishes he had, but Charlie had been in the business a long time, which meant he had probably been skinned by enough publishers. He named a flat fee that was too high for then-fledgling Safari Press and Ludo demurred. Too bad, it would have been a good book!

In spring of 1990, when Askins was eighty-three, we went on a muskox hunt in the Northwest Territories. Askins had never taken a muskox, and he was thinking at his age that he should include pretty much all the bovines in his total. Heck, it's his hundred; he can do what he wants! On that trip Askins shot a fine muskox bull and shot it well, but the real treasure was the three days we spent sitting out a storm in a fishing cabin together with Fred Webb and Art Alphin. My big mistake was I didn't have a recorder because, with absolutely nothing else to do but listen to the howling wind, Askins entertained us nonstop with stories of the old border patrol . . . and an Africa that none of us will ever see again.

Colonel Askins never quite made it to his hundredth buffalo (or bovine). I suppose Bill Askins knows, but I don't know exactly how

*This letter was postmarked from Askins's home address on Blanco Road in San Antonio, a sprawling house with African and Asian trophies, and a huge gun room containing more left-handed rifles than I have ever seen in one place. Oh, perhaps I should have mentioned that, like me, Askins was left-handed.

close he came—close—but although he remained active deep into his eighties, he eventually ran out of time. On 2 March 1999, I was serving at MacDill Air Force Base near Tampa with U.S. Central Command when Bill Askins reached out to tell me his dad had gone on to follow the big herds elsewhere.

So, in large measure this book was Colonel Charlie's concept. I will not be so bold as to suggest I am finishing it for him. His would have been much more colorful and contain more of an older Africa that I never saw . . . remember that by 1986 Askins had done thirty safaris! A number of these were with my old friend Geoff Broom. It was while hunting with Geoff Broom that Colonel Askins was guided by Geoff's young American apprentice, a chap called Peter Hathaway Capstick, but that's a digression. Charlie could be a courtly gentleman, but he could also be irascible. It is something, I fear, that goes with the territory of being a longtime gunwriter. We were at an NRA convention, I think with my boss, Ken Elliott, when a young man dashed up, looked up at the tall Askins and said, "Mr. Askins, I've read your stuff all my life!"

Charlie looked down at him and said, "Son, in the army the only people we address as "Mister" are warrant officers . . . and that's a rank I never held." End of conversation.

I actually saw Colonel Askins only infrequently, mostly when we went shooting together at various ranges and industry events back in the 1980s. Well through his seventies he was scary good—with everything! Geoff Broom recalls that, on safari, he always carried a .22 pistol, using it to shoot francolin and guinea fowl for the pot . . . *in the air!* Trust me, I am unworthy!

So, we are all much the poorer that Col. Charles Askins never quite got around to writing his buffalo book. Whether he would approve of my efforts is open to conjecture. His idea of shooting one hundred buffaloes has driven much of my own hunting for many years, long after his passing.

A great thing about life is one never quits learning. Well, I guess we *can* quit and either rest on our laurels or sit back and pontificate. Both avenues have their attractions, especially at the end of a long day or an unusually tough hunt. Unfortunately, as life progresses and we get older, a point is reached where funerals outnumber christenings. The last few years have seen the loss of several friends and relatives. Not all were older, but all reached points where they became too tired to continue.

Given the fortune to survive long enough, I suppose we'll all reach that point . . . but I'm not quite there yet! I'm still learning, and the older I get, the more I realize how little I really know. The same can be said about my hunts over the years for the African buffalo. I've done a lot of hunting since my first book dedicated to buffalo hunting was published, and I've learned a lot since that time. Thus, what you have before you is a completely updated, revised, and much expanded edition on my hunts for the African buffalo. This is also not the first of my works to see revised editions. After the passage of what seemed due time—and the introduction of many new products—"*Safari Rifles*" became "*Safari Rifles II*" and "*American Hunting Rifles*" became "*American Hunting Rifles II.*"

This is a fine old Mozambique bull with heavy bosses; note the wear on the right tip.

There are parallels with my earlier revised editions and this new one: Fifteen years have passed since I put the finishing touches on *Buffalo!*, so in this volume I've included buffalo hunting that was new to me, in places I hadn't been, for races I hadn't hunted, and in circumstances I knew little about. Of course, there are also similarities: The African buffalo has not changed in fifteen years, nor in many millennia. The "East African savanna buffalo" in Ethiopia has been added for record-keeping, but I doubt the buffaloes have taken note, so it's a stretch to suggest that this volume includes any "new" buffaloes!

There is another parallel as well: While I was satisfied with the two rifle books, I just thought so many new rifles, cartridges, bullets, and so forth had come along that my earlier versions were not as relevant as they could be. Similarly, I was (and am) happy with *Buffalo!* The "new product" angle has little impact on this project, but an overarching theme is the same: I know a lot more now than I did then. It would indeed be a sad commentary if I'd learned nothing in the last fifteen years!

I have continued to hunt buffaloes, perhaps more extensively, even intensively, than I did in the earlier decades of my African hunting career. Without question the buffalo is my favorite African animal and my favorite African hunt. This is not to imply that the buffalo—or his pursuit—is "better" than anything else. We all have different dreams and different ideals . . . and sometimes it takes experience to learn what has the most—and most lasting—appeal. It's been a great journey, and whether it's your first or your one hundredth buffalo, I feel that Africa offers no finer pursuit.

Craig Boddington
Paso Robles, California
February 23, 2019

Africa's Best Hunt

Chapter 1

For me, in the beginning, it was not buffalo that I had an overwhelming desire to pursue. At the outset, what I wanted most was a lion. I cannot say exactly why this was so, but I believe it had a great deal to do with what I read. We all get our dreams from somewhere, and to some extent our ambitions are shaped by what we have read, and that, in turn, spurs our imagination. The body of literature we call Africana is exceptionally rich, and, perhaps, the richest body of sporting literature is in the English language. I voraciously read many of the great and classic African books, and almost invariably these exciting tomes were devoted to the pursuit of dangerous game.

There are exceptions to this, of course. In both Hemingway's *Green Hills of Africa (*1935) and Ruark's *Horn of the Hunter* (1953), the pursuit of the greater kudu is the theme. Collectively, these two books transformed the greater kudu into the icon it remains today. The safaris these books were based on took place in Tanganyika (now Tanzania), a great destination in their respective times, and still a fine safari country today. However, the greater kudu has a spotty distribution in East Africa. In my time we have known that the greater kudu is the most common large antelope across much of Southern Africa and has long been part of the normal bag on short "plains-game safaris." It could thus be argued that both Hemingway and Ruark immortalized hunts conducted in the wrong place!

Both of these excellent books were "first safari" books, semiautobiographical accounts of their authors' (Hemingway's and Ruark's) first experiences in Africa. Despite their unusual focus on kudu, both authors

Few things in life are better than getting in the middle of a big herd of buffaloes!

hunted a large selection of dangerous game, normal back then for a safari of several weeks' duration. Both hunted and took multiple lions in a time when lions were considered vermin. My uncle, Art Popham, took two fine lions on his 1956 Tanganyika safari. As an impressionable youngster I assumed this was normal! In their day, yes . . . but when I first hunted in Africa just twenty years later, things had already changed. The lion had already become a difficult and specialized pursuit.

In those early years of pursuing my dream of hunting an African lion, I failed more than once. I remember wanting a lion so badly I could taste it, and those initial failures ate at my insides. Even through the 1980s, a lion was often on license and available. Sometimes one might be successful and other times not, but the opportunity was there, and a lion safari was not the highly specialized and costly undertaking it is today. I feel sympathy for hunters starting their African careers who, as I did, put a lion at the top of their wish list. One can only hope that today's hunters temper their lists with current realities. For me, hunting in slightly different times, eventually my persistence paid off, and now I can say that I'm content.

In today's Africa a lion safari in a good area is pretty far up the food chain. I can't afford such hunts, but I doubt I would hunt a lion again even if I could. Our realities have to be tempered by our own times and circumstances, and today lions are threatened, with their numbers declining and their habitat shrinking. They are, however, *not* endangered. The distinction between threatened and endangered is important. I believe that lions can and must be managed and that carefully implemented selective hunting is critical in placing value on an animal that rural Africans regard primarily as a dangerous cattle-killing nuisance. So, if hunting a lion encapsulates your dream of Africa, by all means I'd say go for it. It's a marvelous experience, and a scarred old lion is a magnificent creature. I'm happy to have had the opportunity, but my lion-hunting days are done.

Africana literature is especially rich in describing the pursuit of the elephant, the world's largest and, to many, greatest game. As a youngster I discovered the works of W. D. M. "Karamojo" Bell and J. A. Hunter in the school library, and I thrilled to their accounts of hunting great tuskers. Interestingly, neither Hemingway nor Ruark hunted elephants on their first safaris, although in those days they certainly could have. By the time of my own first safari, in 1977, elephant hunting had closed in Kenya, and Tanzania was completely closed—though soon to reopen. In those gloom-and-doom days, commercial poaching was sweeping East and Central Africa, and the handwriting on the wall seemed clear. In those days I never considered pursuing elephant. Not well known was that the better-protected herds in Southern Africa were rebuilding, offering more chances in years to come.

Just as my lion-hunting days are over, I'm fairly certain I've taken my last elephant. My first came in Zimbabwe's Matetsi in 1985, and my "last" was in Namibia's Caprivi in 2015. In between I did a lot of elephant hunting in the Zambezi Valley, and some in Botswana, Mozambique, and Tanzania. Elephant hunting is exciting, exhausting, and really scary . . . and a marvelous experience. Even so, I have no desire to do more of it.

Opportunities have diminished, so elephant "specialists" are increasingly rare today, but historically many of the greatest African hunters considered elephant hunting the finest of all pursuits and left us a treasure trove of fine literature. I missed the great days of elephant hunting by decades. I can't even imagine a time when, with hard hunting in the right places, the quest for hundred-pound tusks was a realistic goal. Those days are over and will never come back, but I have been fortunate to have done more elephant hunting than I ever expected to. I'm happy that the matchless experience of closing with these great beasts remains available to today's African hunters, and I believe there will be elephant hunting for decades to come because the management imperative is unquestionable. I'm equally happy that this chapter of my hunting life is closed; the elephants that must be hunted can be hunted by others.*

For sure I will never take another rhino! It's a conservation miracle that both the black and white rhinos have been brought back from the brink. Both are gravely threatened, but by proper scientific definition, neither is *endangered*. The very limited hunting now done brings in huge funds for management and protection. It deserves our support. That said, hunting a rhino today is a pale shadow of the pursuits for these creatures in classic accounts from days gone by.

---

*I understand the necessity. I've enjoyed the many miles of following the tracks and the moments of sheer terror when you finally get close. Perhaps oddly, I've never felt good about shooting an elephant; too much sadness about taking the life of such a huge animal that, in my younger days, had probably been on our planet longer than I. Regardless of how *you* feel about it, the grim reality is that, distasteful as it might be to antihunters, nonhunters, and all too many hunters, elephant hunting is essential.

Without question the elephant is threatened in many areas, and more right now because of a new wave of ivory poaching. However, elephants are overpopulated in many southern areas. Africa remains a big place, so exact numbers are elusive. Nobody knows how many elephants might persist in the vastness of the Democratic Republic of the Congo (former Zaire). The total continent-wide number currently bandied about is 400,000 elephants, down from ten years ago, and dramatically down from estimates in 1900 and 1940. Here's an odd but important question that came up the other day at a meeting of the International Conservation Caucus (ICC): Just exactly how many elephants would be *enough* . . . and how many lions? If current estimates of 400,000 elephants and 40,000 lions are even remotely close, then how many would be "enough?" What is optimum?

Botswana alone has, by aerial survey, around 250,000 elephants. In arid Botswana this is far too many. Elephants are not currently hunted in Botswana, but when they were, the CITES quota of 350 was never reached. Sport hunting, which I fully support, cannot solve Botswana's elephant problem, but it must be solved or, in time, a massive die-off seems almost inevitable. As I've written before, where currently conducted, elephant hunting is important to rural Africans. Properly managed it can reduce overpopulation, and definitely reduces human-elephant conflict. When overpopulated, elephants are hard on the land and hard on all other species as well. Whether we choose to participate, we hunters must support elephant hunting as an essential management tool.

This is what you're looking for: an old bull with worn horns!

While my days of hunting the African elephant, lion, and rhino are over, I may not be entirely done with the fascinating chess game that is leopard hunting. It's amazing how time flies, and the older one gets, the faster it seems to go. A decade has passed since I took my last leopard, and I've had a couple of failures since then. Of course, that's the way of it with *chui*. Nobody bats a thousand! Leopard hunting takes serious thinking and strategizing, which is what makes it interesting. That said, I hate to sit still. Those incredible moments of crystal-clear excitement when (and *if)* the leopard makes his appearance are worth all the effort—but I don't look forward to the hours in the blind or the days of baiting, dragging, and building blinds.

Leopards are plentiful throughout wild Africa, and probably more numerous than anyone realizes. Clever and wary, they defy counting, and it's most likely that they are present in the suburbs of every city in sub-Saharan Africa. As with lions, I've had my chances, and another leopard hunt is not something I feel compelled to do, but I'll probably try again.

We Western hunters, whether European or American, pursue our passions in a world where deadly encounters are unlikely. Africa, with its Big Five or Dangerous Seven, grabs our imagination. So

The village headman supervises a "meat drop" in Mozambique's Coutada 11. Buffalo meat is an important by-product of the hunt . . . in this area Zambeze Delta Safaris distributes 30 tons *of meat annually to local villages.*

does the great body of literature from the days of the Raj when the dangerous beasts of the Indian subcontinent exceeded those in Africa. Jim Corbett's tales of hunting man-eaters are still among the best in sporting literature, but all those hunts ended a full generation ago while Africa's dangerous game remains relevant. Like moths to the flame, we are fascinated by potential danger, and Africa would not be Africa without her dangerous game.

Classic tales of hunting elephant and lion are legion, and from long-gone times when rhinos were shockingly plentiful there are many hair-raising accounts. In the literature of *Africana*, the leopard seems somehow cheated. My long-held theory is that, in the early years, when safaris were longer, leopards were usually taken in chance encounters. As a technique, baiting didn't come into common play until after World War II . . . almost certainly enabled by widespread use of the riflescope.

Ruark's excellent account of his first leopard in *Horn of the Hunter* differs but little from a modern leopard hunt. Ruark rested on his two and only lions from that first safari. He shot a black rhino on a subsequent safari, and before Kenya closed he would take three elephants with tusks over a hundred pounds each. However, he was enthralled by leopard hunting. He lived just a dozen years after the "*Horn*" safari, but he wrote that he'd taken twenty leopards, a huge number in just a decade.

This brings us to the buffalo, what many think as the most exciting of all the dangerous-game hunts in Africa. We all know that ivory hunters like Bell, Hunter, and Taylor were fixated on elephants and that hunting a buffalo was just a detour to feed the camp. John Burger was different. Unusual among early African hunters, Burger is first and foremost remembered as a buffalo hunter, and his *Horned Death* is a classic on hunting the African buffalo. Of course, he did much hunting of other species, but for years his primary activity was hunting buffaloes to feed sugar plantation workers in colonial Mozambique.

Both Hemingway and Ruark hunted buffaloes on their first safaris. We know from careful reading that Ruark took at least two fine bulls. *Horn of the Hunter* gave us what I think of as some of the best passages ever written on buffalo hunting. This would continue: Ruark, besotted by buffaloes just as much (or more) than leopards, acquired tremendous experience.

Hemingway's experience with buffalo is less clear. In "*Green Hills*" he messed up on one, blaming the heavy trigger on his double rifle. Trust me: Papa Hemingway doesn't have a copyright on messing up on buffalo! He doesn't actually take a buffalo in *Green Hills*, but I have seen a photo of a dark-haired Hemingway with a buffalo and his Griffin & Howe Springfield. There are also photos of a gray-haired Hemingway and his famous .577 sitting next to buffaloes shot on his 1954 safari. Buffalo hunting is a main focus of his short story, *The Short, Happy Life of Francis Macomber* (1936), so I assume that, on his 1933 safari, he spent more time messing with buffaloes than he related in *Green Hills*.

The original textbook on safari hunting, Roosevelt's *African Game Trails*, is also a "first safari" book, although based on a nine-month odyssey, unusual even in those days of extra-long safaris. The Roosevelt party hunted essentially the full range of game that existed in East Africa. Typical of the day, leopards were taken in chance encounters. Lions, elephants, rhinos, and buffaloes were all specifically hunted . . .

and taken in chance encounters. Roosevelt's book gives us an amazing picture of East Africa in 1909, certainly an Africa that will never be seen again.

I can't even imagine the near-pristine Africa that Roosevelt saw, but in some ways even his timing wasn't perfect, especially for our present subject of *buffaloes*. A great rinderpest epidemic swept much of Africa from the 1890s through the following decade, and it took years for the disease to travel the thousands of miles of wild Africa. Across Southern and East Africa buffaloes were nearly eradicated in many areas. It is a historic fact that buffaloes were scarce at the time of the Roosevelt safari and selection was limited.

This may have been partly true at the time of Hemingway's *Green Hills* safari. From careful readings, my impression is that buffaloes were far from plentiful, at least in that area at that time. Fast forward twenty years to Ruark. He had a tough time with kudu, a situation still normal in today's Tanzania, but buffaloes were common with big, old bulls there for the taking.

Skip forward another twenty-odd years to my own early safaris. In the 1970s there were places that held legions of buffaloes, but I wasn't hunting in those places. Remember, my focus was a *lion*. I expected buffaloes to come along as a matter of course, but I found that it wasn't that easy!

Kenya was on its last legs and would soon close; we hunted hard on the slopes of Mount Kenya and saw few buffaloes. A couple years later I hunted in southeastern Rhodesia in what is now part of the Save Valley Conservancy, today one of the best buffalo areas in modern Zimbabwe. When I was there in 1979, the game department had just completed eradicating the buffaloes because of hoof-and-mouth disease. Only a few remnant buffaloes remained in the deepest riverine thickets. We hunted hard and never got a shot. Two years later, under similar circumstances, hunting remnant survivors in thick cover, I got a buffalo near the Bubye River. It was the mid-1980s before I experienced the kind of buffalo hunting that made me a lifelong addict.

I "discovered" buffalo hunting in Zambia, both in the Luangwa Valley and Kafue off to the west, and in Botswana. Zambia was great for buffalo then and remains so today. In Botswana, both the Okavango

Tucked up against a sparse tree in Namibia's Caprivi, PH Dawid Muller and I are plenty close to this herd!

and the Chobe regions were full of buffaloes. This was a time when elephants hadn't yet overpopulated. The Chobe National Park already looked like a nuclear blast zone, but farther south and west elephants were encountered infrequently. Instead, in the course of a normal hunting day we'd run into two or three buffalo herds, not to mention sable antelope, zebra, wildebeest, and usually greater kudu.

Late in that decade—late eighties, early nineties—I hunted in Tanzania three times—in Masailand, Selous, and the west. To this day I've never seen big numbers of buffaloes in Masailand, but it's certainly a place for very big bulls. For me the Selous consistently produced lots of buffaloes while western Tanzania has been less reliable. It's always a matter of luck and timing, but certainly Tanzania remains a fine buffalo country. From the Rhodesia days onward, Zimbabwe has been a favorite destination. In the 1990s and early 2000s I spent a lot of time in the Zambezi Valley, wild country where buffaloes still roam and lions still roar. In the valley in those days we could expect to pick up tracks of bachelor bulls almost at will. Unfortunately, things have changed. The Zambezi Valley still holds lots of buffaloes, but mature bulls are scarcer today than just a decade ago. The quotas have been too high for too long, and Zimbabwe's Lower Zambezi may well be

You can feel the body language when you're getting close . . . the trackers slow down, check the wind constantly, and all eyes scan ahead.

one of few places on the entire African continent where lions have overpopulated.

Zimbabwe remains a great buffalo destination, but the better places have shifted to the big conservancies—Save Valley, Bubye, and the relatively new Nuanetsi. In recent years I've done most of my buffalo hunting in coastal Mozambique, an area that hunter-funded management has brought back from tattered rags—after Mozambique's long civil war—to incredible riches today. This was never a place to look for the biggest bull, and perhaps still isn't, but as the numbers go up, quality is improving, and this is a place to get into huge herds. I love it, and I keep going back because I see it getting better every year, truly a miracle in wild Africa.

The buffalo and its management cannot be compared to the rest of the Big Five. The buffalo is a grazing ungulate that gathers in large herds. They are relatively slow breeders, so wise management is always an issue. Exponential growth is not possible, so with bad management decisions or unfavorable conditions such as drought or disease, a precipitous decline is possible. The buffalo bull needs about ten years to reach full maturity. This is much the same as many other ungulates that are successfully managed around the world, including greater kudu, wild sheep and goats, and elk and red deer. An older buffalo bull is thus a replaceable resource, and in one race or another, the buffalo still has a huge range across Africa.

Population estimates exist in various well-managed enclaves, generally in East and Southern Africa. Overall numbers are not known, not least of all because Central and West Africa are simply too vast. Without question, buffaloes are scarce in some areas and plentiful in others, but not even the most rabid antihunting forces consider the African buffalo threatened, let alone endangered. Buffaloes fly under the radar of the iconic labels now attached to lions, elephants, and rhinos. Their meat is highly prized and always utilized, and they have acquired an almost demonic reputation that, in my opinion, is not entirely deserved.

I would never suggest that hunting the African buffalo is somehow superior to pursuing the greater kudu, or the elephant, or the great cats, nor would I insist that it is Africa's best hunt. It depends on what interests you, and you probably won't know until you have a bit of experience. For me, however, it's the buffalo that keeps drawing me back. Scabby, ridden with ticks, constantly in fear of lions, always testing the wind, the buffalo bull is defiant, arrogant, and absolutely magnificent. For me, personally, the buffalo is Africa's best hunt.

Only a fool is unafraid when closely approaching an elephant, and I have had a lifelong fear of lions—quite possibly from reading Col. John Patterson's *The Man-eaters of Tsavo*. When following a wounded leopard, I know with each step that someone is likely to get scratched. I have no similar fear of the buffalo, but I use caution. I have respect and admiration for this noble creature. For me there is simply nothing like the rush of adrenaline that comes with getting close, smelling the familiar cattle smell, seeing the oxpeckers and egrets darting and swooping, hearing the shifting of dozens, perhaps hundreds of heavy bodies and the soft clacking of horns bumping together, and knowing that a sudden eruption is seconds away. There is also nothing like the suspense and anticipation that comes from hunting this great beast. Always there's the question of where is the bull and where is the *right bull* in that dark mass? Is he there? Will we see him, and if he is there, can we do it right?

I have had a wonderful career and a great life filled with many fine hunting experiences. It would be nice to start over, but as my hunting years grow shorter, there is much I can never experience again, but I will continue to pursue the African buffalo. This ability will diminish as years advance, but I am very much not done yet. I look forward to many more buffalo encounters and to sharing them. For me the buffalo is simply the best hunt and the greatest experience that the African continent and this hunting world can offer.

A Gallery of Beautiful Buffaloes

Chapter 2

1. **A very big Asian water buffalo, taken in 1952 by Dr. Frank Hibben.** Frank Hibben, the 1964 Weatherby Award winner, was an archaeologist and professor at the University of New Mexico; Hibben also served as director of the New Mexico Game Commission from 1961–1971. Hibben believed in "habitat niches" and was responsible for the introduction of ibex, aoudad, and gemsbok into New Mexico. It is not known exactly where Hibben took this whopper of a water buffalo, but at that time it could have come from several places in India or Southeast Asia. (Courtesy of Robert M. Anderson)

2. George Parker with a "red buffalo," northern Angola, 1952. This photograph is appropriate for the beginning of this chapter since 1952 was the year of my birth! I obviously wasn't hunting buffaloes back then, but many years later George Parker became a friend whom I admired immensely. Parker was a lifelong buddy of Col. Charles Askins, who also became a friend. Askins, himself a very tough guy, referred to his friend George Parker as "the tough one." An Arizona native, Parker still holds the record for Coues whitetails listed in Boone and Crockett. Parker took this "red buffalo," actually a dwarf forest buffalo, during a lengthy safari to northern Angola by train, an amazing adventure. Parker used his pet .30-06 Improved on a Model 70 action. On the same safari Parker became one of just a handful of hunters to take a giant sable! George Parker was a great hunter, one of the last of the gunfighters in the Old West tradition; he deserves to be much better remembered than he is.

3. Herb Klein's first and best Cape buffalo, 1953. Herb Klein was the inaugural Weatherby winner in 1956 and an early investor in Roy Weatherby's gun company. A Texas oil man, Klein was foremost among the post-WWII globetrotting American hunters. He hunted throughout Africa widely and took a number of buffaloes, but his first, with a forty-eight-inch spread, remained his best. He took this bull on a July–August 1953 safari to Kenya and Tanganyika with Ker & Downey. The rifle is obviously a pre-Mark V Weatherby, likely in .375 Weatherby Magnum. (Courtesy of Robert M. Anderson)

4. Jack O'Connor's first Cape buffalo, 1953. In my opinion, Jack O'Connor was America's greatest gunwriter! This, his first of several buffaloes, was taken on a safari to Kenya and Tanganyika with Ker & Downey in July–August 1953. O'Connor took this excellent buffalo, over forty-three inches, with the wildcat .450 Watts rifle he had built for this safari. Although he took many of his later safaris with John Kingsley-Heath, on this safari O'Connor was hunting with Donald Ker. (Courtesy of Robert M. Anderson)

5. Herb Klein with a huge gaur, 1954. The gaur or "Indian bison" is the largest bovine in the world! In the 1950s and 1960s, it was just as simple to mount a shikar to India as a safari to Africa. The primary game animal of India was the tiger, but gaur and water buffalo were readily available. This big gaur was probably taken in India or Assam. The rifle is a pre-Mark V Weatherby, probably in .375 Weatherby Magnum. (Courtesy of Robert M. Anderson)

6. Art Popham with a fine Cape buffalo, 1956. Arthur C. Popham Jr. was my uncle, my mother's brother. In 1956 he hunted in Tanganyika on a collecting expedition for the Kansas City Museum of Natural History. This safari was my lifelong undoing; I was only four years old, but I remember quite clearly saying, "I'm going to do that someday!" Uncle Art was hunting with Jackie Hamman in Mto Wa Mbu, a great Masailand concession below Ngorongoro, when he took this bull. As you'll read later, I, too, hunted there in 1993 and took my own best buffalo. I have never measured Uncle Art's buffalo, but it's a great-looking East African buff. The European mount is at my cousin's farm, Carole and Sid McKnight, south of Kansas City. Art was using a .375 Improved on a Winchester Model 70 action.

7. Col. Charles Askins with a Cape buffalo, date unknown. Col. Charles Askins was quite a character. Through her brother, Art Popham, my mom knew Askins and George Parker in the late 1930s and, according to her, she had quite a crush on the dashing Charlie Askins. Gunwriters of the previous generation adopted pet calibers. O'Connor claimed the .270, Warren Page claimed the 7mm, and Askins did his best to stir interest in the 8mm. I believe this buffalo was taken in Zambia, exact year unknown, but for sure it was taken with a wildcat 8mm-.404, one of many 8mm wildcat cartridges that Askins created. This cartridge used a .404 Jeffery case necked down to 8mm, and this buffalo was taken with a 225-grain Speer bullet.

8. George Parker with a big Asian water buffalo, 1958. This is a big "Indian-style" water buffalo with long, sweeping horns. A riding elephant waits patiently behind . . . truly a scene from another era. Exactly where Parker took this buffalo is not known, but in those days there were multiple venues for such game. If the year is correct, then I believe it was taken in Southeast Asia because, at that time Parker's buddy Charlie Askins was serving in Vietnam. Askins was the chief marksmanship instructor for the South Vietnamese army, and Parker visited him and spent an extended time hunting in the region. Some of their adventures are recounted in Askins's book *Asian Jungle, African Bush* (Stackpole, 1959).

9. Bert Klineburger with a big gaur, 1966. My old friend Bert Klineburger was one of the world's greatest hunters. Together with his brother Chris, the Klineburger brothers were pioneers in opening up many of the African and Asian hunting areas we enjoy to this day. This monstrous gaur was taken in Madhya Pradesh in central India in 1966, and the shikar was outfitted by Allwyn-Cooper, a major outfitter in the latter days of Indian hunting. (Courtesy of Robert M. Anderson)

10. A big water buffalo with a 7x57, 2008. Sometimes there's a difference between what you can do and what you should do. One of my all-time favorite rifles is a 7x57 built by Todd Ramirez on the lines of a 1920s "stalking rifle." Having read my Karamojo Bell, I wanted to take a buffalo with it, but I wasn't going to break Africa's minimum caliber requirements. So, I loaded up 175-grain Barnes Super Solids and took it to Argentina on a hunt with Marcelo Sodiro. We found a group of bedded bulls, and I crawled about forty yards to shoot this big bull at the base of the ear. And that's pretty much the end of the story!

11. Bert Klineburger, Marajo Island water buffalo, 1981. Bert Klineburger took this exceptional water buffalo on Brazil's Marajo Island, a large island at the mouth of the Amazon River. Water buffaloes were introduced as a source of meat and milk, and the island still has a large population of these bovines. Most South American water buffaloes have the smaller, curling horns, but the Marajo buffaloes obviously have the wide, sweeping horns of the Indian water buffalo and northern Australia's introduced water buffaloes. The top-ranking South American water buffaloes in the SCI record book are still from Marajo Island.

12. My first big buffalo, 1984. Russ Broom and I were hunting in the Mumbwa West block of Zambia's Kafue region in November 1984. We'd had an awesome safari, but the buffaloes kept eluding us. Late one afternoon circling egrets led us to a herd and I shot a very nice bull. With sunset almost upon us, we took a diagonal approach through some thick *miombo* forest to reach the truck and bumped into a bachelor group with one outsized bull among them. Without hesitation Russ told me to take him. I was using a left-hand-converted Winchester Model 70 in .375 H&H, with a 300-grain Hornady Interlock on top, followed by Hornady solids. This bull was forty-five inches wide with excellent bosses. It was a great buffalo!

13. An Okavango swamp buffalo, 1985. There's nothing really unusual about this buffalo, just a very normal mature bull . . . except for two things: First, it was taken in the Okavango Delta, and while I expect Botswana to reopen and offer at least some buffalo hunting, I doubt the Okavango will ever be open to hunting again. I was hunting with Jack Atcheson Jr. and Ronnie MacFarlane, and we were actually in a *mokoro* or dugout canoe when we saw him on the bank. Jack and Ronnie grounded their poles for stability, and I took the shot. Second, I was using a .416 Hoffman in a time when .416s were still rare. Randy Brooks of Barnes Bullets built the rifle, and I was using 400-grain Barnes Original softpoints backed by the then-new Barnes Super Solid.

14. An almost-a-mistake Cape buffalo from the Selous Reserve, 1988. It was the last hunting day of a three-week safari with Luke Samaras, and I was in the Selous with Paddy Curtis. We had picked up fresh tracks of a dozen or so bachelor bulls relatively early in the morning, expecting to catch them quickly. Four or five hours later we finally caught them bedded on a little knoll . . . only to find they were all immature youngsters! This was the oldest and largest bull, but he's marginal: a sort-of, almost-mature bull, but maybe not quite. The shot was the result of last-day hysteria and the end of a long track. We crawled into them, and when he got up, I shot him from a prone position with my C. W. Andrews .470 using 500-grain Kynoch softpoints. This is a classic example of a tough call!

15. Wide Zimbabwe Cape buffalo bull, 1992. I was hunting leopard with Russ Broom in his Binga concession in the Zambezi Valley when we saw this bull. He was extremely wide at forty-four inches, but we didn't really notice until he was down that he had narrow, skimpy bosses. He's still my widest Zimbabwe bull, and although the width and shape are excellent and although he's an older, fully mature bull, he's a good example of a buffalo bull whose horns didn't come together in the center! I shot him from about fifty yards with the Andrews .470, using Federal Supreme with Woodleigh bullets.

16. My best Cape buffalo, Masailand, 1993. I was hunting in the famous Mto Wa Mbu block in Masailand with Geoff Broom where Ruark hunted on his *Horn of the Hunter* safari in 1953 and where my Uncle Art had hunted in 1956. I'm told it's *still* a very good area for Masailand game. It's just below Ngorongoro Crater, famous for huge buffalo. It was November, the end of the season, and Geoff had never seen this bull or the bigger bull he was with; he believes they were "crater bulls" on a walkabout. He's forty-seven inches wide with decent bosses and great shape, easily my "best-ever" buffalo . . . but you should have seen the buddy! The bigger bull slipped into thick vegetation and didn't come out, so we took the shot we had. Geoff found a set of horns the next year, a bit over fifty inches, and he's certain that's the one that got away. I shot this bull with a Dakota .416 Rigby, then finished him with the Andrews .470.

17. First buffalo in the Save Valley Conservancy, 1995. I first hunted in the area that is now the Save Valley Conservancy in 1979, just after the ranchers had finished eradicating their buffalo! Buffaloes were reintroduced in the mid-1990s as part of the formation of the conservancy. The buffaloes were doing well, but they had a weird bull with a growth on the right like an upside-down eland horn, while his left horn was normal. Worn and broken horns are common, but this is one of the few genuinely "nontypical" buffaloes I've ever encountered. I agreed to take him, and I assume the Whittall family still has the oddball skull at their Humani Ranch headquarters on the conservancy. He was the only African buffalo I've ever taken that was lying down. I used a Dakota Model 10 single shot in .375 Dakota with Swift A-Frame.

18. A very wide Zambia bull, 1996. This was a magic safari. I was on safari with Bob Petersen, Ken Elliott, Gary Williams, and artist Douglas Van Howel, and we were hunting with Russ Broom's outfit, first in Bangweulu, then in Kafue. I was hunting with Angie Angelloz, a great young hunter, and we got onto a group of nine or ten bachelor bulls close to the park's boundary. We'd been waiting hours for them to get up, and when they did, the wind turned and they stampeded away. As they moved toward the park, they caught a wall of scent and stampeded back straight toward us. I think all of them were mature, and I was going to shoot the leader as they came past, but Angie whispered, "Take the second one." They were about thirty yards away, and I was swinging the Rigby .470 like a shotgun. I shot him under the curve of the horn like Geoff Broom had taught me, and the bull slid on his nose for fifty feet. His bosses were narrow, but he was forty-seven inches wide, a great bull.

19. This bull could have gotten even, Zambezi Valley, 1996. I was hunting with Rory Muil in Russ Broom's Binga concession not far from Lake Kariba. We found a couple of bulls moving down a little *korongo*, offering one of the easiest shots ever at a buffalo. I was shooting a scoped .416 Rigby, so there are no excuses, yet somehow I blew it completely. I hit the bull much too far back, not even close to where I thought I had hit him. We jumped him at dark, and then we knew we had trouble on our hands. We picked up the trail at dawn and followed him for eight hours in some of the thickest *jesse* I've ever encountered. This was one of those situations where I'm not sure a charge could have been stopped, but in midafternoon we caught him in a slightly open area just as he was turning to charge. I was embarrassed by my first shot, but I did bring him down. He was a very fine bull, about forty-two inches wide with good bosses and good shape. I felt he deserved a better hunter!

20. Chub Eastman's water buffalo, 1999. Chub and I were hunting with Bob Penfold in his Gan Gan area far off to the east in northern Australia's Arnhemland, which is really remote country and always good for big bulls. Chub's water buffalo was excellent, but what I remember most was the shot. Chub was always a consummate rifleman. On this hunt he was using a .416 Weatherby Magnum, which is a lot of rifle. We were on a steep little ridge looking down, and the buffalo was at the bottom of the slope. He was close, but it meant Chub had to shoot downhill almost into the top of the bull's shoulders. Chub was still with Nosler Bullets and we were using their brand-new 400-grain Partition. The bullet literally flattened the bull, driving it down into the forest floor, where it never moved.

21. Sherwin Scott's water buffalo, 1999. "Scotty" wasn't hunting with Chub and me, but he was in camp. As I recall, there'd been a Shikar-Safari Club meeting in Australia, so a lot of these folks did some hunting before or after. I shared a couple of fine hunts with Scotty. He was an extremely particular hunter, always looking for the very best, and he often found what he was looking for. His water buffalo was superb, but what struck me was that he used his Holland & Holland double .500, hardly a common rifle. More unusual, Sherwin's rifle was chambered to the .500-3¼" Nitro Express cartridge, not the more common .500-3". His was probably the only .500 I've ever seen that was chambered to the longer case.

22. A buffalo for BOB, Zambezi Valley, 2004. In July 2004 I was hunting in the Sapi area of Zimbabwe's Zambezi Valley, east of Mana Pools. It was the first time I'd hunted with Andrew Dawson and I really liked his calm, efficient manner. We were putting the finishing touches on the *Boddington on Buffalo* DVD when we picked up the tracks of two bulls on the old Security Road, which we followed for several hours. We were starting up a gentle ridge when tracker Mukasa saw an oxpecker drop down just over the crest. He stopped and pointed; he knew the bulls were there. When they broke cover, the biggest bull floated through a little clearing, barely fifteen yards away, the most perfect shot imaginable for a double .470. This fine *dagga* bull with good bosses and with tips wearing down was right on the money with a forty-inch spread.

23. Wayne Holt's monster, 2005. It was a very dry year in the Zambezi Valley, with buffaloes commuting long distances between the Zambezi River and good grazing. Wayne Holt (right) was hunting in Sapi with Paul Smith (left) and the pickings were slim. Almost every day we could pick up the tracks of two bulls, but every time we tracked them, they led us miles from the river and into the *jesse*, where it was just too thick to close on them. On Wayne's next-to-last day we followed the same two bulls, but this time they stopped in a thick *korongo*. The first bull broke on the far side, but the second bull charged up the bank, caught us flat-footed, and then turned away. That's when Wayne pasted him with his .458 Lott, visibly stopping him in midstride. With perfect shape and a spread of forty-five inches, this is one of the best buffalo bulls I ever saw from the Zambezi Valley.

24. First buffalo with the new .375 Ruger, 2006. I don't always get these things right. I wasn't totally sure that the world needed another .375, but the .375 Ruger has a clever case design that is intended for smooth feeding in existing actions, and it turned out a bit faster than the .375 H&H. Steve Hornady was hunting with Paul Smith when he brought one of the first Hawkeye .375 Rugers with his new ammo. It was June, primary breeding time when older bulls often satellite the herds. We were tracking a herd when we came up on this beautiful bull trailing the group. Not only did the .375 Ruger work fine on this buffalo, but it also went on to be one of the most successful large-caliber introductions in cartridge history.

25. A big Zambezi Valley bull for Donna, 2006. We were hunting in Dande North, the northeastern corner of Zimbabwe with Paul Smith. It was Donna's turn when we picked up the tracks of a big herd in the late morning. The tracks were from the night, so I thought this would be a long hike, but we caught up to them in little more than an hour. Paul quickly spotted a really fine bull with huge bosses and big curls, but other buffaloes were shielding him, so there was no possibility of a shot. The situation stayed that way for hours! Finally, in the late afternoon, the herd moved off. We got onto them about three more times before this bull, trailing the herd, stopped in a little meadow. Donna was shooting a Ruger No. 1 in .450/.400-3" with Hornady's first run of modern factory ammo. That hunt made me a believer in the .450/.400 for buffalo!

26. Brittany's Lemco bull, 2008. We were on the huge Lemco Conservancy, now called Bubye Valley Conservancy, in Zimbabwe. Like in the Save Valley, buffaloes had been eradicated because of bovine disease and then reintroduced. They'd been there for a while, were doing well, and the area was producing great bulls. Daughter Brittany had suffered through a very tough and unsuccessful buffalo hunt in the Zambezi Valley, so Andrew Dawson wanted to give the lowveld a try. The cover is thick, so it's not easy buffalo hunting. I think it was on the third day when we caught this beautiful lone bull in his bed. Britt was on the sticks and ready when he got up, and she pasted him perfectly. She was using a Ruger No. 1 in .405 Winchester, a strong action, with 400-grain Hornady bullets loaded up to about .450/.400 velocity. Performance was perfect!

27. A fine Mozambique bull for the Turnbull, 2008. I'm often asked about hunting buffaloes with a big lever action. There's no reason not to, but I've only done it once. I was hunting in coastal Mozambique's Coutada 10 with Willem van Dyk Jr., son of my Kenya hunter, using a Winchester Model 1886 by Doug Turnbull in his proprietary .475 Turnbull cartridge. The rifle is powerful and accurate, but the traditional buckhorn sights probably aren't perfect in the Zambezi Delta's open floodplains. We found this excellent bull lying down, and I studied the shot for a long time. When he finally got up, I was comfortable and confident to make the shot. This buffalo is still one of my best Mozambique bulls.

28. Buck Buckner's big bull with a classic double, 2009. Eldon "Buck" Buckner was a longtime friend of Jack O'Connor's and is one of our leaders in the Boone and Crockett Club. He's done a lot of African hunting, including a safari with me in Mozambique a few years ago. In 2009 he went to Tanzania on a "buffalo-only" hunt with two very special rifles, and he took two very special bulls. At 102 yards, this was a fine shot with a double rifle. The bull is 43½ inches, which is good, but its deep hooks and big bosses make it even better. Buck used a John Rigby .450-3¼" Nitro Express on this magnificent bull. (Courtesy of Robert M. Anderson)

29. A big bull for Buck with O'Connor's .458, 2009. Buck Buckner collaborated with Robert M. Anderson on the breakdown of O'Connor's firearms in Anderson's biography, *Jack O'Connor: The Legendary Life of America's Greatest Gunwriter*. In 1969 O'Connor took his one and only elephant in Zambia. Upon his return he got the itch to return for a big elephant bull, so he had a .458 Winchester Magnum built by Fred Wells and stocked by Clayton Nelson. It's a distinctive and unusual rifle, with a half-octagon barrel and a full rib. O'Connor never went on that elephant hunt. He sold the rifle to Henry Kaufman, who later sold it to Buck Buckner. Buck took this forty-inch bull in Tanzania with Jack O'Connor's Wells-Nelson rifle. I suspect Professor O'Connor would approve! (Courtesy of Robert M. Anderson)

30. A big Rungwa buffalo for Ron Bird, 2010. In October 2010 Ron Bird and I were hunting in Michel Mantheakis's Rungwa concession in central Tanzania. Ron's primary quest was for a lion, but although we were knee-deep in lions, we couldn't find one that met Tanzania's six-year-old rule. We encountered buffalo herds daily, but buffalo hunting was secondary to bait replenishment, so when we needed bait, we couldn't be too picky. One morning we caught a group of bulls headed toward a waterhole. We followed, catching them in open ground. Using his .375, Ron shot the largest bull. He took this fine East African buffalo, right at forty-five inches in spread . . . and took his lion on the last day!

31. The heart attack buffalo, Uganda, 2011. We were hunting Nile buffalo with Christian Weth along the northern edge of Murchison Falls National Park. Late one blistering hot morning a couple of villagers came to tell us they'd seen a lone bull headed north, away from the park. We found the tracks easily enough and followed them up and over a couple of ridges. Even though I was feeling the heat and uncharacteristically short of breath, we continued to follow the tracks up onto a forested plateau. We found the spots where the buffalo had twice bedded, and then we saw him in a third bed. I shot him as he rose. I was doing a "high five" with the government game scout when the world spun and the ground rose up to meet me. The next thing I remember is being splashed with water, and after I had recovered a bit, I crawled over to the bull. He was a very old and classic Nile buffalo. I thought about him a lot in the weeks of recovery that followed.

32. J. C. Bell takes the Big Boss, 2012. In my experience, buffaloes with really huge bosses are rare. A friend of mine was filming a group of bulls and his PH was exhorting him to "shoot the big boss." His cameraman was clueless, having no idea which bull was the boss of the group, and no shots were fired. J. C. Bell didn't have that problem when they ran into this awesome bull in the *miombo* forests of Coutada 11 in Mozambique. He shot it well—but not perfectly—with his .375, and the buffalo instantly charged! His PH was behind a tree and couldn't help, so J. C. stopped it at a couple dozen feet. Although not wide, the huge bosses are exceptional. Obviously, this was a memorable hunt, especially since it was J. C. Bell's first buffalo!

33. Water buffalo in the Philippines, 2013. My buddy from Macedonia, Saso Ivanov, and I were hunting on Luzon with Jay Carlson. It was an odd hunt as well as very hot and very tropical. You can't bring firearms into the Philippines, so we "borrowed" a worn M14 from the local garrison, with slug-loaded shotguns for backup! This excellent bull was feeding in a small jungle of a valley, so we approached to a matter of feet and I let drive with military ball ammunition. Fortunately, that old M14 functioned perfectly and the bull went down on the spot. Taking turns, Saso and I shot several water buffaloes . . . and that's the way they all went!

34. A snappy double on swamp buffaloes, Mozambique, 2016. After a shot is fired, buffalo herds often don't go very far. Provided that first shot is good, it isn't unusual to get a second opportunity. The first time I saw a "double" from the same herd was in Botswana's Chobe in 1989 when Ed Weatherby and I were hunting with Steve Liversedge. It's much less common, however, to have two bulls down close together and in the same photo! We were in Coutada 11, Donna hunting with Gert Boosye and I was with Mark Haldane, both of us shooting .375s. We saw Donna's bull go down, and then another good bull stepped to the edge. These are both nice swamp bulls, Donna's a bit wider, mine with more drop. They went down close together, with a total of three shots fired.

35. A big Nile buffalo for Steve Hornady, Uganda, 2017. Steve and I hunted together in Zambia back in 1983, so we go back a long way. In March 2017 we were hunting with Christian Weth in Uganda's Karamoja district on the edge of the Kidepo National Park, an amazing area for bachelor bulls. In a time of plenty, how do you know when to shoot? Steve wanted one good Nile buffalo, and we'd seen and passed a number of mature bulls. As we approached, I could see that this bull had excellent bosses and a bit more drop and curl than is normal with typically "flat-horn" Nile buffaloes. It did, however, have one tip that was clearly worn. We maneuvered close and Steve wanted my opinion, but I also wasn't sure. I guess the proper decision was reached, for this was Uganda Wildlife Safaris' best bull of the 2017 season!

36. A really ugly buffalo, Mozambique, 2017. In October 2017 I was hunting in Coutada 11 with Mark Haldane and his Zambeze Delta Safaris. Late in the hunt we went to the swamps one more time, and it occurred to me that if we got lucky, this would be, as near as I can reckon, my hundredth buffalo. My friend Gordon Marsh had taken two bulls earlier in the hunt, one with his .375 and another with his Sabatti .450/.400-3". Back in 2005 I'd convinced Hornady to develop a modern load for the .450/.400-3", together with a run of Ruger No. 1 rifles. Relatively mild in recoil and extremely effective, the cartridge has been a great success. I have sort of a paternal interest in it, and Gordon was kind enough to loan me his double. We checked it on the range, found it perfect, so off we went. I wasn't looking for a big bull and this one certainly isn't, but as I said, he's probably my hundredth buffalo. His horns are narrow and ugly, but he's absolutely mature, and, as usual, the .450/.400 with DGX did a great job. I like to think that Col. Charles Askins would be proud.

37. A really good-looking buffalo, 2018. In October 2018 I was back in Coutada 11 in Mozambique with Mark Haldane. Slowly, over time, I believe the buffalo bulls in the Zambezi Delta are just getting better and better, but luck is always a factor, as are your expectations. Earlier in this hunt my daughter's fiancé, Brad Jannenga, was hoping for a "wide bull" and took a fine buffalo with a forty-two-inch spread. These days I often don't look for big horns as my focus nowadays is on mature bulls, but in those big herds you either take—or leave—what is offered. This particular herd had several really nice bulls, but, as usual, most of them were a bit too young. I was shooting a Sabatti in .450-3¼", another favorite, when this beautiful bull stepped out of the herd. We couldn't resist!

38. A dwarf forest buffalo at last, Cameroon, 2019. Christophe Lemée guided me to this nice "DFB." As they say, big things come in small packages! These are really small buffaloes in both body and horn . . . but oh, so difficult to obtain! I'm pretty sure it took me sixty days of very hard hunting to take this bull, and this was the first real chance I ever had. As with most animals, you must be in the right place at the right time: This area was on the northern edge of the forest, an area where they can only hunt for buffalo in late March and early April, before the grass gets too long. The rifle is a Sako Model 85 in .375 H&H with Leica scope, a very nice "camp gun."

Learning Curve

Chapter 3

When I first hunted buffalo, I had no clue what I was doing. Needless to say, I didn't know that! As I'd read *everything*, naturally I felt I had to be an expert. I could shoot very well, probably better than today. For sure experience counts, but I was steadier forty years ago, and in better shape than I am today, or ever again for that matter. These things are all important; only a handful of PHs can actually *do* a lot of buffalo hunting in a given year, so studying is valuable. Print media was king when I was young, and the buffalo had inspired generations of good reading and good writing. Today we have a lot of excellent and some not-so-excellent videos, available on television and over the Internet. The good stuff is just that, *good*, yet while helpful and useful, it's not exactly the same as being there.

Shooting is important. Buffaloes are killed primarily by shot placement. On the surface it should be easy because the target is huge. All that's really necessary is to hit a basketball within a hundred yards—simple. However, I am convinced that dark animals somehow confound the aim. It doesn't matter if it's a black bear, boar, or buffalo; there's something about black animals that make achieving a precise point of aim more difficult, especially when they're in harsh shadows.

Relatively few of us screw up so badly as to shoot at the whole buffalo. Most of the time we have clues: legs, head, ever-switching tail, and the horizontal lines of belly and spine. We can usually figure out which is the front half, but that's not good enough. We must learn to visualize a basketball against that dark mass. While it isn't hard,

My initial exposure to buffalo hunting in the seventies was in marginal areas; I didn't become besotted with buffaloes until the mid-eighties. Russ Broom and I took these two bulls in Zambia's Kafue region on the same day in November 1984.

it's not as easy as it sounds. In large part this is because, often, we overstudy the problem. When a hunter goes after a first buffalo, that person is in near-panic mode. We've read and seen the sensational, and we're afraid. In our subconscious is the thought: *This thing is gonna kill me*. Sure, it might, but the probability is low. Even so, it's not easy to put the jitters and buck/buffalo fever aside.

By the way, this is not only OK; it is as it should be. If you're not extremely nervous when you go after your first buffalo—or first several buffaloes!—you're too cool a customer for me. You need something else to get your adrenaline properly flowing. Consider an Everest ascent, or, since I'm terrified of heights, maybe hang-gliding will do it for you. Come to think of it, I'm *still* plenty nervous when I go in on a buffalo. I respect the animal, and I understand the potential consequences if I mess up.

These days I can control my emotions fairly well—my hands shake *after*, not *during*—but I was very nervous for a long time. In part this was because I'd probably read and studied too damn much, but I also had the poor luck—and bad performance!—to wound and lose my first buffalo. This is not an uncommon calamity, but it changes the game the next time you get on the horse. Now you're not just afraid of the buffalo; you're terrified of screwing up again because now you know it can happen. Trust me, it can! You've done a million instant replays, and you're probably not exactly certain *how* you screwed up.

A screw-up is hard to swallow, but it might not be your fault. Possible is the very rare instance of a genuine bullet failure. If that is the case and you hit the basketball and wound the animal, this usually becomes a matter of how far and how long you will have to track. Buffaloes do not possess magical powers. With the assumption that you are using one of the dozens of adequate calibers and suitable bullets, if you hit the basketball in the right place, the buffalo will be dead. Hit high, low, forward, or back, and there is a reasonable chance that buffalo will never be seen again, or it will kill someone. The former is far more likely than the latter.

I think this business of black animal in black shadow coupled with excitement are the primary reasons for poor shots on buffaloes. The target is always huge—if you can see it—and the range is never long. I don't think we need to worry about wind deflection, and if holdover is an issue, you're too far away to be shooting at a buffalo. Wobbles are an issue since relatively few shots at buffaloes will be from dead-steady positions. If that is the case, shooting sticks will help. On the other hand, it takes a lot of movement to set up sticks, and sometimes, especially at close range, it isn't possible to use them; other times the ground is too uneven or there's too much vegetation. So, shooting sticks, although useful, are not a *panacea* for placing good shots at buffaloes. I've often taken a quick rest off a handy tree, and sometimes, at close range, I've had to stand up and shoot. Ultimately placing a good shot on a buffalo is a skill and no different from anything else: Practice and learn to get quickly steady and comfortable from a wide range of positions. In field shooting, one of our old Marine Corps mantras is perfect: *Adapt and overcome!*

If you do a lot of buffalo hunting, it's inevitable that you'll take some close-range shots from an unsupported standing position. This is never desirable, but it will happen! Over the years I've also taken several buffaloes from kneeling and sitting positions. I *think* I've taken just one buffalo from a proper prone position. It was 1996, the Save Valley Conservancy was new, and its newly reintroduced buffalo

A close encounter like this is unusual, but there are times when the only option is to raise the rifle and fire.

population had just increased to where a small quota was possible. There were some good bulls around, but Roger Whittall and I had seen a really cool (and rare) freak buffalo. This animal had one normal horn and the other was pointing straight-down like an upside-down eland horn. We knew which group he was in, so on a hot midday we crawled into their bedroom. It was really miserable creeping on our hands and knees over blistering scorched ground.

We got within sixty to eighty yards of the bedded herd with our bull inside a tight cluster. It was a horrible situation: His head was to the right, and he was snoozing away on his side with his legs to us. Honest, this is a terrible shot and should be avoided because it's very difficult to be certain where the vitals lie because of the animal's position on the ground. Ideally you wait for them to get up. We waited a long time in the broiling heat with our elbows, hands, and knees skinned raw. Eventually I crawled into a clear spot and took a NRA prone position, made the sling tight on my arm, and grounded my elbows and body.

I was shooting a Dakota Model 10 single-shot in .375 Dakota. No matter what, there would be just one shot. This was a classic situation where the dark animal and dark shadows confounded both the aiming point and the visualization of the vital zone. We had time, so we crawled this way and that. Roger and I eventually agreed that the fork of a dead snag just short of the buffalo formed an ideal "V" with the base pointing the way. I took a deep breath and pressed the trigger. The group wasn't large, but it doesn't take many buffaloes to make a lot of dust and noise! I had no idea what I'd done, or failed to do, but when the dust settled we found our bull down and dead fifty yards away.

I hope you know that in my writing I try to be both honest and modest about my shooting. I'm competent—better than some and worse than others—but I'm hardly infallible. It's been my experience that most shots at buffaloes are technically simple; this one was difficult and, I admit, a bit risky. It goes in my notebook as one of very few "post-graduate" shots at buffaloes . . . it was a reasonable opportunity, but I needed to be very, very steady and certain.

When I was a young hunter, the unfamiliar "dark animal" issue combined with pure anxiety complicated my early shots at buffaloes. There was more. I grew up as a Western hunter, accustomed to glassing and stalking in relatively open country. I was a whiz at crawling through sagebrush to stalk pronghorns and mule deer, but as a young hunter I had almost no exposure to close-cover hunting, and please note: Much buffalo hunting is in close cover. The target is just as large, but I had no experience trying to pick out a buffalo through intervening cover. Doesn't matter that it's big and black—in the early days I can't tell you how often I just couldn't see the buffalo. Mind you, this also applied to other species. I just didn't have the experience to find the bits and pieces of an animal through the latticework of thornbush.

I don't know how you learn this except through trial and error. Depending on where you come from, you might be good at it. Elk and deer hunters from the Pacific Northwest are used to still-hunting in rainforest-like habitat. Eastern whitetail hunters could be good at it, but it seems to me that still-hunting, stalking slowly through thick cover, has been largely supplanted by stand hunting. Hunting from stands is a skill unto its own, placing reliance on patience and powers of observation, listening as well as watching. Done right, stand hunting isn't easy and can be exhausting, but I'm not sure it serves as preparation for much of anything else except stand hunting, which is not uncommon but specialized in Africa. You don't hunt buffalo from stands!

The powers of observation of African trackers—and some experienced and skilled PHs—are amazing. You've tracked for hours, and then one of the team stops and points. Depending on the cover, you may be sixty yards or a matter of feet from a buffalo. Maybe they've seen an out-of-place black spot, a horizontal line, or glint of horn. Often, it's a matter of texture as much as substance, but whatever it is, these guys know it's a buffalo even if you can't see it. In thick vegetation it's not just an anomaly but a major breakthrough if you, rather than the trackers, see a buffalo first. Although comment is unlikely, they will be personally and professionally embarrassed if this happens. Most of the time you can't beat them, but you can learn to pay attention, watching their body language, freezing when they stop instead of blundering forward.

Then there are the little things, which are not so little if you're the one who steps on a stick at the wrong moment. I also wasn't very good at learning to walk slowly and quietly or to always pay attention to the wind. African trackers are the masters, moving through thick cover almost like ghosts. I've found that especially when you're in close contact, it's a matter of almost sliding along rather than stepping.

All too often we unthinkingly choose the wrong gear. Soft, quiet shoe soles are amazingly important. The aggressive Vibram soles we might choose for traction in hilly country can be ridiculously loud when stalking. Once, when I was wearing typical hunting boots, a PH complained about the noise I was making, so I put on soft-soled shoes and even I (pre-hearing aids!) could hear the difference.

Clothing also matters. In most areas PHs wear shorts. This is not necessarily for keeping cool but because thorns catch on cloth while bare legs slide through silently. The tradeoff is you get scratched, but for sure shorts are quieter. This is not a universal truism. In swampy country long trousers and long sleeves are essential because of leeches, and in the forest zone there are just too many biting ants to leave flesh exposed. Soft cotton is generally quieter than synthetics. The differences are subtle, but when it comes down to taking just another few steps to open up a shot, you need to be as silent as possible. Learn to watch where you place your feet and pay attention to the placement of each foot. Once again, you probably can't beat the

Learning to walk quietly is one of the most important skills in buffalo hunting. Watch the trackers and PH, follow their body language, and try to step where they step.

experts, but you can make their jobs easier . . . and make your own hunt more successful.

Although I've done a great deal of buffalo hunting, it is a gross overstatement to say I'm an expert at it. As we said in the Marines: I'm not fit to carry the jockstraps of good African trackers or experienced PHs. It's still their turf, and I'm not even a gifted amateur.

That said, I'm a whole lot better at it than I was forty years ago!

As I said, always it's a matter of *seeing* buffalo, but that's just the beginning. The next step is to recognize a good bull when you see one. The former is always difficult; the latter you can learn over time. At first you'll find it quite difficult to tell the bulls from the cows. Both have similar horns, so this initial learning curve is steep. Given the chance to observe buffaloes, you'll catch on quickly. As with instantly knowing a buck whitetail from a doe, you'll see it in the bigger, blockier body, and often by the placement in a herd. When buffaloes are moving, the bulls are often in the rear, sometimes in the front, but rarely in the middle. Cows tend to be blacker and "slicker." Mature bulls often appear gray and scabby, and are more likely to be caked with mud. On more open ground you can readily see the penis sheath—but in thick vegetation you have to get pretty close to view this part of the bull's anatomy.

Next, to become a skilled buffalo hunter, you must be able to quickly tell whether a mature bull has a hard boss. Honest, you have to look at a lot of buffaloes to consistently do this accurately. This is a gentle learning curve that takes a lot of time. It's easy to rule out the youngsters with green, hairy horn bases. Sorting the seven- and eight-year-olds from fully mature bulls two or three years older, however, is art rather than science. This takes years of study, and in that marginal "almost there" zone, even the best and most experienced hunters will err once in a while.

The actual hunting of buffalo hasn't changed much in my time, and probably hasn't changed much in the last century. When I was just beginning, in the 1970s and 1980s, I was bumbling in my attempts, but through trial and error I got better. By the turn of the millennium, I thought I had this buffalo stuff figured out pretty well. At that time most of my buffalo hunting had been done in thornbush country, a lot in Tanzania, Zambia, and Zimbabwe. I'd done some buffalo hunting in the forest zone, and early on I hunted several times in northern Botswana. Hunting buffaloes in the Okavango's mosaic of channels and palm islands was different, but my opinion was that buffalo hunting was buffalo hunting. This was and is absolutely true!

You'll find a lot of variables when hunting buffaloes. Vegetation varies a lot. In the south mopane is the dominant tree, so we call it mopane forest. Farther north the soil becomes sandy, and we call it *miombo* forest. Above the forest zone and below the Sahara, Terminalia becomes dominant and we call it Terminalia forest. Density varies tremendously, and for me this makes the biggest difference in buffalo hunting. From south to north and east to west, buffaloes will vary in horn shape and color as you move from one subspecies to another. Habitat also causes variations in buffalo behavior: True forest buffalo almost never form big herds and are generally found in small family groups, similar to the water buffaloes. But whether this is a true difference or based on local habitat and food sources, I simply can't say. I can say that, regardless of race or subspecies or local density,

A group of bachelor bulls taking a nap in open acacia forest in Uganda's Karamoja region. When buffaloes are lying down, the best approach is usually to be patient and wait for them to get up.

the thicker the cover the more difficult the hunting. We'll discuss this in greater detail later.

I'm convinced it's the thick cover that makes hunting the dwarf forest buffalo so much more difficult. You must get very close in order to get a shot—and, typically, the thicker the cover, the noisier it is to make a final approach. Exactly the same is true of hunting buffalo on the slopes of Masailand's densely forested mountains. These are plain old southern Cape buffaloes, same as the buffalo found in the Selous and Serengeti. Buffalo densities are generally much higher than off to the west in the true forest zone, but the hunting is still very difficult because it's hard to get close enough because of the noise factor.

I don't buy into the local beliefs that forest buffaloes and northwestern savanna buffaloes are "more aggressive" than southern Cape buffaloes. Heck, knowledgeable PHs in Tanzania have told me that their "mountain" buffaloes are more aggressive than the buffaloes on their plains. There may be a greater incidence of problems, but I can't buy that the buffaloes are different; I think it's more a matter that, as cover gets thicker, you must approach closer to get a shot. The closer you need to get, the more likely you are to run into trouble. That's my story, but I can't prove it.

The last dozen years I've hunted buffaloes in coastal Mozambique, specifically in Coutadas 10, 11, and 14 surrounding the Marromeu Reserve. Here the vast majority of buffaloes—one of the greatest concentrations on the continent—are found on the floodplains and in papyrus swamps. Much smaller numbers of buffaloes, generally in smaller herds, have shifted out to the surrounding *miombo* forests. It's the same buffalo, but hunting them is so different that locally the outfitters refer to them as "swamp" and "forest" buffaloes, although obviously they are all southern Cape buffaloes. Hunting them in the forest is extremely difficult because through most of the season it's extremely noisy there, so it becomes sort of like stalking over a layer of corn flakes. Although I tried many times, I never got a buffalo "in the forest" until 2017. While it's difficult hunting, the good news is that there are now more buffaloes in the forest than ten years ago, and they are increasing; quite a few are tracked and taken each year, just as they are in thornbush and woodland elsewhere.

While you won't catch me saying that the "swamp buffaloes" are different, *hunting them* is different. It's no secret that I wrote another book on buffalo hunting, now nearly fifteen years ago. I'm not at all displeased with that book, but I know more now than I did then. Perhaps my greatest regret in that earlier volume comes under the heading, "You don't know what you don't know." When that book was published, I had done very little swamp buffalo hunting; now, with more understanding, I can say that I've found it to be neither better nor worse but a vastly different experience. Some will like it better, others not as much, but it's different enough that it deserves a chapter later in this book.

There are also differences in the habits of the swamp buffaloes. Herds tend to be much larger. It's hard to come up with an average because we do see groups of fifty or sixty buffaloes—but it's more common to see herds into the hundreds. I've even seen—probably temporary—gatherings into the low thousands. More interesting, bachelor groups are rare and most herds contain several mature bulls. I can't explain this. We do see occasional lone bulls and bachelor groups, but not enough to reliably seek them as is done in so many areas. We hunt the herds, reasonably secure in the knowledge that a big herd will hold mature bulls.

While approaches and methodology vary, it's still buffalo hunting, no matter the locale. Mozambique has emerged as a major buffalo hunting destination, far more important than it was at the turn of the millennium. Other things have changed as well. Botswana has not "closed," but at this writing "safari hunting" on government land is suspended. That means buffalo hunting is closed. Whether open or not, Botswana has changed. In the 1980s Botswana rivaled Zimbabwe for shorter buffalo safaris, and there were oceans of buffaloes in big herds.

I assume Botswana still holds plenty of buffaloes, but nothing like thirty years ago. This is almost certainly a byproduct of her elephant overpopulation, which has impacted all species. Establishing protections for lions and leopards hasn't helped, and her long-nurtured roan and sable populations have suffered mightily. I believe Botswana will reopen in some fashion by 2020, at least in part because her quarter-million elephants simply must be somehow managed. Even so, I doubt she will become an important buffalo destination because the big numbers are no longer there.

Tanzania, Zambia, and Zimbabwe remain important buffalo countries. Over the years I've spent a lot of time in Namibia, but it's only been recently that I've hunted buffaloes there. Because Namibia is so arid, buffalo habitat is naturally limited. Unlike her neighbors and competitors in South Africa, Namibian game ranchers are not allowed to breed buffaloes because of concerns over bovine diseases. Thus, Namibia has relatively few buffaloes and quotas are short. Against that, genetics are spectacular in areas such as Caprivi (now called the "Zambezi Region") and isolated areas such as the Waterberg. Meantime, South African game ranchers have really gotten the jump and have been breeding disease-free buffaloes at a frantic pace. South African genetics are also exceptional, and as the number have come up, age class distribution has improved and prices have come down. South Africa is now extremely competitive for buffalo safaris, but I'll write more about that in the next chapter.

Elsewhere on the continent relatively little has changed. For the western subspecies, Benin, Burkina Faso, and Cameroon are solid. The Central African Republic is also good, but at this writing unstable, but that's not new; C.A.R. has periodic issues, but it's a wild and remote country and one of my favorite places when it's safe—just pay attention to the status of the country before you go there. The Congo is currently the best place for dwarf forest buffalo. I hunted there in May 2017, and

Given a choice I'll always use a rest, either sticks or a natural rest. Sometimes, however, extra movement can't be risked, so it's wise to spend a lot of range time practicing unsupported standing.

although I got beaten (again), it wasn't for a lack of buffaloes! Gabon was also very good for this smallest and most difficult of buffaloes. It has recently reopened, but at this writing, the buffalo is not on license.

Another small but important change is, having now been open (again) for about a decade, wildlife numbers are coming up fast in Uganda. Uganda is thus "the" place for Nile buffalo. Moreover, her buffalo hunting is spectacular, especially up in the northeast. Ethiopia's buffaloes have been, I think properly, reclassified from Nile buffalo to "East African savanna buffalo." Hunting is solid there, and this is the only place for this race of buffaloes, but despite the huge size of the country and almost unlimited habitat, overall numbers are low, outfitters are few, and the quota is small.

There are other opportunities for buffaloes here and there. I still think Angola will eventually reopen, but there has been little recent momentum. More positive is South Sudan, especially in East Equatoria in the southeast where Nile buffaloes are plentiful. Africa is Africa and change is constant. I expect little impact on buffalo hunting, but I know now that my own learning curve will never flatten out!

The 96th Buffalo, an Education

Chapter 4

When I take a fresh track, I expect to close with buffaloes, but I don't necessarily anticipate a shot. To some extent that depends on my frame of mind, and, specifically, on how picky I'm feeling. This, in turn, depends on how long the hunt has progressed, how much time remains, and how this particular hunt fits into my goals. If I'm hunting with someone else, maybe Donna, a friend, or one of my daughters, it may be more important for somebody else to get a shot and, perhaps, a better buffalo. In my world, unfortunately, business also enters the picture. Perhaps I have a special rifle or a new cartridge that I'm itching to try. Always of concern, of course, is the story. Perhaps we're filming a TV episode where it's necessary to take a shot. While these may not be good reasons to end an animal's life, they're my reality.

So, unless it's somebody else's hunt altogether and I'm just following along, I can't imagine taking a buffalo track without desiring to close on the herd, sort out the bulls, and take a shot if we find a buffalo that suits my fancy on that particular day. Honestly, I'm not usually looking for the biggest bull in the area. Chances are I'll never have another buffalo mounted. The meat will be utilized, of course, and certainly I'm only looking for a mature bull, preferably an *old* bull, but these days I'd just as soon leave a monster for someone who will take it home and appreciate it.

That decision must wait until we find the buffaloes. When a fresh track is taken, this is likely, but you really don't know what's going to happen . . . and for sure you don't know what kind of bulls might

This is one of the most beautiful buffalo bulls I've ever seen! He's in a disease-free breeding herd not far from Kruger National Park; South Africa's genetics for good horn quality are second to none.

be in the group. Whether you'll be lucky depends a lot on the wind. Wind can change and moving buffaloes can change direction. It also depends on how far the buffaloes will travel and what the vegetation is like when you close. You never can predict how these variables will affect the hunt when you set out, but when I start a fresh track, I expect to see the group and have some chance to sort them out.

I was hunting with Diekie Muller, and on the first day we found fresh tracks shortly after dawn. The cover was fairly thick, but at that time of day the wind was constant and probably would remain steady for several hours. I doubt we'd gone half an hour when we heard branches break ahead, typical sounds from feeding buffaloes. So far this was going perfectly . . . and a bit too easy. Six hours later, with the winds swirling in the midday heat, we gave it up. We had a visual on these buffaloes a half-dozen times, always in very thick bush. They were a group of bachelor bulls, exactly how many we were never certain, but there were between six and ten. From the glimpses we got, there were some really good bulls among them, but we never had a chance for a shot. OK, that isn't true. Once, in the late morning, we had a too-young bull feeding broadside at ten yards. There were other bulls just beyond him, close but completely hidden . . . and then they all crashed away.

A few days later and not so early, we had picked up two bulls and followed them a long way. On that day the cover was a bit more open, scattered mopane thickets interspersed with small clearings—all in all very good country for tracking buffaloes. The tracks meandered; our buffaloes were looking for a place to lie down. We knew we were very close. Then, as so often happens, one of our trackers made a miraculous spot, correctly interpreting a dark patch in black shadow as a bedded buffalo. We had them, and Diekie Muller set up the sticks. In that moment I felt a swirl of breeze kiss the back of my neck, and instantly they were up and running, clattering away into the distance.

Hunting is unusual in that it is a solitary sport. There may be witnesses, whether hunting buddies or "helpers" such as guides and trackers, but there are no teammates and no gallery. There are game laws, which I consider inviolable, but there is no rule book. There are, however, ethics, which I consider a personal matter. What matters ultimately is that you can look at yourself in the mirror. There are also concepts such as fair chase, native range, and free range. These are difficult concepts to define with absolute precision.

In June 2017 I was hunting buffaloes in South Africa's Limpopo province, one of the centers of South Africa's game-ranching industry. Just twenty years ago buffaloes were extremely scarce and prices for the few available surplus bulls were outrageous. Thanks to active breeding programs—and huge investment in disease-free breeding stock—this has changed. Today buffaloes are very common in the Limpopo and, literally, found and hunted countrywide, though certainly not present on all properties. There are exceptions here and there, but most South African buffaloes are restricted, if not confined. To put a point on it, they are behind game fencing. It's up to you and your reflection in the mirror to determine exactly how much acreage is "enough."

Yes, you are correct: It's impossible to establish even an approximate size because so much depends on the vegetation and terrain. It can be said, fairly I think, that the vast majority of South African buffaloes are not free range. Whether the concept "native range" applies or not poses a question. Most of South Africa, except where too arid, is original buffalo habitat. However, most buffaloes were gone before the nineteenth century turned to the twentieth, eradicated to make way for ranching. Only remnants remained in deepest sanctuaries that became parks, such as the Addo and Kruger. Both areas, and few others, still hold native-range herds.

Buffaloes on private land have been reintroduced. Whether they can offer "fair-chase" hunting depends on your sense of the term. In North America the Boone and Crockett Club, our oldest conservation organization and the traditional keeper of North American records, drew a line in the sand decades ago: If an animal is behind a game fence, it cannot go into the club's records, regardless of acreage or habitat. Period. This is a strict interpretation for record-keeping purposes, but I'm sure we're all aware that game fencing is common in Namibia and South Africa and in other parts of the world, including Argentina and New Zealand . . . and let's not forget Texas.

I try hard to avoid high fences. How you feel about them is up to you; we have free choice whether to go in the gate. The late Bob Penfold, a great South Pacific outfitter, preferred the term "wild and free." South African buffaloes are not "free," but I quickly learned that they can be extremely "wild"! I didn't expect my buffalo hunt in South Africa to be difficult, but I was learning fast, and at least in my mind I was there to learn.

It's not my job as a hunting journalist to rain on anyone's parade, but until 2017 I'd avoided South African buffaloes. Fences were one reason. Until that hunt, most of my buffalo hunting had been totally free range. The only exceptions were on a couple of Zimbabwe's big conservancies, Bubye and the Save Valley. At the times I hunted on them, each area encompassed around a million acres. Again, if we take the strictest interpretation, then to have a fence is to be fenced. It's an absolute in the same way that you cannot be "a little bit pregnant." You either are or you're not; you either have a fence or you do not. Moreover, the average private property in South Africa that holds buffaloes is a whole lot smaller than the conservancies in Zimbabwe!

Pieter Slabbert of Bandur Safaris and his tracker confer on fresh buffalo tracks. Located in the Limpopo Valley, Slabbert is among a new generation of South African outfitters specializing in buffalo hunting.

There were other reasons I had avoided hunting buffaloes in South Africa. There are plenty of free-range options that exist elsewhere on the continent, so I didn't see the point. That's not quite all, however. With numbers low and surplus bulls scarce, I had two other concerns. First, with limited supply, prices were too high; genuine free-range buffalo safaris in Mozambique and Zimbabwe were half the price of the South African trophy fee alone. It didn't make sense to me, but it did have appeal for folks who had concerns about their safety while hunting in other countries.

Buffalo genetics in South Africa are exceptional, no doubt enhanced by selective breeding programs. Genetics mean nothing, however, unless the bulls are allowed to mature. Up until a decade or so back, my final concern about South African buffaloes, from so many photos I saw, was that, with limited supply and increasing demand—at

An awesome breeding bull in typically thick Addo thornbush in South Africa's Eastern Cape. Most South African buffaloes are in private herds, now found in literally all parts of the country. This bull is on Barry Burchell's Frontier Safaris's property, inland from Port Elizabeth.

any price—many bulls were too young. They were wide and beautiful, but they were nowhere near hard-bossed and mature.

So, I wrote off hunting buffaloes in South Africa, but that was then and now is now. The properties are still fenced, but as numbers increased, prices fell . . . and then there are the great genetics. Today, price-wise, South African buffalo hunts are competitive with Mozambique and Zimbabwe, and trophy quality is excellent—and just getting better as numbers continue to increase and more bulls grow older. In my writing and many speaking engagements, I damned with faint praise. I didn't have much to say about South African buffalo hunting, and the changes went right over my head. I was aware prices had dropped, and I was seeing more and more photos of great bulls. I figured if I was prepared to knock it, I'd better take a look or keep my mouth shut.

So, at an SCI fundraiser at Dennis Anderson's place in Southern California, I bought a South African hunt. It wasn't exactly a buffalo hunt, but I knew the outfitter, Diekie Muller, and we agreed to upgrade to include a buffalo. I figured it would probably be a bit too easy, but at least I'd get to see what it was all about.

Five days in and it wasn't looking so easy! Some days it took longer than others, but we found fresh tracks to follow every day, and we caught up with buffaloes every day. Not only did we not shoot; we never had a chance for a shot. We were hunting in a place up the road from Diekie's camp. By Limpopo standards at several thousand acres, it was pretty large. This is not large at all as buffalo areas go, but most of it was thick thornbush. As we tracked day after day, it felt large enough! After a day or two I felt success was just a matter of time. Eventually I came to the sobering realization that, although the buffaloes were there and weren't going anywhere, I might well run out of time before I got a shot.

Partly it was the uniformly thick cover, which always makes buffalo hunting difficult, but I also had to accept that these buffaloes were extremely switched-on. In years gone by I've hunted buffaloes in a couple of areas that were being heavily poached. On the Upper Chinko River in 1994 the place was being cleaned out by poaching gangs coming in from Sudan. Every day we heard AK-47 shots from one direction or another, and we tried to stay as far away from them as we could. By hunting hard we took most of the available species in the area, including Derby eland.

Meanwhile, the buffaloes had gotten the message. The few groups we tried to follow took us for miles, and when we finally caught up, they proved almost impossible to approach. Another time, in 2006 in southern Tanzania, I saw a similar situation. Ivory poachers had worked the area over, and although the antelope species were relatively untouched, the buffaloes were crazy wild. The groups we followed took us inordinately long distances, and when we caught up, they seemed impossible to approach.

The situation with the South African buffaloes was different. There was no poaching going on, and very little hunting pressure. The buffaloes were traveling normally, watering and feeding and moving into bedding cover, yet they were extremely wary. Hey, it always depends on wind and cover. If the wind is against you, there's no chance, and sometimes they would stop in cover so thick that no approach can work.

On the afternoon of the sixth day we had a nearly perfect situation. We were looking for fresh tracks when we saw several bulls feeding. We managed to slip past them and get around the wind. Hindsight being so perfect, we might have tried a direct approach, but we were sure they were feeding into a small meadow, so we waited for them. With distant sightings through brush and the occasional grunt or stick breaking, we knew exactly where they were, so we held tight while the clock ticked toward sundown.

Eventually it became clear we were going to run out of time, so we crawled a couple hundred yards and set up. About the same time, the buffaloes finally made their move, coming down a little rise and crossing the head of a gully within easy range. Just to make things more interesting, I was using a big .460 Smith & Wesson revolver mounted with an Aimpoint, which meant I was totally underestimating these buffaloes. We set the sticks up for a sitting position, and I had the red dot on a fine bull that was about sixty yards away . . . but I decided I had left it too late because there was too little light to be sure. I passed on the shot.

That's buffalo hunting. No matter how perfect things almost are, there isn't always a shot. However, during that frustrating week, we got thwarted so many times—when everything seemed *almost* right—that I realized I was overlooking some things. South African buffaloes don't have limitless expanses to roam, but this changes the nature of the pursuit, in some ways, in their favor. First, they know every rock and tree in their limited habitat. More important, they know the prevailing air currents and exactly where to bed to their best advantage. Also, although on most properties only a couple of buffaloes will be hunted every year, they don't know that every kudu or impala hunter isn't after *them*. They know humans are bad news and learn very well how best to avoid them.

There's another factor that only came to me recently. On any given property, the buffalo range is limited, but so are the buffaloes. Private

Preparing a braai *at Diekie Muller's camp. One of the advantages to South African buffalo hunting is it is often conducted from the same comfortable camps as plains-game safaris.*

PH Diekie Muller did a fine job on my South African buffalo hunt . . . and wound up stopping a serious charge after I messed up the shot! The hunt was much more difficult than I expected, and I completely underestimated the situation.

herds are not large, perhaps into the dozens, and almost never into the hundreds. This means that, of necessity, you often must track the same groups multiple times. This can happen in wild country, too, and the result is the same. The best chance for a shot is the first encounter. Whether you blow it or the stalk gets blown for you, by shifting wind or whatever, odds decrease with each encounter, with the buffaloes becoming progressively warier and harder to approach.

After my hunt with Diekie, I spent some time at other buffalo properties, including Pieter Slabbert's Bandur Safaris and at Stanley Pieterse's place. Pieter had a buffalo hunt going and I accompanied them for several days. The experience was similar to mine: thick cover, buffaloes that were difficult to approach, things becoming more difficult with each encounter. At Stanley's place, well, his buffaloes were on parade, and I got some great photos, so it always depends on luck. Then again, we weren't actually trying to shoot one!

Like most South African operators, Diekie Muller hunts on multiple properties. We had other options, but after five days I was getting stubborn. These damn South African buffaloes weren't going to beat me! Except they did. After getting so close on the sixth evening, I caved in. On the seventh day, with me running short on time, we went to a different property where we could find some "new" buffaloes. The landowner's son told us where we should look, and even so we hiked for about three hours before we located a small group.

Oh, Lord, it was a perfect setup! The buffaloes, a small group of bulls, were on the uphill side of a grassy clearing with thick brush above them and below us. Diekie set up the sticks and we agreed on the biggest bull, which was on the right of the group and quartering nicely to me—I clearly saw the red Aimpoint dot vivid on his shoulder. I started the trigger press, and in that moment, after all that effort, I blew it! The buffalo turned to his left, my right, and I swear the hammer was falling, but I couldn't call it back. I tried for a second shot, *anywhere*, but I was too late. My bull mixed with the group as they all ran up the hill into the thick brush. Diekie, on binoculars, said, "That looked good. How did it feel?"

After all his effort, I hated to tell him, but I *knew*. So, wishing he was right, I told him the ugly truth. "Too far back, he moved out of the shot."

Unfortunately, I was exactly correct. We saw the bull again twice that day, once in a close encounter in thick riverine vegetation where there was no way to be sure if it was the same bull. Again, we saw him just before dark moving along a strand of cover, but we couldn't be sure it was him. We took the spoor again at dawn. Sometimes we saw sporadic blood, most times not. I guess this is a small advantage with these buffaloes; their range is not unlimited. They can't leave the country, but they can—and this one did—circle endlessly. At midday the next day, we again saw blood, just a smear on a leaf or stalk every thirty or forty yards, headed downhill into dense thickets along the major watercourse. By then we had some help, so my team

Most private herds in South Africa are fairly small, but trophy quality is excellent. Look at the bull coming over the rise behind these younger bulls!

tried to work out the direction of the blood while Diekie and his lead tracker looped ahead.

Diekie and his tracker made it to the bull first. We heard a grunt as the buffalo rose from his bed, then Diekie's prized .470 Krieghoff boomed once. Short pause, then the second barrel thundered. Diekie had seen a suspicious dark spot in black shadow under thick thorn. Carefully, he took two steps forward, the buffalo rose, grunted once, and launched himself at Diekie. The first shot was perfect, just beside the bull's right eye. When I got there, it was all over. I measured six yards from the buffalo's nose to Diekie's shoelaces.

In the postmortem my shot was exactly as I'd called it, too far back. Penetration from the .460 S&W was absolutely adequate, but a bullet must hit the right spot. This was all my fault, totally, and without question it was a serious charge. If Diekie hadn't used his Krieghoff .470 properly, the buffalo would have run over him and might have killed him.

My theory is that "buffalo are buffalo." Across Africa lots of folks maintain "their buffaloes" are more aggressive than elsewhere. Usually I think the big difference comes down to the average distance in encounters; thus, forest and western buffaloes have a fierce reputation because, in closer cover, you bump into them at such close range. However, albeit fenced and products of selective breeding programs, the South African buffaloes are serious opponents. Diekie Muller is a careful and experienced hunter and a good tracker, but this was not his first charge nor, since then, his last! I had to leave before Pieter Slabbert's client got a shot. Like my hunt, it happened on the seventh day, and, like my hunt, this one also required a follow-up that ended in a charge.

I will not say South Africa buffaloes are *more* aggressive than any other African buffalo. Place the first shot right and no further discussion is needed. However, the Limpopo thornbush is serious stuff. There is also that which we don't like to talk about: These buffaloes are essentially livestock, handled and moved now and again, and probably not happy about it. It is not impossible that they have either lost respect for man or acquired hatred for our kind.

Another factor is that most South African buffaloes are taken by inexperienced plains-game hunters who "upgrade." Add to that, most South African PHs have limited experience on dangerous game. No slurs are intended.

This was my 96th buffalo, and I screwed up the shot. It happens. Diekie Muller and Pieter Slabbert are among few South African PHs who, with opportunities growing, concentrate on buffalo. They have guided a lot of clients to buffaloes and know how to handle bad situations, but in their part of Africa buffalo hunting and, thus the opportunity to gain experience, is fairly new. Few South Africans have the experience of PHs to the north who grew up hunting buffalo.

For sure I am not done hunting buffaloes, but whether I will hunt another South African buffalo is up for question. The genetics are superb, perhaps unmatchable elsewhere, and the prices are now competitive. Once you are behind the gate, the experience differs little. For myself, whatever African hunting that remains ahead for me, I'd probably just as soon not go through a gate. I concede, however, that I have been wrong about South African buffalo hunting. The experience can be and should be good, and these buffaloes offer a sound option. This is sure: Whatever you think of them, South Africa's buffaloes think of themselves as real buffaloes. Neither the hunt nor the animals should be underestimated.

Changing Culture

Chapter 5

More than forty years have passed since my first safari. African hunting has changed, and buffalo hunting has changed. The physical actions involved with hunting the African buffalo and the methodologies employed haven't changed much, if at all. However, the sociology of buffalo hunting has changed, and the priority given to hunting buffalo has changed. The value of a buffalo and the cost of a buffalo safari have risen dramatically.

Mind you, the buffalo has always been an important part of the African scene, easily the most available and, excepting the leopard, the most widespread of Africa's dangerous game. In days gone by, average safaris were much longer, allowable bags were more generous, and safaris weren't nearly as specialized as they are today. All these assertions must be taken in context. The epic Roosevelt safari lasted about nine months. This was not normal even in 1909, nor was a bag running into the hundreds normal. Even in that altogether different time the Roosevelts were criticized for excess. I offer no defense here, but there is a mitigating factor, which is the expedition was under museum sponsorship "for science." Also, in the East Africa of 1909, few game laws existed to guide hunting ethics and promote restraint; consequently, there was very little restraint.

Those of us who consider ourselves "Africa nuts" generally believe that a "safari" as we know it started with the Roosevelt expedition. That's fair enough, especially since several of the local settlers engaged to shepherd the Roosevelts remained as part of the fledgling safari industry in East Africa. In 1909 Philip Percival was just a youngster,

The days of longer "truck-mobile" safaris are pretty much over, with most hunting now done from permanent camps. This was, perhaps, the largest safari of all, the huge convoy that attended the filming of Howard Hawks's Hatari *(starring John Wayne) in 1962.* (Photo courtesy of John Dugmore)

but he came to be called "the dean of professional hunters," and as almost the permanent president of the East African Professional Hunters Association, he was largely responsible for instituting the traditions, mores, and game laws that guide us to this day.

The EAPHA was the first organization to establish "minimum calibers" for dangerous game; their original rule was .40-caliber for thick-skinned game, which technically outlawed the .375 for buffalo. Not all rules were universally followed even "in the day." For instance, hunters were not allowed to shoot within specified distances of a vehicle or a water source . . . and dalliance with a client was worth one's license. Clearly a victim of my generation, I originally described this last deadly sin as "dalliance with a female client." Unfortunately, this poor choice of words would have suggested all PHs are male and heterosexual, neither of which is true. So please forgive me my politically incorrect language, but allow me to keep that wonderfully archaic word "dalliance" rather than requiring millennium-speak such as "unprofessional or improper relationship."

Many restrictions became local law as colonial game regulations matured, but in 1909 that remained in the future. My assumption is that the Roosevelt party could have shot as many buffaloes as they desired—along with most everything else. "Most everything else" included nine northern white rhinos out of "Rhino Camp" in northwestern Uganda. Although a century plus a decade ago, the northern white rhino was already considered scarce; this was one of the most criticized extravagances of the Roosevelt expedition.

In actual fact, the Roosevelt safari shot relatively few buffaloes, but this was a matter of timing rather than intent. From the 1890s through the first decade of the twentieth century, a great rinderpest swept much of sub-Saharan Africa. It took years to reach East Africa, impacting some species—including buffalo, eland, and greater kudu—much more than others. It is possible that the kudu's spotty distribution in East Africa is the result of the species being nearly eradicated in the early years of the twentieth century. That's a personal theory, but for sure the Cape buffalo was scarce at the time of the Roosevelt safari and much less plentiful in East Africa than in decades to come—including today.

After World War I, what we call the "safari industry" started to take shape, as did the mythical "typical safari" of the day. It was certainly *not* the nine-month Roosevelt safari that romped across Kenya, Uganda, and a fair portion of Sudan! Safaris were longer, but not *that* long. Considering much greater travel time, a thirty-day safari was fairly short; and safaris of sixty to ninety days were common; in other words, safaris were counted in months rather than weeks. There were restrictions, licenses, and in most cases bag limits. Costs were laughable by today's standards, but the time and expense of steamship travel must be factored in. I don't think it's incorrect to say that an African safari between the World Wars was the province of the wealthy.

As for the bag, this depended on the area and, as today, hunters' preferences. This was a time when elephants with heavy ivory were available. Not necessarily readily—for sure there weren't hundred-pounders behind every bush—but elephants with big teeth could be pursued with some chance for success. As in years to come, there were "specialists" who offered hunts for big elephants, and famous names such as Denys Finch-Hatton and Bror Blixen were certainly among them. Even then the search for big ivory was specialized and time consuming.

But not everyone wanted to hunt elephants, and relatively few back then wanted to hunt leopards. A leopard might be taken in a chance encounter, but it was rarely hunted specifically. While lions were often primary pursuits, in some areas the lion remained classed as "vermin" into the 1950s. Buffaloes were certainly an important part of the menu, and most areas offered the opportunity to take multiples.

However, "collectors" as we think of it today were uncommon; choices of antelopes to be hunted were largely driven by availability in the areas to be hunted rather than a specific wish list, and general knowledge and recognition of African wildlife was far less prevalent than today. Ernest Hemingway's "Green Hills safari" in 1933 was, at least in some ways, typical of the era. The actual length of Hemingway's safari is uncertain; chances are it was not quite as long as he hinted at in his writing. (Ruark would do the same on his *Horn of the Hunter* safari almost twenty years later.) We could call Hemingway's safari a month-long affair and wouldn't be too far off.

Their PH, Philip Percival, was at the top of his game and in high demand; however, since Hemingway wasn't yet wealthy, his safari was largely financed by his father-in-law, who was. In those days East African safaris originated in Kenya, but the actual hunting was done in Tanganyika. By then vehicles were in common use, so it was common to "kit up" in Nairobi, then drive southward into northern Tanganyika.

Hemingway didn't hunt elephants, and apparently didn't spend much time looking for a leopard. His safari took multiple lions, and he also took a black rhino, which were plentiful in those days. We aren't quite certain how many buffaloes Hemingway hunted because *Green Hills* gives us only glimpses but not a day-to-day account of his hunts. We know Hemingway wounded and lost a buffalo, blaming the heavy trigger on his double—but we don't know for certain if he took other buffaloes—or how many. I wish we had a clearer picture of Hemingway's buffalo hunts, which took center stage in his fictional *The Short, Happy Life of Francis Macomber*.

Allow me two comments about this story: First, it invokes two events that were already serious no-no's: The PH's dalliance with Macomber's wife—you knew I'd find a way to use that word, didn't you?—and chasing a herd of buffaloes with a vehicle. Clearly other past, present, and future PHs have committed both transgressions, but it wouldn't have been in Philip Percival's nature to do so. Percival was a stickler for the code of ethics he largely created, and he probably wasn't any too pleased—conjecture on my part—to be part of Hemingway's literary legacy that clearly spoke of ethical violations. It is widely held by people who knew Philip Percival that he didn't care for Hemingway, and he went out of his way to steer clear when Papa returned to Africa twenty years later.

In the 1980s, Botswana competed with Zambia and Zimbabwe in the short "buffalo-and-plains-game" safari market. That is a much younger version of me and Jack Atcheson Jr. (second and third from left) after a ten-day safari in the Okavango with Vira Safaris.

During Hemingway's 1933 safari, he focused on two key antelope species, the greater kudu and the sable. Both, especially his search for a kudu, occupy major portions of *Green Hills of Africa* (1935). This is interesting because it was unusual for those times when safaris would typically focus on the hunting of dangerous game.

Fast-forward to 1952 and Robert Ruark's *Horn of the Hunter* safari, which gives an excellent picture of a typical post-WWII safari. By then Ruark and his wife, Virginia, could fly Pan-Am into Nairobi, get fitted overnight for proper safari duds, and then begin the trek south toward Tanganyika. According to the late Harry Selby, he was "assigned" the Ruark safari, not specifically requested. In 1952 John Henry "Harry" Selby was just a few years into perhaps the most remarkable career as a PH in the history of African hunting. For sure the Ruark safari launched him into legend and stardom, both as the central figure in the best-selling *Horn of the Hunter* (1953) but also as the model for Ruark's fictional hero, Peter McKenzie, in his blockbuster novel *Something of Value* that followed in 1955. Selby, soft-spoken and self-effacing, never seemed fully comfortable with the fame. Without question, he would have been a highly successful and probably legendary PH with or without Ruark. However, in a filmed interview in 2007 he told me he was just one among several equally competent East African PHs, any of whom could just as easily have been tasked with the Ruark safari.

In *Horn of the Hunter* we get the impression that the safari was lengthy. This is a common journalistic trick; especially on short hunts

I took this nice, old buffalo with one horn-tip broken in the Selous Reserve in 1988. Tanzania is among the few places that still offers multiple buffaloes on a license . . . but there are no guarantees!

it's rare that I give a chronological account precise enough to allow a day count! Selby recalled that the *Horn* safari was just three weeks. Perhaps he was mistaken and it was a bit longer, but it was not a three-month affair. Safaris of such length certainly existed long after World War II, but with travel time greatly reduced, a safari of about three weeks was customary . . . and would remain so until the 1980s.

The norm was a "general bag" safari including some mixture and multiples of the Big Five, along with available plains game. At that time air charters were unheard of and roads were terrible. There was little specialization, especially in the plains game department. After consulting with the client, the PH would select an area based on the game desired. Using trucks on the safari would allow the hunters access to multiple areas and expand the available game; however, there would be no rambling through Kenya, Uganda, and Sudan—not in a month or less!

Like Hemingway, Ruark chose not to hunt elephants on his first safari. He saved that—and black rhino—for subsequent safaris. He did take two lions, which was normal for the day, yet according to later writings, Ruark never took another lion. Interestingly, on that first safari he did take a leopard over bait using a scoped rifle. He got badly bitten by the leopard bug, which you could take in two ways because years later Ruark was badly mauled by an Asian leopard in India. We all build our "wish list" of game for different reasons. We know that Selby became famous for his success on leopards, so I wonder if Selby pushed Ruark into hunting leopard on that first safari or if Ruark came to it on his own?

Like Hemingway, Ruark became obsessed by the greater kudu, and his trials and travails with this antelope occupy a major portion of the *Horn of the Hunter*. He also spent a lot of time hunting buffaloes and took multiple fine bulls. The portions of "*Horn*" devoted to buffalo hunting are some of the very best on the subject in the entire body of Africana. In this book Ruark gave us perhaps the best known and most descriptive picture of the African buffalo when he said, ". . . he looks at you like you owe him money."

Well into the 1970s the normal three-week African safari included two to four of the Big Five. At least one buffalo—and usually multiples—were included on license. A permit to take a lion—by then one to a customer!—was often included, and some safaris would also hunt for leopard and/or elephant. This analysis is an oversimplification because the status quo that had held for so long throughout Africa was about to be overturned: By this time the winds of change were sweeping throughout Africa and with them came political change and widespread commercial poaching that threatened key species, including elephant, rhino, and leopard. Kenya and Tanzania remained the most popular destinations . . . until they suddenly weren't. Few saw these changes coming.

Tanzania closed all hunting in 1973, reopening four years later. Kenya closed elephant hunting in 1973 and closed all hunting in 1977. By then there were many other options. Harry Selby had opened Botswana in the early 1960s, accompanied and followed by other East African PHs. At the time Tanzania closed, options included Angola, Botswana, C.A.R., Chad, Mozambique, Rhodesia, Sudan, Uganda, and Zambia. Other losses came fast. The Portuguese pulled out quickly, leaving an unstable mess; consequently, hunting ground to a halt in Angola and Mozambique. Idi Amin came to power in Uganda, and the country became dangerous. Chad closed hunting in 1977. After Kenya closed, a number of her outfitters limped along in Sudan, but instability worsened and by 1983 Sudan was finished.

By the early 1980s options were generally limited to Botswana, C.A.R., Rhodesia (now Zimbabwe), newly reopened Tanzania, and Zambia. The safari industry had lost much ground, but the changes in the game populations were worse. Continent-wide the black rhino was nearly gone. Elephants had been nearly eradicated across much of East and Central Africa, leaving primarily the southernmost herds. The leopard was also impacted, especially given that leopard coats had become a high-fashion statement; in 1968 more than eight thousand leopard skins landed in New York. This rate of import was not supportable and far exceeded the current continent-wide CITES quota for sport-hunted leopards. Leopard hunting was far less successful then than now, and we forget that under the U.S. Spotted Cat Act and then our Endangered Species Act, Americans couldn't import leopard trophies from 1973 until the early 1980s.

In that period, the late 1970s and well into the 1980s, options to hunt elephants were limited and diminishing fast. It was still fairly common for a safari to have a lion on license. Most of us didn't realize it at the time, but lion numbers were also dwindling and success was low. I squeaked into Kenya in 1977 just before it closed. That safari was fairly typical of a dying era: twenty-one days, a truck-mobile safari with a staff of sixteen, and a lion as the primary goal. I didn't get my lion, but that wasn't unusual. The cost was three hundred bucks a day, trivial by today's standards.

Buffalo hunting remained constant, with multiple buffaloes the norm. In the last days of Kenya, one had to purchase specific licenses for each animal to be hunted. I bought two buffalo licenses; I don't honestly recall if I could have purchased more, but I could afford two. When Kenya closed weeks later, it no longer mattered. Unlike elephants and the great cats, buffaloes remained generally plentiful and most areas allowed more than one. A Ugandan hunting license allowed *five* buffaloes. In the 1980s I did several hunts in Zambia and Botswana; both were awesome buffalo countries back then. Hunting buffaloes wasn't a free-for-all, but it wasn't "one to a customer" either. Those days were coming soon, but hadn't happened quite yet. I was first in Tanzania in 1988; the situation then was much as it is now, with some of Africa's most detailed licensing. A three-week license allowed

This ancient buffalo looks like we "owe him money," Robert Ruark's great line that perfectly describes the African buffalo.

three buffaloes, with government fees increasing for the second and third. Tanzania was and is a very expensive safari destination, but once you get past the price of admission, many of her license fees, including for buffalo, were and are reasonable.

Mind you, whether one, two, or several, the legal authorization to hunt and harvest buffaloes isn't exactly the same as putting them in the salt. This depends on timing, effort, and plain old luck. I figured out fairly early that I really *like* hunting buffalo. It doesn't really matter if I get one or not, but I can't get enough of mixing with the herds . . . and I'm not done. So, over the years, when possible, I've gravitated toward areas where I might have the opportunity to take a second buffalo if things work out. This isn't gonna happen all the time.

Zambia is an awesome buffalo destination, and as a country it's yielded some of my all-time-best bulls. I've hunted there five times, but I never saw a mature buffalo on my first hunt there in 1983. On that first Zambian hunt, now thirty-six years ago, we hunted *hard* for buffalo, but couldn't make it happen. As I said, Tanzania is unique in today's Africa, offering three buffaloes on license with a definable structure. I don't mean to sound greedy—though perhaps I am where buffaloes are concerned!—but on the seven occasions I've hunted in Tanzania, I've always held at least a passing thought that I would take every buffalo allowed on license. It has happened, but not every time.

This buffalo bull has fairly narrow bosses, but what a wonderful spread! Bulls like this have always been exceedingly rare, but they still pop up now and again. This bull was photographed in Kenya in the 1960s. (Photo courtesy of John Dugmore)

Tanzania can be a wonderful place to hunt buffalo, but I've also been skunked there. Again, timing, effort, and *area, area, area!*

The opportunity to take multiple buffaloes also does not ensure that they keep getting bigger one by one! Having multiple buffaloes on license gives one the flexibility of looking for a nice bull and then looking for a better one. It also helps if there is a disaster when hunting, which, unfortunately, does happen. One of the real tragedies with the "one-to-a-customer" situation most common today is that if a buffalo is hit and not recovered there may be no *reclama* at any price.

Multiple buffaloes on license allow for a "spare" buffalo to be used to feed the camp or to provide bait(s) for cat hunting. As quotas and bag limits drop, the buffalo may be the only large animal left where a second animal is possible on a license. In some areas with high buffalo populations, there may be a quota for buffalo cows; on cat hunts there can be critical times when baits must be refreshed. These are not situations when it makes sense to look for big bulls!

In the 1980s, general-bag safaris remained common in Botswana, Tanzania, Zambia, and Zimbabwe's wilder areas. Elephant hunting was closed in Botswana and Zambia, but either leopards and/or lions were often "on license" along with multiple buffaloes. With the fur trade long since shut down, leopards recovered and hunting became more successful. However, finding a good lion has become increasingly difficult. Few of us understood how rapidly lion populations were diminishing in the face of increasing encroachment by humans and their cattle, but lion hunting was not yet the specialized undertaking it would soon become. What Ruark described in the 1950s as "the high cost of lions" was escalating rapidly.

Although the options for each country were reduced, the 1980s were wonderful times to hunt buffaloes. Botswana, Tanzania, Zambia, and Zimbabwe were fantastic, with high populations and big herds. This was not everywhere, never everywhere, but in wilder, less-settled areas of which there were still plenty. Buffaloes remained part of the bag on longer safaris, but during this time, two-week hunts became common, and they still included more than one of the Big Five. The "ten-day-buffalo" safari, now with a buffalo as the primary quarry, also became popular. We were still in those innocent pre-Internet, pre-cellphone days, but even so, life was becoming ever more hectic in Western civilization. A ten-day hunt could be squeezed into a normal two-week vacation period. Jet transportation was ever faster and more effective, and charter aircraft increased access and greatly reduced travel time.

Zimbabwe is not a large country, and her buffalo habitat lies on the periphery. Commercial flights primarily land in Harare and Victoria Falls, with some flights into Bulawayo. The entire country is within possible driving distance of these airports, or a short charter away. In the 1980s the "ten-day buffalo safari" became the mainstay of Zimbabwe's fast-growing safari industry. Perhaps oddly, it wasn't until the 1990s that I did such a hunt in Zimbabwe. Botswana offered strong competition in the 1980s, with high buffalo numbers and elephants not yet overpopulated. Zambia's operators were also in the running, offering shorter safaris with buffalo as a primary goal. All three countries offered a significant mix of plains game on license along with at least one buffalo, and often an extra buffalo could be had as well.

In the 1980s I did three, ten-day "buffalo-and-plains-game hunts" in Botswana. Buffaloes were so plentiful that we never spent time looking for tracks. We looked for herds, usually encountering two or three per day; we only tracked when moving herds outpaced us and we had to catch up!

Note, please, that I haven't yet said a word about Namibia and South Africa, the two countries that now have the largest and strongest safari industries. Together they host at least 60 percent of the entire continent's annual hunting safaris. The majority of these hunts in both countries are shorter "plains-game" safaris, with no dangerous game. This type of hunt barely existed in the 1970s!

I first hunted in both South Africa and Namibia in 1979. Namibia, then South-West Africa, was just a sleepy backwater. As a former German colony, it was popular with German hunters, but largely unheard of in the U.S. South Africa's game-ranching industry was in its infancy, and there was limited opportunity. How things have changed! My guess is both countries now hold twenty to thirty times more wildlife than forty years ago. The seven-to-ten-day plains-game safari is now the most common in the industry. Offering the opportunity to take a half-dozen or more varieties of antelopes, pigs, and zebras, the plains-game safari is the best bargain in the hunting world!

In 1979, however, buffalo hunting, which must remain our primary subject, was almost nonexistent in both countries. In South Africa remnant buffalo populations were almost entirely in parks and reserves, and arid Namibia contains only limited buffalo habitat. As discussed in the previous chapter, South African game ranchers got busy breeding disease-free buffalo herds on private land. The buffalo is a slow breeder; consequently, this process has taken decades and continues. Even so, buffaloes are now fairly common. In time the ban on breeding buffaloes may be lifted in Namibia, but even if this happens, Namibia is unlikely to ever catch up. On the other hand, Namibia produces fine buffaloes in some specific habitat enclaves, and unlike South Africa, most are free range.

So, for different reasons, both Namibia and South Africa are solidly in the buffalo business today. Botswana is out, with safari hunting on government concessions currently closed. Hunting on private land remains open, but few buffaloes are found on private

Michel Mantheakis (left) and Ron Bird with one of three buffaloes taken by Ron on a safari in Tanzania's Rungwa area. This is an older bull with a broken horn, taken because we badly needed lion bait. One of Ron's bulls was superb; the other two were taken as needed.

estates in Botswana. Also, due to the overpopulation of elephants, buffalo numbers—and all antelope species—are much reduced from what I saw back in the 1980s.

Both Tanzania and Zambia have remained premier destinations for longer safaris, taking advantage of their wide range of species and numerous indigenous rarities. However, both countries offer superb buffalo hunting in the right areas. Most operators in Tanzania and Zambia offer shorter buffalo safaris. Operating costs are high in both countries, so these buffalo packages are usually not the most economical.

Safari companies in Mozambique and Zimbabwe, on the other hand, are pretty much on a "buffalo economy." Cat and elephant safaris offer some gravy, but the bread and butter is the ten-day buffalo safari. The number of customers an outfitter can schedule is primarily based on the buffaloes available for harvest. Thus "one buffalo bull equals one safari" is the normal rule, so it's usually one bull to a customer.

How the available harvest quota is determined varies from area to area, but today it is more likely to be determined by game counts. Today's safari operator rarely establishes quotas in a vacuum; rather, he consults with government representatives and, depending on the area, often with nongovernmental organizations (NGOs) such as World Wildlife Fund and African Parks. We can only hope that the harvest quota is science-based, but people have conflicting agendas. African governments want the revenue, and local communities want their share, and the meat, of course.

Then there are imponderables. The Zambezi Valley areas where I was hunting and filming a lot fifteen years ago when I wrote *Buffalo!* had high buffalo populations. On any given day we would cut the tracks of multiple groups of bachelor bulls. The quotas didn't seem high, and at the time they appeared sustainable. There were rumors of meat poaching, but I don't think that was an issue in most of the Zimbabwe Designated Safari Areas (DSAs), areas where habitation is not allowed and villages are far away. The imponderable was too many lions, rare in today's Africa.

The late Ian Gibson, killed by an elephant in 2015, pointed this out to me. We were in Chewore South, an area where it was no trick to see a thousand buffaloes in a few days. Ian said, "Craig, look at the herds and count the calves." I did—and saw that a herd of two hundred would have almost no calves.

There was still a quota of four male lions in the area, along with forty buffalo bulls, but in deference to political correctness, they had taken lionesses off quota. Separate prides of lions lived along every river, of course targeting buffaloes, their preferred prey. The handwriting was on the wall: Recruitment was down, and the once-plentiful groups of bachelor bulls were being eaten.

I went back a few years later and we still saw plenty of buffaloes, but mature bulls were scarce. It's a complex science between prey, predator, and hunter, and every area is different. Zimbabwe has great buffalo areas, especially the big conservancies in the south. Mozambique has come up from almost nothing after her long civil war ended in 1990; today Mozambique has awesome buffalo areas, but they're not everywhere. Buffalo culture has changed, but the biggest change is "one buffalo bull equals one safari." It's an area by area situation, and continent-wide, the only good buffalo areas are those that are being carefully managed.

Shoot Old Buffaloes

Chapter 6

One of the best-known photos from the Roosevelt safari shows Kermit and his father with a buffalo bull, both wearing pith helmets and displaying double rifles. They're sitting comfortably together on the buffalo, a pose that would drive today's social-media-Nazis insane. Hey, those were different times, so ease up!

The bull is wide with a beautiful curl and may well have looked at Kermit and Theodore as if they owed him money. Unfortunately, it's a young bull with excellent potential, and the bosses are very soft. I have no idea what young Philip Percival thought of this buffalo. I do know that in most present-day safari companies any professional hunter who brought such a buffalo into camp would be severely chastised . . . and possibly fired.

Again, those were different times. As I've mentioned, the Roosevelt safari took place in the wake of a great rinderpest pandemic. Buffalo numbers were low, and the selection was probably limited. Of equal importance, "trophy consciousness" was far different in those days. London taxidermist Rowland Ward started tabulating records and published the first record book in 1892. Back then methodology was simple, with no reflection on mass and no indication of age. Published photos were still uncommon, so exactly what references might the Roosevelts have studied to learn exactly what a mature buffalo was supposed to look like? Through the course of their long safari, Kermit shot a female bongo in the Kenya highlands, and his father shot a Derby eland cow in far-off

This is a very old bull that was living alone near a waterhole in Zambia's Kafue. It's risky to take a single track, but we gave it a try. We had followed for less than an hour before finding him bedded.

Sudan. With these extremely difficult species that was the best they could do . . . and I suspect they were both "Dee-lighted!" with those successes. It was a different time.

Today we have no excuses. With a century's worth of good references, we know that a buffalo bull's maturity is easily judged by the hard, helmetlike growth at the base of the horns that we call the "boss." As with all horned animals, not all buffalo bulls grow spectacular horns. Diet and minerals matter, but genetics is probably the greatest influencer. Now forty years into selective breeding of disease-free buffaloes, South African game ranchers are the experts, and are producing spectacular specimens.

The ethic behind selectively shooting mature bulls, however, is not about inches of horn or even appearance. In the wild, some buffaloes grow bigger horns than others. Some are narrow, some have flat horns while others have a lot of drop and curl, and mass varies.

Some buffalo hunters like width while others prefer horns that drop well down and then curve up. These are usually not the widest bulls, but I like the drop and curl. Still others go for mass.

So far, we're missing the point, which is: Buffalo bulls establish most of their width and eventual shape when young. Precocious youngsters may *look* spectacular at just four or five, *but* their bosses are not fully formed, and their bases are soft and covered with hair, much like the Roosevelt buffalo. Bosses become fully hard when a bull is about nine years old. This obviously varies somewhat; it isn't about precise years but about the complete formation.

When hunting buffaloes and sorting through a big herd, one will often see spectacular young bulls with extremely wide horns and appealing shape. A PH worthy of his license will immediately say, "No, he's "soft" or "green" or, simply, "Sorry, he's just too young."

The southern Cape buffalo is one of those animals wherein our primary hunter's yardstick of quality is total width or "outside spread." The mule deer is another, likewise the moose. In the American West a "thirty-inch mule deer" is the Holy Grail. With moose it depends on where you are, but when you say "sixty-inch moose," most hunters know what you're talking about. With Cape buffalo a forty-inch spread is the magic number. One good thing about spread is it's probably the easiest characteristic to judge, but also incomplete. With antlered animals, it says nothing about tines or length, and with buffalo it says nothing about shape, mass, or boss.

So, you've done your homework. You're looking at a bull frontally, and you're seeing lots of beautifully curving horn well past the ear tips on both sides. In your dreams you've coveted a forty-inch bull, and you know the bull you're studying is at least into the mid-forties. Your PH says you can't shoot him—you're crushed and confused and maybe a little bit angry. You want that buffalo! What possible harm can there be in removing him?

Here's the problem: That beautiful young bull you're looking at may not have had the chance to breed and pass along his superior genetics. Buffalo bulls fight viciously for breeding rights, using their horns and their strength. Their ability to compete successfully more or less coincides with full maturity, roundabout nine years old. This, too, varies. Buffalo bulls are sexually mature when they're about three years old. In unnatural situations where too many mature bulls have been removed, young bulls can breed. During primary mating season, usually June in southern Africa, a youngster will certainly try to slip into the herd while the old boy isn't looking. He may be successful now and again, but he's years away from being a prime breeding bull.

His time as a herd bull is actually quite short, perhaps just two or three years. Around the age of eleven he'll be bested by a stronger, newly mature bull and enter into at least partial retirement. At this stage horn wear will exceed growth. His needle-sharp horn tips will become blunted and recede, and his bosses may start to flake away. At this point we can call him an old bull. In a perfect world this is the kind of

Dr. Kevin Robertson and Simon Barr with the ultimate "old buffalo," a true "scrum cap" bull with both horns worn almost to the boss. Barr took this bull with a Rigby Big Game in .416. Few buffalo bulls live to this age and such bulls are rare; I've only seen one live scrum-cap bull. (Photo courtesy of Simon Barr)

Take a close look at the boss of J. C. Bell's first buffalo, taken in Coutada 11 in 2012. Although not especially wide, bosses this big are unusual . . . I've never taken a bull with bosses anywhere close to this heavy!

buffalo bull we should strive for; he has done his breeding and passed along his genes. If he lives long enough, he may wear one or both horns completely off, leaving only the skullcap of his bosses. Since African PHs are more likely to follow rugby than American football, such bulls are often called "scrum" or "scrum-cap" bulls after the leather rugby helmet. Few buffalo bulls live that long, so such bulls are uncommon. I've only seen a couple, but for those of us who truly believe in the credo of "shooting old bulls," then a scrum bull is the ultimate prize.

One year when we were hunting in Sapi in the Lower Zambezi, there were two ancient bulls living along the Mana Pools Park boundary. One had one horn intact while the other was either broken or worn right to the base; his buddy was a scrum bull. We called them "Teacup and the Boxer." We could never quite catch them outside the park buffer zone, so we didn't get a shot at either one. In that area they were on borrowed time—I'd be surprised if lions didn't pull them down in a matter of weeks.

Swift Bullets' Bill Hober took this ancient bull in a sawgrass flat in coastal Mozambique's Coutada 11. Although tip wear is minimal, the entire horn is polished smooth. Hober used his original John Rigby .416.

As a hunting culture we are extremely horn-conscious, especially we Americans. European hunters place much greater emphasis on age, and they actively seek old, downhill animals. I admire this ethic and regret it isn't more widespread. Even so, I think it's unrealistic, if not unreasonable, to expect a hunter who has saved for and dreamed of a beautiful buffalo bull with wide, curling horns and a heavy helmetlike boss to be equally happy with a worn-down, broken-horn old warrior. We can all agree that the oldster is a better management choice and perhaps a worthier adversary, but this is a cultural conundrum and one that I am hesitant to force on another hunter. This is a tough call for a PH to make!

Let's not forget, moreover, that the African buffalo isn't anywhere near threatened or endangered. As I've said before, shooting a buffalo is somewhat like hunting a lawyer. Buffaloes and lawyers are mean, ugly, and nasty. Both look at you like you owe them money . . . and they're plentiful and easily replaced! While it's a whole different deal with lions, which are threatened and have entirely different social structures, I have no interest in mandating the shooting of only old bulls. With buffaloes, I'm content with planting the seed: It's best for the buffaloes and for the future of hunting them to shoot old (or at least older) bulls. Also, it depends on the bull and his potential—or lack thereof. There are many bulls with narrow or otherwise ugly horns that will never be big, and some areas have nontrophy or "cull" permits to address this issue. The point is to avoid shooting young bulls that will mature into great bulls and pass along their genes.

The mantra "shoot old buffaloes" properly belongs to my friend, colleague, and fellow buffalo nut, Dr. Kevin "Doctari" Robertson. Long an outspoken leader in advocating shooting old buffaloes, Kevin became concerned when he saw the diminishing numbers of mature bulls in the Zambezi Valley areas where he was hunting.

This cultural dilemma for hunters has genuine and practical concerns when it comes to judging (and measuring) buffaloes for the record books. This is because current measuring criteria *do not* reflect age! The measuring system for buffaloes under SCI's record-keeping system is fairly simple: Run a tape along the outside curl, bridge the skull gap between the horns, and continue along the outside to the other horn tip, thus deriving a total length of horn measurement. Measure the two bosses from the edge of hard horn in back to the edge of hard horn in front, each at its widest place, and at a right angle to the long axis of the horns. Add these three measurements, and you have a total score. The SCI minimum is 100 inches or "points." This is a high minimum. That's OK with me; not every animal should make any "book," but it takes a darned good buffalo to meet that minimum, and many older bulls with worn tips will fall short.

Rowland Ward, a much older system, originally measured outside spread only, and by this criterion, its minimum was 42 inches, clearly a very good, wide bull and a high standard. The Rowland methodology for buffalo was recently changed and is now based on outside spread

This is a beautiful young bull, easily into the midforties . . . but he's still a youngster—probably about five years old—with much growing and breeding ahead of him. It's a very tough call when you must pass a bull like this . . . but young bulls with such potential must be allowed to breed.

plus the width of the bosses. By the new system, Rowland Ward's minimum is now 64 inches. In simplest terms, this means that a bull with a forty-inch spread and good (but not awesome) twelve-inch bosses meets the minimum (40 + 12 + 12 = 64). This is a *very good* buffalo. What I like about Rowland Ward's system of using outside width (and now combining it with bosses) is that an older bull with worn tips isn't penalized . . . nor is the taking of a young bull with long, sharp tips rewarded!

Under SCI, however, the preponderance of the score obviously goes to total horn length, which unfortunately favors younger bulls with long, sharp tips and lots of curl. Think of it this way: The boss measurements of a big bull with huge bosses will only contribute thirty-something to the total score (high twenties more likely); the rest, seventy-plus inches, must come from length, so older bulls with heavy, worn horns are penalized.

Robertson came up with what I thought a very good idea as an alternative system: He suggested doubling the boss measurements to give greater weight to wide bosses. There is a precedent for this since SCI's measuring methodology for fallow deer doubles the paddle measurement to give greater weight to this defining feature of the species. Robertson's method on buffalo has the added advantage that no buffaloes would require remeasurement; boss measurements are on record, so the scores could be easily modified.

The late Irvin Barnhart long held the Africa chair on SCI's record book committee, and he took a look at Robertson's method. According to his analysis, doubling the boss measurements would clearly elevate scores, but it did little to change actual record book placement. I really hate that obviously young buffalo bulls occupy some of the top places in the book, but I'm darned if I can come up with a solution, and after much reflection I think Barnhart was probably correct that fiddling with boss measurements wasn't the answer.

The thing is, the actual *size* of the bosses isn't a matter of age if you take hard and green boss materials together, and, furthermore, big bosses—though desirable—aren't common . . . . Yes, the bosses will fill in as the bull matures and the soft bases become hard horn, but a bull with "average-normal," twelve-inch bosses can be fully mature, and there's no way he will ever grow sixteen-inch bosses. By the same token, the unusual bull with huge eighteen-inch bosses had those exceptionally wide bosses long before he reached maturity. However, Rowland Ward and SCI specifically state that *green boss materials should not be measured.* Once the skull and horns are boiled and cleaned, the soft green material falls away and at that point it is easy to measure hard materials only.

Thus, it isn't only the size of the bosses that matter, but the fact that they are *fully formed, hard, hairless horn to the edges*. While I admire big bosses, I have never shot a buffalo bull with really outsized bosses. One Zambia bull had fifteen-inch bosses, which is big, but I've never taken a bull with eye-popping sixteen-inch (or better!) bosses. I have seen (and passed) some young bulls that had exceptional bosses, but, despite their impressive helmets, they were too young and their headgear was still soft.

Brad Jannenga wanted a wide buffalo, and he got exactly that with this forty-two-inch bull. This is a tough bull to call: The bosses, though fairly narrow, are grown together, but there's still some hair on the front surface. He isn't "old," but I'd call him mature.

Hard bosses have become a big focal point for hunters and outfitters and, as a consequence, quite a few are now "enhanced" during the mounting process by taxidermists. Because there are now so many buffaloes with putty-enhanced bosses, Rowland Ward made the decision last year that no buffalo would be accepted under its system if the horns have been enhanced in any way. This decision was based on the fact that it is impossible for measurers to differentiate where artificial materials start and real horns stop.

The size of a bull's bosses is, thus, just one more characteristic of his horns. You'll probably see the width and the curve first, but chances are your PH studies the bosses first. At this stage he doesn't really care if the bosses are small, medium, or large; his priority is making sure that the bull is mature and that the bosses are hard. That comes first, and then he's going to look at the rest. However, really big bosses stand out and grab your attention.

Over the years I've seen few buffalo bulls with bosses into the upper teens. Only the occasional buffalo has it all: Wide horns, deep curls, lots of mass *and* exceptional bosses. These are rare, and it's probably only fair to say that most bulls I've seen with tremendous bosses were fairly narrow. In 2012 my friend J. C. Bell was part of our group in Mozambique's Coutada 11. It was his first safari and his first buffalo. The bull's bosses were tremendous, and the spread was wider than it looked because those huge bosses throw you off. This was a really great buffalo! This bull also gave J. C. a full-on charge in close cover. His PH was blocked, so J. C. stopped it at a matter of feet—all in all, it was quite a way to start one's African hunting career!

As Jack O'Connor said, "the big ones look big." A buffalo with exceptional bosses stands out and you see this readily, usually because there's more shine since there's more surface to reflect light. Again, however, really big bosses deep into the teens are rare. If there's a "norm" on a mature buffalo bull with obviously good bosses, it's probably about twelve inches back to front. Above that we're talking large. Below that doesn't mean it's a poor bull; again, like spread, the boss is just one characteristic. One of my widest buffaloes—a really impressive Zambian bull with forty-seven-inch spread and nice shape—had skimpy bosses that were eleven inches at best.

Buffalo bulls look really cool when the bosses are almost grown together. This is common with really heavy bosses because there's only so much room on the skull, but as a characteristic it has nothing to do with age or overall quality. Many southern Cape buffalo bulls at full maturity will have a gap between horn bases of up to two inches while many others have horns that have nearly grown together.

In 1992, hunting with Russ Broom in the Binga area near Lake Kariba, I shot a bull with a forty-four-inch spread, my widest Zimbabwe buffalo. He was a fine buffalo and fully mature; however, not only were the bosses skimpy but they were also not even close to coming together. Honestly, we saw the spread and checked close enough to be sure he was mature, but the bosses are *terrible.* He was in a group in some thick vegetation, but that's not an excuse because I would probably make the same decision again. No matter what animal you're hunting, you want a mix of all the characteristics. With

In a perfect world this ancient "scrum cap" bull would always be the perfect bull to take! Unfortunately, this is not the kind of buffalo bull that most hunters dream about! (Photo courtesy of Kevin Robertson)

the Cape buffalo look for spread, shape, mass, and bosses—and the bosses must be hard.

It takes experience to determine mature from immature. As a visiting hunter, this is your PH's job, not yours, but it is your job to support his decision. At this writing I know of no legal restriction on shooting a wide-horned youngster, except I believe it's the wrong thing to do. *You* will have to explain it to buddies who may know better, but your PH will suffer most of the grief. These days PHs who bring immature bulls into camp can expect ridicule from their peers, and many outfits levy a hefty fine. So, if your PH says a bull is too young, go with it. By sparing that youngster you're probably not altering Africa's herd dynamics, but one buffalo at a time will make a difference.

A U.S. Supreme Court Justice once said, regarding pornography, "It's impossible to describe, but you know it when you see it."

Absolutely judging the maturity of a buffalo bull is much the same. It's very easy to recognize a too-young, immature bull with the lower surfaces of the horn bases covered with hair and appearing soft and green. It's equally easy to identify an old warrior with his hard bosses, worn-down horns, scarred and scabby body, and bald patches on his face and neck.

Ideally, this is the kind of buffalo bull we should be shooting, but it's not always easy to sort them out, especially for younger professional hunters because you need to look at lots of buffalo bulls in order to make the call quickly in a shifting group. It depends, too, on the area, and I'm not sure I can explain this. For instance, in Zimbabwe's Zambezi Valley we always checked herds for mature bulls, and, in June, the primary mating season, we would often find older bulls trailing herds as "satellite" bulls. The tracks we looked for and preferred to follow were bachelor groups of two, three, and sometimes a half-dozen bulls. In that area we could count on most of these *dagga* boys being mature bulls.

In coastal Mozambique, almost inexplicably, bachelor groups of mature bulls are uncommon. There are lots of buffaloes and lots of herds. For example, the Zambezi Delta complex around the Marromeu Reserve holds more than 25,000 buffaloes . . . and it's an area that has few lions. So, there are plenty of bulls and plenty of mature bulls. However, older bulls there seem to stay with the herds rather than splitting off into bachelor groups as they often do in other places. Thus, most of the herds contain mature bulls.

It's one thing to track a group of a half-dozen bachelor bulls with the reasonable certainty that most are mature and that one or two might be what you're looking for. It's a bit different to crawl into a herd of several hundred buffaloes and try to sort them out. Most of the time you never see all the bulls in a big herd, and many of them are only glimpses in a shifting mass.

Properly seeing the boss to judge maturity isn't just a matter of hard or soft, which is difficult enough. It's also a matter of color, texture, and light reflection, which is much easier to discern in sunlight than on a cloudy day. The old boys are easy, and so are the young bulls whose bosses are visibly not fully formed. I suppose a purer purist than I would say the answer is simple: Just find an obvious old-timer and ignore the rest.

On the other hand, that pure purist probably hasn't dreamed of this buffalo hunt for years and scrimped and saved to get there. Also, this all comes with experience. The average buffalo hunter may have looked at photos and video but hasn't had the chance to study a lot of live buffaloes. At some point you have to trust your PH and believe that his intentions are the same as yours: To shoot the oldest, nicest buffalo you and your hunting team can locate.

Old or young is fairly black and white. There isn't really a gray area; the boss is still soft or it's hard, so the bull is mature or he isn't. However, the most difficult bulls to judge are the recently mature "herd bulls." Exact age varies, but these are generally eight or nine-year-old bulls. Their bosses may be fully hard, but perhaps not as corrugated as they will be in future years. Horn growth and thus length are at their maximum, and horn tips are usually sharp.

Note, please, that I am not advocating taking such bulls. In a perfect world it's better to take bulls a couple years older. In this imperfect world, I prefer to be a realist. Availability, of course, depends on local populations and herd dynamics, but you can assume that ten-year-old bulls far outnumber twelve-year-old bulls (and so forth). You can also assume that, whether nine, ten, or eleven years old, a bull that is genuinely hard-bossed has had the opportunity to breed and pass along his genes. If left alone, he may breed with many more cows, or he may soon be ejected from the herd, but there need be no shame in taking such a bull. The motto to "shoot old buffaloes" is a perfectly valid ideal, but in the real world of hunting buffalo, I'm satisfied with striving to "shoot *older* buffaloes!"

Tracking

Chapter 7

It is often said that tracking is the purest and most classic way to hunt buffalo. Maybe, but here's the truth: Nobody sets out to track buffalo! When you are hunting buffaloes, you are always looking for buffaloes. You might see black forms at a distance and occasionally nearby. In dry country you may see the dust of a moving herd, and birds—red-billed or yellow-billed oxpeckers or white cattle egrets—are often a dead giveaway. Your hunting team is, of course, constantly looking for tracks, but the reality is that finding and following tracks is essentially a fallback position.

If you see buffaloes or hard evidence of buffaloes close-by, then you judge the terrain, get the wind right, and begin the approach. That said, there are many places where finding tracks to follow is far more likely than actually *seeing* buffaloes. It depends on the terrain and vegetation, and also the local buffalo density. Buffaloes always leave tracks, and tracks can usually be followed, but it's a mistake to adopt a romantic or preconceived notion that any given buffalo hunt will be a tracking hunt. On any buffalo hunt, in any area, you can run into buffaloes at any moment.

As I've said before, it's a sad thing to take a buffalo cheaply by making a fast shot from the hunting car. When such a chance is offered, it will be a great temptation for both hunter and professional hunter. Shooting from the vehicle is often illegal and always unethical, but, also important, it robs the hunter of the excitement of closing with the buffalo, which is perhaps the best part of the experience. Far worse is chasing buffaloes with the car. I've rarely seen situations where this might be even theoretically possible, but once in a while buffaloes may be caught on a short-grass savanna. (Re-read Hemingway's *The Short, Happy Life of Francis Macomber.*)

I've seen many situations where nice bulls are surprised at short range while you're driving. It's tempting to take a shot in such instances, but I've never succumbed. Also, I've been fortunate to hunt with PHs whose sense of ethics wouldn't brook such nonsense. As for chasing a buffalo in a car, aside from minor nuisances like legalities and concepts of fair chase, warthog and aardvark holes make such nonsense dangerous to the point of suicidal. Thank God I've never seen it done, but I've heard accounts, so I fear it occasionally happens. Good way to break the car, if not one's neck, and obviously very poor sportsmanship!

When buffaloes are spotted from a vehicle, whether near or far, the better option is switch off, sit quietly, and let them move off. After you guess the direction they're going and read the wind, you can then begin an approach or stalk. Whether the buffaloes are spooked or just drift away, this could turn into a tracking hunt, but at least you know where to find fresh tracks!

Seeing buffaloes can happen anywhere at any time, but while your team is looking for buffaloes, you bet they're also looking for tracks! Because of the general density of thick mopane scrub forest, most of my Zimbabwe buffaloes have been taken by "pure" tracking, which means finding fresh tracks and following. My experience in Tanzania and Zambia has been a mixture of sometimes tracking and at other times sightings. The latter provides a shortcut in the hunt. This has also been true in the Terminalia forest or "savanna" zone in Central and West Africa. Often the country is open enough or has enough relief that glassing and stalking is possible. The thicker the vegetation, the less likely you are to see buffaloes and the more likely you are to find tracks and follow them. Nobody passes fresh tracks and keeps looking for buffaloes standing around waiting to be shot. When you find tracks, you stop to evaluate. If they are fresh and conditions are favorable, you follow them.

The buffalo is a large, heavy hoofed animal. His tracks will be clear in the dust of a road or on a trail or in damp soil near water. The

"Rolling tires" is one way to find tracks. These buffaloes have crossed a dirt road over the top of a vehicle. If it's your vehicle or another vehicle from your camp, you now have a good time frame for when the buffaloes were there.

practicality of following depends on how many buffaloes there are, the general soil conditions in the area—soft, sandy, rocky—and the skill of the trackers. I've tracked enough buffaloes that I can probably follow a mixed herd under most conditions. Bachelor groups are harder, but a half-dozen bulls should be fairly easy to follow. As the numbers diminish, it becomes more difficult, especially on hard or rocky ground. Because their cloven hoofs have relatively sharp edges, buffaloes are generally easier to follow than elephants, whose much greater weight is spread over their large pads, and they are much easier to follow than lions. That said, following just two or three buffalo bulls across mixed terrain becomes serious tracking, and following a single bull is very difficult.

Strategy comes into play. Your professional hunter and his tracker must weigh the odds, and their experience and judgment are part of what you're paying them for. The "normal" buffalo hunt today is ten days, so every day is ten percent of your hunt. In really good areas, combined with good conditions (and luck!), you might sometimes have a couple of opportunities per day, but when you take a buffalo track, no one can predict what might happen. You might catch up

Buffaloes must water almost daily, so waterholes are good places to check for tracks.

in minutes or a couple of hours, but when you take a track, you are pretty much committing that day to that group. Obviously, there are no sure things. The buffaloes might walk away from you, the wind might change, and the tracks of a small group might be lost.

There's also no assurance that the bull you seek will be in the group you're following! A mixed herd might or might not have a mature bull with them, but you probably have to go look, especially if it's a larger group of, say, sixty or more. Depending on conditions and the progress of the hunt, your PH may be reluctant to commit to just one or two bulls since the chances of losing the tracks are significant and since you have no ideas what their horns look like. A bachelor group of three or more greatly increases the odds. You will probably follow if the tracks are fresh and the wind is favorable, but there are still no guarantees.

Long before you make the "follow" or "don't follow" decision, you will spend some time studying the tracks. Buffalo bulls leave much larger tracks than females and calves. With mixed herds, the trackers will look for bull tracks on the edges because bulls traveling with herds usually trail or move slightly to one side or the other. Big tracks are good indicators, but maturity and quality can only be judged by sight. The age of the track is critical to the decision as is the time of day when you find them. All tracking is based on the assumption the buffaloes will stop; otherwise you can never catch up!

Buffaloes feed most actively in the early morning and late afternoon, which are also the periods when they are likely to go to water. They may also water at night, but generally speaking they don't move long distances in darkness, which is when they alternately bed and feed. Typically, they will cover the most ground in the early morning hours, moving toward heavy cover in the late morning, where they will bed and chew their cuds until the late afternoon.

To age a track is an imprecise art depending on soil and wind: Are the edges sharp? Have leaves and other debris drifted into the tracks? Skilled trackers will study tracks first and then they will look for dung. Buffalo defecate frequently when moving and feeding, and, of course, the more buffaloes there are, the more dung they will leave. To age dung is also not a precise science. Depending on temperature, humidity, and sunlight, a crust forms quickly; even the best trackers may need to follow for some time before they're fairly certain how far behind you are. With just a few bulls, it may take a while to find dung. Leaves and cut stems from feeding are also indicators, but as you follow the spoor, the trackers will test the interior of the dung piles. When it's still warm from the buffalo's body heat, you know they aren't far ahead.

Depending on time of day, it isn't necessary to have smoking fresh spoor. On the premise that buffaloes don't usually move far in darkness, in the early morning you can decide to follow a set of tracks made during the night with some confidence. Depending on the conditions and also on the difficulty you're having locating buffalo, in early morning you might decide to take spoor estimated to be from the previous afternoon. As your hunting day wears on, tracks must be ever fresher before you commit. This is not only because the buffaloes are farther ahead of you but also because the older the track, the more difficult it becomes to age! Late afternoon, when they've gotten up and are moving slowly and feeding, is a great time to track buffaloes, but an afternoon track must be very fresh because you only have a few hours of daylight left in order to close. On the other hand, following buffaloes late in the afternoon is good even if you don't close; just mark the spot where you left them and pick up the tracks again early the next morning. Now your chances of closing are very good.

Mixed herds with calves usually don't travel great distances. Older bulls traveling alone or with a few peers, usually don't, either. Older

This dung is hot! Freshness of dung is critical to tracking, but how rapidly the dung crusts and dries depends heavily on temperature, humidity, and sun. When the dung is warm from the buffalo's body, you know you are very close.

Checking the freshness of dung is the best way to tell how old a track is. An area like this with lots of dung shows that a group stopped here. Buffaloes defecate frequently, but you usually have to follow for a while before finding dung to check.

bulls become somewhat habitual and sedentary, feeding and watering in much the same areas and retreating into the same thick sanctuaries to bed at midday. Of course, anything can happen, and if lions get involved, all bets are off.

One of the big fallacies in buffalo hunting is the way we throw this term "*dagga* bull" around. Whether alone or in a herd, a buffalo bull is not automatically a *dagga* bull. *Dagga* is the Shona word for mud. All buffaloes love to roll in mud, but what is implied by the term is an older bull, mostly past breeding and at least in semiretirement. In many areas these older bulls are ejected from the herds and join other older bulls. However, this is not consistent.

In coastal Mozambique today, as we shall see, there are lots of buffaloes and plenty of mature bulls. I've done much of my buffalo hunting there for the past decade. If I were a lot smarter perhaps I could explain this, but we rarely see bachelor groups of older bulls! There, for whatever bovine rationale, the older bulls tend to stay with the big herds, and that's where we find them. Once in a while, randomly, we'll bump an old *dagga* bull cruising through the sawgrass. Swift Bullets' Bill Hober shot one a couple of years ago in a thick patch of sawgrass, but it's rare to see them alone. As a theory, perhaps it's because these buffaloes live a soft life, forming into big herds out in the swamps where there's plenty of grass and water . . . and almost no lions.

That's Mukasa with the shooting sticks, Andrew Dawson's great tracker. Part of the experience of hunting buffaloes is to watch a good tracker work his magic!

My point is that a bachelor bull is not necessarily an old *dagga* bull. Younger bulls also form into bachelor groups, and these can move around a lot. One of the longest tracking jobs I recall was on my last day in the Selous Reserve in 1988. It was still early when we picked up the very fresh tracks of a dozen bulls. Jackpot! Except they just kept going. OK, the wind shifted once, but the tracks were very fresh at the start and never got old. These bulls just kept walking. We expected to catch them quickly, and, foolishly, we weren't carrying any water. Even great PHs can get caught up in the excitement, so take some initiative and make sure that doesn't happen to you! Seven hours later, hot and parched, we found them bedded peacefully on a tiny knoll and crawled into them. None were old, most were immature, and only one was acceptable . . . but it definitely was not a "*dagga* bull."

The buffalo's first line of defense is always its sense of smell, so even before the trackers age the tracks, they're studying the wind. Regardless of how long ago the buffalo passed, there's no telling how close or far away they might be, so you're not going to follow unless the wind is favorable. In areas where there are lots of roads, you might circle to see if they've crossed the *next* road. Or you might simply leave the tracks and walk in a circle. Windy days make all animals nervous and are tough for hunting. Ideal, I suppose, is a steady breeze of ten to fifteen miles per hour because a wind of that intensity seems unlikely to change on a whim. The problem in much of Africa is that toward late morning, as the day heats up, the breezes typically become unstable and start to swirl. The trackers are watching the wind all the time. Often, as breezes shift, the trackers will stop in hopes the wind will stabilize—or they will lead you away from the tracks, circling or half-circling to keep the wind right.

When on the move, buffalo herds are noisy, breaking branches and lowing and snorting. The trackers will endeavor to keep the wind favorable, especially when they think they're getting close. Even when the herd is at rest, you'll probably hear the buffaloes before you blunder into them, but bachelor bulls, especially a small group, are very quiet. As the day wears on, timing is against you, too. In the morning there's always the hope of catching up while the buffaloes are moving and feeding. On the move they are noisier and less vigilant; once they get comfortable and lie down, they're warier, and there's usually at least one suspicious old cow on full alert. In these midday hours the wind is at its least stable, and I can't tell you how many times I've been on the edges of a bedded herd only to feel a slight kiss of breeze on the back of my neck. Seconds later the whole black mass explodes into pounding hoofs and a pall of dust.

Provided you start with decent wind and pay attention, my experience is that, when tracking, you will usually catch up at least once. You may track less than an hour, or it may be four hours. The norm or average is probably somewhere in between; whatever, that's the easy part. It's slow, steady walking and not strenuous; it's a wonderful chance to see the trackers do their work. The hard part is closing and seeing the bulls in the group. Getting a shot depends on

While tracking, you are always on the lookout for audio and visual clues. Buffaloes are fairly noisy while moving and feeding, and this old bull is carrying two sentries: a red-billed oxpecker and a white cattle egret.

your luck, how picky you are, how thick is the cover, and whether the wind is holding.

Often midday is approaching by the time you approach the herd. It should be time for them to lie down. If you're fortunate to make contact with a bedded group or if you catch them as they're starting to lie down, I'm convinced the best tactic is to back off, find some shade, and wait them out. This can be really hard, so patience is a huge virtue! They should lie down between ten and noon, and they should get up again about three. Remember that midday is the time when the wind is usually the most erratic, but by the late afternoon it should stabilize, which is a strong argument for waiting and trying to catch them when they get up and start to feed again.

Conditions vary from place to place and year to year, but it always comes down to time and opportunity: There is only so much time and there can only be so many opportunities. As I wrote in chapter 3, the "estate" buffalo hunting in South Africa isn't as easy as one might think. It's mostly tracking. The thornbush is thick and the buffaloes are wary, but one might have tracks to follow every day. There, I suppose a seven-day hunt is OK, but in general I think a buffalo safari should be ten days. Maybe you'll get lucky in the first couple of days, but then again, maybe you won't, and you can't expect opportunities or finding tracks to follow every single day.

I'm actually in Namibia's Caprivi as I'm writing this chapter, hunting with Dawid Muller of Daggaboy Safaris, one of Namibia's few genuine buffalo experts. I shot a buffalo yesterday, on my second day, and we were talking about this. I have time to burn, but if movement is slow, there's a disproportionate difference between seven and ten hunting days. Dawid only sells minimum ten-day buffalo hunts; likewise it is the same for so many of my buffalo hunting mentors, including Andrew Dawson, Paul Smith, and Mike Payne in Zimbabwe and Mark Haldane in Mozambique. You don't always need the time, but if you do, those extra days make a huge difference.

We once caught a really dry year in the Zambezi Valley. Most water was right on the river, and there was little grazing until you got to the thick *jesse* a long way south. That meant the buffaloes had to make a long commute between water and grass, so every track was a matter of miles. I was hunting in the Sapi area next to Mana Pools with Wayne Holt, then of Hornady, and Paul Smith, who was our PH. The farther you must track a buffalo, the greater the chance of something going wrong! We had tracks to follow most days, but they led us from the river south for miles, so if we caught up at all, we hit them in thick *jesse* about the time the winds began to swirl.

There were a couple of small herds and several bachelor groups, but there were two bulls, one with huge feet, watering at the same place every night. I think we tracked them four times without a glimpse. On the ninth morning we tracked them again and followed until nearly noon. Tracking was really tough on the hard-baked ground, and they were just two bulls. We'd lost them before, and I think they understood the game. This time, instead of going all the way into the hopeless *jesse*, they led us into a dark, dry riverine just short of the thicket line.

The wind swirled and one bull did an "exit, stage right." From the quick rear-end view he gave us as he crashed away, he looked pretty good, but we didn't have much time to think about him because his big buddy broke seconds later. This bull was "exit, stage left"—from deep thornbrush in the bottom of the gully straight up the gentle sandbank right toward us.

Why in the world he didn't run over us I'll never know. It wasn't really a charge because the African buffalo doesn't do "mock charges." He just decided to run in that direction and we were in his way. He got most of the way up the bank, but then he put on the brakes and turned away. At that moment, Wayne anchored him with his .458 Lott. He was a giant with a 45-inch spread, arguably the best bull I have seen taken in all my time in the Zambezi Valley.

Swamp Buffalo

Chapter 8

Want to hunt buffaloes in a swamp? Pack your gloves and kneepads and be ready to get your feet wet! Unlike the dwarf forest buffalo and the several races of savanna buffalo, a "swamp buffalo" is just a plain old buffalo that happens to live in a swampy area. The African buffalo must have grass and water, and provided both are sufficient for his needs, he can be found in almost all of Africa's many habitat types except the great deserts. While he doesn't mind lots of water, the buffalo isn't exactly semiaquatic like the sitatunga. Even so, you will find him in varying densities in most of Africa's great swamps; in fact, a swamp is the natural habitat for the *Syncerus* genus!

Classic swamp buffalo habitats include Botswana's Okavango, Namibia's Caprivi, Mozambique's Zambezi Delta, Tanzania's Moyowosi/Kigosi complex, and Zambia's Bangweulu. There are many others, but common to all is a mosaic of islands and channels, usually interspersed with floodplains. When water levels are low, the latter are grassy plains or short-grass savannas, inundated during and after the rains. Both the Okavango and, to its northwest, Namibia's less famous Kwando/Linyanti system are special cases, essentially inland deltas. Both are fed by and become much swampier during Africa's rainy seasons, but they are also fed from typically heavy rains in the Angola highlands far to the northwest. This water takes weeks to filter down the river systems, arriving in August long after the rains have stopped. In Maun, gateway to the Okavango, the water level is carefully monitored and a traditional festival ensues when the rivers start to rise.

*In Botswana's Okavango we used dugout canoes—*makoros*—to move along channels and hunt on the palm islands.*

At this writing the only hunting remaining in Botswana is plains game on private land. I fully expect Botswana to reopen buffalo and elephant hunting, perhaps by the time this volume sees the light of day. Regrettably, it appears unlikely that the Okavango Delta will again be open to hunting. For many years photographic safaris and hunting operators worked together in reasonable harmony, but eventually Botswana's increasingly lucrative ecotourism industry gained supremacy. The last Okavango hunting was in 2007, and regardless of which direction Botswana's new administration pursues, hunting in the Okavango will probably not resume.

There are still many great areas to hunt buffaloes, so it's not the end of the world, but it's regrettable because hunting buffaloes in the Okavango was a really special experience. I did several hunts there in the 1980s when the Okavango was still in its heyday, and it was magic. We hunted from *mokoros,* traditional dugout canoes, poling quietly along the clear-flowing channels and tracking from one palm island to another.

The Okavango was my unforgettable introduction to Africa's swamp hunting. Over the years I've hunted in many of Africa's swamp habitats, sometimes for buffalo and sometimes for sitatunga, lechwe, crocodile, hippo, and other swamp dwellers. When I wrote *Buffalo!,*

I didn't give proper credence to how different this hunting is from tracking and stalking in drier habitats. Unfortunately, you don't know what you don't know! The last dozen years, long after I wrote that earlier book, I've hunted annually in the swamps and floodplains of the Zambezi Delta in coastal Mozambique.

Aside from being a unique experience, this region is important to modern buffalo hunting. In the 1960s the mouth of the Zambezi held an amazing concentration of buffaloes and other game, but there were lots of options then, and buffalo quality—probably because of overpopulation—was considered poor. After the Portuguese pullout and during the long civil war that followed, the buffaloes and most other species were nearly eradicated. When the shooting finally stopped, outfitters moved back in, but there wasn't much left.

The Marromeu Reserve is the heart of the Zambezi Delta. An estimated 40,000 buffaloes roamed there in 1970, but by 1990, the population was below 1,200. The last quarter-century has wrought a seeming miracle. Protected purely by hunting outfitters and funds from visiting hunters, the Marromeu buffalo population had reached 25,000 in 2016. This is again one of Africa's great concentrations, and it's probably a sustainable number. Instead of ugly, stunted buffaloes, every herd now contains beautiful bulls, and the horn quality is increasing. Slowly, but noticeably by the year, buffaloes are expanding from the Marromeu core into the surrounding *miombo* woodlands, and major live-trapping efforts are re-establishing buffaloes into other areas, including the critical Gorongosa Park complex to the west.

Although it's a beautiful slice of wild Africa, the Marromeu complex isn't gigantic, perhaps totaling some five million acres. The reserve proper, which is not hunted, is the core and epicenter, surrounded by numbered Coutadas (hunting areas) 10, 11, 12, and 14, all lying south of the Zambezi and north of Beira. The area is really three habitats. Although well south of the main channel, the Marromeu Reserve is the Zambezi Delta, a treeless swamp of papyrus-lined channels interspersed with often flooded sawgrass flats and short-grass savannas. The papyrus channels and swamps are perfect habitat for sitatungas and lechwes, but in Africa's sometimes weird distribution of wildlife, neither species ever got there. The southern

Cape buffalo is the primary, dominant, and most plentiful species in the swamps, but there are also a few waterbucks, warthogs, bushpigs, elephants, hippos, and crocodiles.

Surrounding the swamps are vast grassy floodplains, just slightly higher and dry for part of the year. These are home to large numbers of pigs, reedbucks, and waterbucks as well as herd animals such as Lichtenstein's hartebeests, Selous zebras, and Livingstone's elands. Some sable herds make their home on the floodplain, but most sable antelopes make their home in the third habitat—several million acres of *miombo* woodland stretching north to the Zambezi and to the west. All the above-named species as well as nyalas, the great cats, and a full complement of pygmy antelopes are found in varying densities in the woodlands.

When the civil war ended, all wildlife was scarce and the continued existence of some species was uncertain. Today all are thriving, with the exception of lions, apparently common in the 1960s, but now scarce in this region, and no one seems to know exactly why. There are a few, but one of the current hunter-based initiatives is reintroducing lions into the area. There are always unintended consequences in life, and the reintroduction of the lion may, over time, change buffalo hunting.

Just a decade ago, when I started hunting in this area, buffaloes were extremely scarce in the *miombo* forests. Today they are relatively common and seem to be increasing. My personal annual "brother-in-law survey" reveals more sightings in the woodlands every year. Much more empirically, buffaloes taken in the woodlands are increasing as a percentage of the outfitters' quotas. The annual aerial survey, under the aegis of the World Wildlife Fund (WWF), only counts buffaloes in and around the reserve, so buffaloes in the woodlands are an uncounted bonus!

Hunting bulls in the *miombo* sand forest is no different from hunting them in any other woodland setting throughout much of Africa, but it's so different from the swamp hunting that, typically, both the local hunters and their visitors tend to refer to them as "swamp buffaloes" and "forest buffaloes." Both are, obviously, southern Cape buffaloes, exactly the same animal, yet the hunting experience

The big Hägglund BVs make buffalo hunting easier in the Zambezi Delta, but the real point behind the investment is meat recovery as one trailer can easily recover two buffalo bulls.

is altogether different. A common feature of the low-lying, relatively flat *miombo* forest is slight depressions or "pans" that collect water, promote lush growth, and are irresistible draws for both grazing and browsing species. Only when pressed for time do we drive into the pans; usually we stalk them from a few hundred yards because you never know what you might catch there—at any hour of the day.

Most of my sightings of buffalo in the forest have been at pans, but most of the time it's a matter of finding tracks and following them. This is no different from tracking buffaloes anywhere else, except the woodland hunting there is some of the most difficult I've done. This follows from two factors. First, the coastal Mozambique woodlands are extremely thick, and, second, the leaf litter is thick and noisy. It's actually more like following true forest buffaloes in the forest zone rather than tracking in Zimbabwe's mopane forest—which can be thick but not *that* thick or *that* noisy!

Swamp hunting is something else again. Once you get out there, the concentrations are amazing, so, honestly, it's a fairly easy and extremely successful way to hunt. The problem is that you have to get there. It's usually hot, sometimes wet, and there's no shade. In the Marromeu complex, Coutadas 10, 11, and 14 all have slices of swamp along the boundaries of the reserve; Coutada 12 is primarily *miombo* forest. I've hunted in them all and taken buffaloes in all. Because of heavy rains, the season runs a bit later than found in much of southern Africa; it's still very wet into August.

In the Zambezi Delta there are no natural vantage points to look for white cattle egrets circling the buffalo herds. PH Debbie Visser had her trackers carry a long pole so they could lift her up to glass.

Swamp buffalo hunting is practical throughout: Go early and you're going to get wetter, but later it starts to get very hot. I am not especially bothered by heat, so I like to go late. October has been my favorite time because I think that time is better for key antelope species like nyala. For buffalo it doesn't matter much, but it does get hot. If you're lucky, you might get cloud cover and a nice breeze, but I've seen temperatures of 130 degrees Fahrenheit out there, and there is no shade. Proximity to the Indian Ocean is a blessing because it means that it cools down at night, and even in October a campfire is welcome!

The first challenge of hunting the swamp buffalo is getting to him! No wheeled vehicle can cross the papyrus channels. Early in the season some river systems allow access by boat, but as the water levels drop, not even a *mokoro* can get there. I have done hunts out there on foot. Tony Wicker, longtime proprietor of Coutada 14, prefers to do it this way: Drive to the last possible crossing, glass from the last climbable tree. Then walk and wade, with enough help to carry out the meat. This is an awesome way to hunt buffalo, but it's not for everybody.

The Argo, the Canadian tundra vehicle, is used by several operators. Honestly, in the heat and the swamp they're a maintenance nightmare—never go out there with just one Argo!—but they allow access. The biggest problem with the Argo is its limited payload for meat recovery. My buddy Mark Haldane of Zambeze Delta Safaris (ZDS) has hunted in Coutada 11 for twenty-five years. He started on foot and with *mokoros*, shifted to Argos, and a few years ago discovered the big Hägglund BV, developed in Sweden for military use. It's a monstrous tracked thing with a four-seat van, followed by an open articulated tracked trailer. You feel like Erwin Rommel or George Patton going buffalo hunting, but it works! Intended for Arctic use, it took some smart mechanics to modify the radiator systems to a tropical climate. In addition to the full hunting team, the trailer can haul two buffalo bulls—in a pinch three—out of the swamps.

Obviously, meat recovery and distribution are important to the whole concept of conservation and sustainable use. Today, thanks largely to the BVs, ZDS annually distributes over thirty tons of meat to the local villages. Breakdowns are not impossible, so they prefer to attack the swamps with two BVs carrying at least two hunters, PHs, and trackers. Once you get out there, the vehicles can separate. Some days no buffaloes are taken, but two-buffalo days aren't uncommon, and I've been in on a few three-buffalo days. Mind you, these are long, hard days. Depending on the water level, the swamp vehicles are staged as close as possible to the last island, rarely less than a slow, bumpy, three-hour run to get in reasonable proximity of where buffaloes might be. Toward late afternoon everybody starts watching the clock, for it's the same three-hour run to get out. Getting caught overnight in the swamp isn't a great idea.

There is another reason that hunting buffaloes in the swamp isn't for everybody. Between the hours, the pounding, and the heat, nobody can take it day after day. When there's a group in camp, "swamp days" are done in rotation. Some hunters do it once, get their buffalo, and are happy to say "been there, done that." Maybe I'm a little sick, but I love it out there, and I know of no better chance to get into big herds! No,

I can't do it every day—but on my annual ten-day hunts there, I go to the swamps three or four times, and look forward to each foray.

Even though the Okavango is long closed, the Zambezi Delta is hardly Africa's only area for hunting swamp buffaloes, and I suppose every area is a bit different. Boats with tall observation towers were used along Botswana's Chobe River and are in use in Tanzania's Kilombero Valley, southwest of the Selous Reserve. I'm a bit of a latecomer to Namibia's Caprivi (now officially the Zambezi Region); I've done just three hunts there, all recently. The buffalo hunting there is excellent and horn quality is exceptional. The country is also gorgeous, in many ways much like the Okavango, but more grass and fewer trees. Unfortunately, my experience there has been during a protracted dry period, so instead of following the buffalo across channels from island to island, my hunting there has been "feet dry" in seas of grass or on raised mopane hummocks. There was a bit more water in July 2018, so if better rains continue, I might still experience a real and proper swamp buffalo hunt in Caprivi. At this writing, however, the majority of my experience with swamp buffalo has been around the Marromeu Reserve.

One thing common to swamp buffalo hunting is that tracking is not the primary tactic. Yes, we tracked buffalo in the Okavango. In Mozambique we're looking for tracks while transiting in the swamp vehicles, and if a herd gives us the slip, we will surely track it. However, some channels are deep, and they are always inhabited by crocodiles, hippos, and occasionally elephants. So, we're generally hunting by sight. Elevation is key. Where there are trees, agile trackers and younger PHs scramble up—I don't do a lot of tree-climbing anymore!

In the Marromeu there are no trees, so elevation is limited to standing up on a vehicle. PH Debbie Visser, who generally attacks the swamp on foot, has her trackers carry a stout pole. She stands on it and they hoist her up, gaining her about ten feet of elevation. The swamps are very flat. Visibility is limited by sawgrass just tall enough to hide a buffalo herd, and the horizons are blocked by strands of tall papyrus. This problem is easily solved: Out there, although we might see a herd of buffaloes as a distant black line, we're not really glassing for black forms—we glass for birds!

Strands of papyrus can offer good cover for stalking; here Mark Haldane is spotting and has a good bull in view.

White cattle egrets constantly swirl and circle over the herds, diving and landing and moving with their buffalo hosts. By using binoculars, we can spot the swooping birds from at least a mile away. Some caution is needed, for the birds might just as easily be circling elephants or hippos, rather than buffaloes, and you don't want to blunder into either. You watch for a while and check the wind. The birds give you direction, and in time, through a break in the green sea, you'll see buffaloes moving under the birds.

This is where the hunt starts! So far it sounds too easy and it has been, but there's much more to come. With an approach planned, rifles and ammo are gathered and packs are filled with water. This is the time to put on your kneepads. For most of my African hunting, I wear shorts, which I find to be cooler and quieter. I tried that in the swamps and gave it up. The sawgrass is aptly named, for it cuts. I'm cursed with far too much machismo to worry about a few scratches, but leeches are another thing.

I now wear long sleeves and long trousers, and I secure the trouser cuffs over my shoes at the ankles. I wear light leather gloves, not only

This is plenty close enough . . . now it's time to locate a good bull!

against the sawgrass, but also for crawling on spiky ground. Mark Haldane himself convinced me of the value of kneepads. Seemed kind of wimpy, but if you get caught on a hard-baked, short-grass savanna, your knees will be raw in minutes. I gave in and got a set of lightweight rugby kneepads. Most of the time bugs aren't all that bad out there—until dusk, that is. I carry a head net for when the mosquitoes swarm, and it's also useful to reduce face shine during a close approach. Bug dope, sun block, and a brimmed hat pretty much completes my swamp gear.

As with any approach, you never know exactly what you're getting into. I've done a few that were feet-dry approaches. More often a channel or two must be crossed, and soft mud must be slogged through. No different from most situations, you usually start with a herd that's moving and feeding, but by the time you circle and close, they're ready to lie down. The sawgrass flats are deadly, for they are just tall enough to hide an entire army of buffalo, and it's difficult and dangerous to approach in that stuff . . . and usually impossible to sort out a bull. Fortunately, the herds usually move *through* sawgrass because they prefer to lie down on the wide-open short-grass savannas. I suppose this is for security so that they can see danger approaching, but there's also good grass for nibbling. In the short grass you can see them clearly, which makes it ideal for sorting out the bulls—but there is very little cover. Ideally, some strands of sawgrass or fingers of papyrus will offer cover for a close approach, but sometimes you have to belly crawl across open ground under the midday sun. It doesn't always work—sometimes it does, and sometimes it doesn't.

There are no lions out in the swamps, little or no poaching, and light hunting pressure; consequently, these buffalo are usually calm. Out there they gather into big herds, several hundred into a thousand, and perhaps they feel some security and safety in numbers. No, you can't crawl right up to them, but if you take your time and use whatever cover there is, even the sparsest tufts of grass, I'm often surprised at how close we get.

That said, unless you get lucky and catch the herd right on the edge of sawgrass or papyrus, shooting is rarely point-blank. The rules don't change, and nobody takes long shots, but out there, shots average farther than they do in closer cover. I'd call it a ninety-yard average. This means that some shots will be fifty or sixty yards, and others will be closer to one hundred and fifty. I have used iron sights out there, but you're pushing the limit. Better to use a scope or red-dot sight, and by all means carry sticks, preferably sticks that can be shortened to sit behind or kneel against.

As I've said, the majority of this hunting is in herds, and they are often very big herds. Unless needed for a follow-up, we don't use solids, and we don't use the hardest, deepest-penetrating softpoints like the homogenous-alloy bullets. Preferred are bullets that expand well but are unlikely to exit—good examples include Swift A-Frame and Hornady DGX. Other than a bit more distance and the sheer size of the herds, shooting and shot placement are no different from any other situation when hunting buffaloes. The real hard part, however, is sorting out a bull. This is very tricky, especially if you're new to the game, and it can take a huge amount of patience. The harsh sunlight on a shifting black mass doesn't help!

Once you get into position on a more or less stationary herd, you have won, and, unless the wind shifts or you make a mistake, they're probably not going anywhere. So, slowly and carefully, you must study the herd, pick out the bulls, and try to find a good one. This is the part I love the most, and it's both exciting and frustrating.

If they're bedded, you can study them to your heart's content, but you may need to wait until they get up before you can see them all. If they're feeding or milling, they are not static.

You'll get glimpses of bulls, and then you'll lose them again. You and your PH will confer. It usually isn't productive to count fifty-six buffaloes from the right or left, so you have to be creative. See that cow in the center with an egret on her back? Look two buffaloes to her left. See that reddish calf on the edge, about a third from the right? There's a big bull just behind. Often the mature bulls will be in a knot at one edge or another. Just wait. As they shift, a good bull may reveal himself. The trick, then, is to lock onto him and hope that he comes to one of the edges where he will offer a shot.

Of course, your targeted bull may never come to the edge, and in larger herds it's unrealistic to believe you will ever see all the bulls. What's important is to be patient and stay focused, and as your PH points out one buffalo or another in that black mass, pay attention and make sure you are able to isolate the animal he's talking about. The biggest risk is shooting the wrong buffalo, so you need to be sure—and if you aren't sure, don't shoot. You can always locate this herd again or find another herd or try again on another day. What you can't do is call back a bad shot.

I've had a lot of experience with this and I've seen a lot of buffalo bulls, so I'm pretty good at picking them out, being ready, and taking a fleeting opportunity when presented. However, I've been with a lot of first-time buffalo hunters in these big herds, and most of them have taken very fine bulls. It's just a matter of patience—and not minding the heat.

This is *not* the classic *dagga*-bull hunting you've read about! In some ways it's more exciting, and as I've said, for unknown bovine reasons, most herds contain mature bulls, and some of them are very old. Why we see so few bachelor bulls in this area is another bovine mystery, but we do see them now and again. A couple of times I've been sitting on the BV, watching while another hunting team made a stalk, and saw some very nice lone bulls cruise by.

Then there was the time when I was hunting with my friend Zack Aultman, and he was to shoot first. Earlier in the day his wife, Debi, had taken a gorgeous bull, so we were trying to make

This is a good example of the kind of buffaloes coming from the Marromeu complex today. John Stucker took this fine forty-inch bull in 2016.

it a two-buffalo day. Zack was having serious eye trouble, so it was difficult for him to sort out a bull. (Trust me, even with perfect vision it isn't easy!) We got onto a couple of herds, but it simply wasn't happening for Zack.

Now it was late afternoon. Our Cinderella cutoff was approaching, but we saw another herd on the horizon, so we decided to give it one more go. They were on a small, short-grass savanna between two big sawgrass flats. We circled one of the flats to get the wind right and then crawled along the edge, pitching up about eighty yards from the herd. *Perfect!* We were just starting to sort them out when a lone bull stepped out of the sawgrass we'd just crawled through and strolled toward the herd. I'm very glad we didn't run into him while we were on our hands and knees in the mud! He was a very good bull. The sticks went up, Zack anchored him, shot him again, and that was it.

Sometimes, as it happened that day, the herd doesn't run. With the herd still there after Zack's shot, PH Dylan Holmes got me on the sticks. A few seconds later another nice bull stepped clear on the right side of the herd. I shot him and was just about to shoot again when he tipped over, back of horns flat to the ground, nose straight up in the air. Caution on the walk-up is mandatory, but when you see a bull in that attitude, there's no reason to shoot again. So, in the matter of a few lucky seconds, we had turned it into a three-buffalo day!

It isn't always necessary or desirable to take more than one buffalo at a time, but, as I said, we usually go to the swamp in teams. So long as the meat can be recovered, sometimes it works out. I've seen it happen here and there across Africa, but a second opportunity tends to be most common when encountering large herds, and in Mozambique's swamps big herds are the name of the game. After a buffalo is taken, they may run a bit and stop, allowing a second approach—or they may simply mill a bit, and occasionally they'll advance closer, surrounding the stricken bull. If a second hunter is present, the order must be established, and the second gun needs to be ready if an opportunity presents itself.

The biggest caution is that, before a second bull is taken, it's essential to make sure the first one is down and out! The tall sawgrass offers one of the worst conditions I've seen for following a wounded buffalo, though the flooded papyrus is worse. One bull to follow is always bad, but more than one is a nightmare scenario! Caution is mandatory, but I've seen quite a few double plays out there. In 2016 Donna took a nice bull; we lost it momentarily in the press of buffalo bodies, and then we saw it go down. The herd didn't run, so I jumped on the sticks and shot another nice bull a few seconds later. When the herd moved off, our two bulls lay still just a few yards apart. This was a nice but unusual coincidence.

On Open Ground

Chapter 9

It is often suggested that tracking is the most proper form of buffalo hunting. As an alternative, I've just expended several thousand words on swamp hunting, which is rarely tracking, but it sure is exciting and *fun!* To some extent it depends on the cover and your luck. As I've said, you can always run into buffalo.

In October 1993 Geoff Broom and I were hunting in Mto Wa Mbu in Tanzania, a classic Masailand concession near Lake Manyara. It's essentially a broad valley with a range of hills on one side, and taller hills on the other side below Ngorongoro. Mto Wa Mbu was one of Ruark's blocks on his *Horn of the Hunter* safari, and I'm told it's still an exceptional block for most of the East African antelopes. I'm not sure it's a particularly good area for buffalo, but that depends on time of year, the rains, and your luck. I was there in October before the short rains, so the plains were dry and dusty. Geoff warned me that the buffalo had pulled back into the high country where grass and water remained.

On the first afternoon we took a track leading up into the hills along a narrow ridge. With maybe an hour of good light, we spotted a herd a couple of ridges away. On that first glance, through good glass, we saw a great bull that would go mid-forties. By the time we got on them, sundown was approaching. We were close—we were *there*—except we couldn't find that bull in the herd. So, with light going and a great bull more or less located, we left them, figuring we could get back on them the next day.

Shortly after dawn we were back on the same ridge. Hindsight being a wonderful thing, it might have been smarter to take their

We're glassing from a prominent ridge above the Zambezi Valley. Distant sightings of moving buffaloes can offer a shortcut to tracking, so it's always wise to look.

tracks, but our ridge led to another taller ridge, and we saw a small herd in thick vegetation near the crest, moving from left to right. There were forty or fifty animals, and this herd was about the same size as the group we'd seen the night before. They were about a half-mile off, easily reachable up a series of gentle inclines. Naturally we assumed it was the same herd—the next assumption being that beautiful bull we'd seen would still be with them. I'm still not convinced either assumption was incorrect! Keeping the wind right, we went after them.

By the time we reached the crest, they had vanished, but along the way we had jumped a fantastic lesser kudu. I had one on license and the trophy fee was a lot less then than it is today. I still wish I'd shot him, but I didn't need another lesser kudu, and we were after buffalo. We left the kudu and had no trouble finding the tracks of the buffalo herd. We followed them laterally along the edge of a big plateau for an hour or so, catching them bedded in thick vegetation. There they were, a dense clump of buffaloes in deep midday shade. We crawled back and forth for three eternities—rarely were they more than sixty yards away—but we just couldn't spot that spectacular bull. When you have a dense mass of buffaloes in thick vegetation, it's very difficult to see them all, so to this day I don't know if that bull was there and we couldn't see him, or if he'd left, or if we'd gotten onto the wrong herd.

Eventually we spooked them on purpose and then ran with the herd, hoping that if he was there he would show himself. They spooked easily enough, ran a bit, and then turned to face us. We still couldn't see him, but we still weren't completely certain he wasn't there. We advanced, spooking them good this time, thinking we must surely see him at the tail of the herd as they took off. Nope, just a couple of immature bulls and no big boys to be seen. This time they ran over the ridge, down across a *korongo*, and left their dust hanging on the crest of the next ridge. We decided to follow them a bit farther, and by then we didn't so much want that bull, but we wanted to know if he was there and if we had missed him.

I still don't know. When we got to the crest of the next ridge, the herd was long gone, but when we glassed to our left and down into a deep cut that led to the plains below, we saw three bulls. I'm certain they had nothing to do with the herd we were following, but all three were mature and two were spectacular. We immediately forgot about the herd and began an approach. It was the end of the season, and no one had spotted these three bulls prior to this, so I suspect they were Ngorongoro Crater bulls on walkabout, and we just happened to have blundered into them. The largest of the three pulled a very clever exit, but his slightly smaller buddy remains my best-ever buffalo bull.

Just a year later I was hunting with Paul Roberts and Patti Pugh, then of Rigby, in the Selous Reserve with Luke Samaras. On this particular day I was out with Luke's son, Jasper, an older teenager at the time. The Selous holds lots of buffaloes and we were there at a particularly good time; most days would yield sightings without us struggling to find tracks. On that particular day I don't recall if we'd seen fresh tracks or not, but we'd turned away from riverine cover and were driving along a track in powdered red soil with a low hill rising to our left when we saw red dust rising at the base of the hill. I was confused for a moment—Jasper wasn't—and our trackers understood immediately. *Buffalo!* We were in relatively open bush, so elephants were unlikely, and in that area nothing else travels in large enough herds to raise that much dust.

So we got our equipment together, checked the wind, and began an approach. In just a few minutes we were able to get in front of the herd. We found a bit of cover on a brushy termite mound and almost immediately the herd began passing in front of us, very close. We let them pass while we sorted them out, and toward the rear of the herd we saw a very good bull on our edge of the mass. Paul Roberts had just introduced the .450 Rigby Rimless Magnum, their traditional .416 Rigby case necked up to .458. This was its maiden voyage and our purpose was to take two or three buffaloes apiece with the new Rigby cartridge. This was not a giant bull, but he was fully mature and plenty good enough. This bull stayed on our side, and I doubt he was twenty yards away when he passed the base of our termite mound. At the shot the whole herd reversed in panic, and, instantly, stampeding buffaloes exploded around us, veiled by a curtain of dust. There was no chance for a second shot.

We let the hoofbeats fade into the distance and the thick dust settle, and then we descended from our perch and walked along the edge of the tracks. Hardly fifty yards along, just beyond another big termite mound, we saw our buffalo stretched out, as if in full flight. Ready, I came a bit closer, saw no movement, and then shot him again from behind with a 500-grain solid. Given the attitude of the buffalo, today, honestly, I probably would ask one of the trackers to throw a stick before I wasted a bullet or messed up more meat. That was a long time ago, however.

Also, this was Jasper's first "solo" buffalo as a PH, so I'd promised his dad we'd be careful. Jasper did a lot more hunting and was a very good young PH—but he didn't do many more buffalo hunts before he was badly hammered by a wounded buffalo. He survived, barely, but extreme internal injuries ended his buffalo-hunting career. The buffalo hunt we did together couldn't have gone more perfectly or been more uneventful, but you never know.

Even further back, in 1984, Geoff Broom's son, Russ, and I had a truly charmed safari in the Mumbwa West block in Zambia's

During the dry season, moving buffalo herds raise a huge pall of dust. Just remember that while dust clouds can be elephants, they are likely to be buffaloes!

Kafue region. Lord, we'd taken my best lion, my best sable, a great Livingstone's eland, and good specimens of other common game—but we couldn't find a buffalo. We tracked a couple of herds, losing them across the boundary into the Kafue National Park, and one morning, on the park boundary road, we hit a bachelor herd with a great bull staring at us less than fifty yards way . . . except they were standing on the wrong side of the boundary.

Russ kept saying we'd catch them out of the park, but time was growing short, so late one afternoon we drove into a short-grass savanna with a big tree line on the far side. Russ pointed out some white birds circling on the far side of the trees. This time I definitely didn't get it. The swooping birds were the white cattle egrets so important to our Mozambique buffalo hunting—but I didn't know about that back then. Russ, of course, instantly keyed on the birds. He immediately hissed "*Buffalo!*" and stopped the car. I had been looking for black animals while he had been watching the birds!

By the time we got unlimbered, circled the wind, and got around the tree line, the buffaloes had moved on. Possibly they had heard the vehicle, but we quickly found their tracks. You can't always pick your timing, no more than you can determine where you might see buffaloes, but given a choice, late afternoon is the very best time to pursue them. Buffaloes are always at their calmest in that golden hour surrounding sunset. That's when they're traveling their slowest and covering the least distance, and then, before dusk, they gather tightly together for security because during the night the lions rule their world.

This is a group of buffaloes moving through an open savanna. Buffaloes must have grass, and they often lie down in open areas for security.

This became a very special afternoon. We followed the herd for less than a half-mile and caught them in another clearing, and I took my first really nice buffalo bull. It was about forty-one inches with good bosses and a nice shape. After my shot, he got into the herd, and there was no chance for a second shot, but we followed him only a couple hundred yards before we found him down and dead. Sunset was on us, so we took a diagonal route straight toward the truck through *miombo* woodland and ran smack into a small bachelor group. Russ instantly spotted a big bull, giant in both body and horn, and told me I had to take him. "*Now!*" he said. At my shot, the bull dropped on the spot. So, on the same day, I took a really nice bull and my first *really big* buffalo bull.

Fresh tracks are good, but it's just as good—and maybe even better—to see buffaloes, or see clear evidence that buffaloes are close-by. Because of the generally thick bush, hunting in Zimbabwe is mostly tracking, but your team is looking for everything, not just tracks. Isolated rocky kopjes and huge stone monoliths are common landforms both in the Zambezi Valley and the lowveld, and they make ideal vantage points. It's common to climb them and glass for a while. Honest, the thick bush doesn't reveal a lot of secrets, but it's not uncommon while glassing to see elephants, various antelopes, and sometimes buffaloes.

Andrew Dawson and I were once trying to get a buffalo for my daughter Brittany on the Lemco Conservancy. We clambered up a huge monolith of black basalt, and, sure enough, after a little while we spotted a big, lone buffalo bull cruising through the brush, maybe five hundred yards away. We marked his progress carefully and made a line to intercept him. Heck, we not only didn't find that buffalo . . . we never found his tracks!

Whether it's dust, a sighting, or birds that reveal buffaloes to be close at hand, things don't always work out. In fact, I can't even give you what the odds are. Anything can happen, and nothing is certain. Any sighting can quickly yield a shot, or it can turn into a long tracking job. I can't remember exactly when or where, but I know it was early in my hunting career and I was still desperate to take a good buffalo when, early one morning, we saw a huge herd spread out on the edge of a big clearing, just starting to drift into the tree line. Perfect! Early morning is also a very good time for hunting buffaloes because that's when they are moving along and feeding slowly, and the winds are usually calm.

We were probably three hundred yards away, so I doubt the vehicle disturbed them. We did everything right, drove on past, quietly gathered our rifles and ammo, checked the wind, and came into the tree line with the wind in our faces. We found their tracks easily, but they never stopped, and we never caught up. The dung stayed fresh and hot but we never saw them again. After a couple of hours, the wind turned against us and seemed steady, so we gave up, which is usually the right thing to do.

Most of the time actual sightings are random, but your hunting team is always on the lookout for birds and dust—as well as actual buffaloes. They're also listening. It hasn't happened often, but a feeding herd is noisy, and I can remember a few times when we've moved into buffaloes based on sound rather than tracks or a sighting. Regardless of how you get there, getting among them is the goal. To me it's all interesting, but it starts getting really exciting when you're closing in on them, when you have their cattle smell in your nostrils, and when you can start sorting the bulls.

The swamp hunting I've done, especially in Mozambique, is unique in that we're generally looking for moving herds or birds swooping above them, and we don't worry too much about tracks. No matter how you locate the buffalo, usually fresh tracks are extremely important, but I have hunted in a few places where the country was so open that tracks weren't all that important. I'm sure these open vistas occur all over Africa, but a couple I've experienced include Namibia's Zambezi region (Caprivi Strip) and Uganda's Karamoja district.

As I've said, my hunts in Caprivi have taken place during a protracted drought, not under normal conditions when it's probably a lot more like the Okavango. Hunting in the Caprivi occurs on communal lands joined into conservancies. Most of the hunting areas are relatively small and are bordered by parks, and hunting depends on game movement in and out of sanctuaries. This changes the game; there's no point starting a track with the likelihood that the buffaloes have moved through the area and are already across the boundary. Park boundary hunts occur all over Africa—and the world—and are a bit different in that patience is necessary. You have to wait for the animals to move in. In Caprivi there's a lot of buffalo movement, both from the parks and from Botswana, but it's probably not going to be a classic tracking hunt.

On the plus side there are lots of buffaloes, trophy quality is superb, and hunting pressure is very light: Of course there is no hunting in the parks, there is little poaching, and the hunting quotas are very conservative. There are lions, but in my view they exist in about the right numbers. Combine all factors, and, despite how open the country looks, I've been amazed at how close you can stalk to a Caprivi buffalo!

Success depends on the skill and experience of your hunting team, but when these things come together, it's fantastic. In the Caprivi, I've been hunting with Dawid Muller and his longtime tracker, Da Silva. Time and again we would glass buffaloes—whether a big herd, a splintered herd, or a group of bulls—in a sea of grass. Every time, it appeared to me an approach was highly unlikely to succeed. Working the wind carefully, using whatever cover was available, and, unknown and mysterious to an outsider, following the preferred pathways used by the buffaloes to enter and exit those seas of grass, we have consistently gotten very close. Time and again, with careful maneuvering and amazing insight into bovine behavior, we would find buffaloes feeding or simply moving directly to us.

Because arid Namibia has limited buffalo habitat, with small numbers and a conservative quota, buffaloes there are more limited and

White cattle egrets are constantly swooping and diving above buffalo herds. In coastal Mozambique, this is what we're looking for: white birds on the horizon.

more expensive than, say, in Mozambique or Zimbabwe. No outsider has huge experience with them and mine is limited. Dawid Muller, hunting in the Wuparo Conservancy adjacent to Nkasa Rupara National Park, has retained his area for more than a decade and takes about a dozen to fifteen buffalo bulls a year. In Namibia these are large numbers, meaning he and his team have more experience than most. They should know how to hunt them and they do. I've taken just two bulls with them (so far!), but both were within twenty-five yards in improbably open grassland. We've turned down others at rock-throwing range. Maybe I'll eventually figure out how they do it!

In March 2017 Steve Hornady and I hunted with Christian Weth's Uganda Wildlife Safaris in the Karamoja district, which is in the extreme northeast. This was not my first time in Uganda, nor with Christian's outfit, but it was my first time to the area made famous by Walter Bell. It turned out to be dramatic country of open acacia flats surrounded by high, rocky ridges—and not what I expected. It was dry and between the sparse acacias was short-grass savanna. The buffaloes had little cover, but they had grass and water, so they seemed perfectly content.

This was also a park boundary hunt; the hunting area is just south of the Kidepo National Park, which, in turn, runs north to the Sudan border. Kidepo has a large population, perhaps 7,000 buffaloes, but during dry months there's more water in the hunting area to the south than in the park. I have no doubt that almost any month exhibits different weather patterns, so it's dangerous to make generalizations, but in March 2017 it was very dry.

Contact! When a herd is in sight, now begins the approach phase, the most exciting part of any buffalo hunt.

At that time we found most of the movement out of the park was by bachelor groups. There were small mixed herds—twenty or forty or a hundred—but, unique in my experience, we saw nearly as many bulls as cows and calves combined! It was improbable and strange, but we could work our way slowly through the open acacia, and we would see bulls. Once spotted, we could pick a couple of trees to use as cover, and darn near walk up to them.

Over the years I've had easy buffalo and hard buffalo hunts, but combining unusually open ground with a strange influx of bulls, without question this was the easiest buffalo hunting I've ever seen. Still, it was *not* a sure thing. These buffaloes didn't stand around and wait to be shot, and there were several bulls worth a second look that gave us the slip. However, there was no tracking, nor any reason to track, and there was no reason to watch for birds or dust. This was pure glassing and stalking, and it was a totally different and unusual experience.

Nile Buffalo

Chapter 10

The Nile buffalo, *Syncerus caffer aequinoctialis*, is the race that begins the African buffalo's westward transition from, essentially, big and black with large horns to, ultimately, small bodied and red with increasingly modest horns. The Nile buffalo is tied to the huge Nile drainage, a vast chunk of northeastern Africa. It's a complicated river system that includes the White, Blue, Albert, and Victoria Niles, plus innumerable smaller tributaries. The Nile buffalo is thus the buffalo of Egypt—some remain in the south—and certainly of vast Sudan, northwestern Uganda, and traditionally southwestern Ethiopia.

We like our boundaries to be clean and precise, but the Nile buffalo causes us problems because its range and changing physical characteristics are anything but neat and orderly. Before Sudan banned hunting, the outfitters tried to separate the buffaloes into savanna and forest, red and black. It's a huge country, and on the western border the buffaloes probably are more like the Central African savanna buffalo. It's cleaner to say that all buffalo in Sudan are of the Nile variety, but that may not be accurate. Anyway, it's a moot point because southern Sudan hasn't been open to hunting since 1983. If hunting opens again, and I think it will, primary opportunities are in the southeast in East Equatoria province, and buffaloes there should be unarguably Nile.

Uganda is a problem. In the northwest her buffaloes are clearly classic Nile, not dramatically smaller in the body, but with flat horns and with a significant percentage of red and brown animals in the

My friend Mike Adams took this gorgeous Nile buffalo in Uganda's Karamoja region. The spread is an amazing forty-seven inches. The "flat" horns are typical of Nile buffaloes.

herds. In the northeast, the Karamoja district, categorizing is more difficult. Uganda is not a large country anyway, and in the northeast, looking north, you have Kenya to the right, Sudan to the front, and Ethiopia at the "two o'clock" position. Uganda probably has a mix of Kenya buffalo in the northeast and pure Nile buffalo in the northwest, but drawing the lines are difficult, so I'm happy to give Uganda to the Nile buffalo, and, right now, Uganda is the only place where the Nile buffalo may be hunted.

I doubt that Kenya, which is also a relatively small country, will ever again open to hunting, but we have always considered all Kenya buffaloes to be the large southern Cape buffalo. Up in Kenya's northwest corner and adjacent Uganda, either Kenya buffaloes are tainted with Nile buffalo blood . . . or vice versa. Boundaries, being human inventions, must be drawn *somewhere*, so I'm OK to keep with tradition and consider all Uganda buffaloes as Nile and all Kenya buffaloes as southern Cape.

Ethiopia has a lot of theoretical buffalo habitat, but her actual population is low and the hunting quota tiny. In the period between the closing of Sudan and the reopening of Uganda, Ethiopia was the only place the "Nile buffalo" could be hunted. The Ethiopian buffaloes are smaller in both body and horn than the buffaloes of Sudan and Uganda, and earlier hunters considered them to be different. More recently, while Sudan and Uganda were closed, we were happy to call Ethiopian buffaloes "Nile"—but they cannot compete in horn size and in record book listings. Jason Roussos did the research—I've seen his work—and it makes sense. SCI agreed, and the buffaloes of southwestern Ethiopia now have their own category: East African Savanna Buffalo. So as not to deviate from our discussion of the Nile buffalo, we'll save this discussion until later.

How does the Nile buffalo differ in both appearance and hunting from the widespread southern Cape buffalo? First, they're said to be a bit smaller. I think this is true, but actual weights of most African buffaloes are a subject for debate and exaggeration. After all, how many buffalo carcasses are actually weighed whole? I would wager a guess that not many are. Also, weight will vary with the area and is dependent on food, minerals, and—I suppose—genetics. As I've written elsewhere—and often—the business of the Cape buffalo being "one ton of black fury" is malarkey. It's possible that somewhere there may have been an outsized buffalo bull that actually weighed a ton in the wild—but I've never seen one. Fifteen hundred pounds is about right for a mature bull at his peak, with outsized bulls perhaps weighing two or three hundred pounds more—and some a bit less.

I do think some areas typically produce slightly larger or slightly smaller buffaloes. The buffaloes we hunt in coastal Mozambique seem a bit smaller than those found in the Zambezi Valley. Selous Reserve bulls seem smaller in body than Masailand bulls, while mature bulls in Namibia and South Africa seem slightly bigger. None of this is hard evidence, just my impressions, but I'm comfortable suggesting that the average mature southern Cape buffalo bull runs a bit over three-quarters of a ton.

My guess is the Nile buffalo is probably 10 percent lighter. Given the variance among individuals, the size difference is hardly noticeable—and may not even exist. I've seen some really big-bodied bulls in Uganda's national parks, and they sure look like "real buffalo" to me! Actually, any and all differences between southern Cape buffaloes and Nile buffaloes are kind of subtle—but there are differences.

Even among southern Cape buffaloes, the bases of the horns forming into the characteristic boss isn't universal. At maturity some bulls retain a wide gap between the bases, and other bulls grow skimpy, wimpy bosses. However, the boss is a defining characteristic of better and maybe even the "best" Cape buffalo bulls. As we move west across Africa and encounter the other races, the classic helmetlike boss becomes less and less prevalent. Also, the horns tend to drop less, curving upward instead of down from the skull.

Although I certainly haven't shot all that many, I've seen a lot of Nile buffalo bulls in Uganda. To my thinking these Ugandan buffaloes are the most similar to the southern Cape buffalo, which makes sense because they're right next door, just across the border from Kenya and directly northwest of Tanzania. At least in Uganda, most Nile buffalo bulls seem to have classic bosses. I can't be sure about what they look like farther west, in Sudan, because hunting in Sudan was before my time. Plenty of photos still survive, however, so I think Sudan, and especially western Sudan, is where the major transition toward the savanna and forest races occurs.

It's been my observation that Nile buffaloes can't be defined solely by the characteristics of smaller size or the absence of bosses at the horn bases. Take time to study a few of them, however, and two distinct characteristics will be obvious: First is color. In herds you will see a noticeable percentage of brown, red, and even tan animals. Most of these will be females and youngsters. In Uganda, the only place I've seen Nile buffaloes, I don't think I've seen a mature bull that was anything but black. However, all mixed herds I've seen, including in Karamoja, where Kenya was just a ridgetop away, contained at least a few light-colored animals.

From the standpoint of the folks who keep the records, the more definitive characteristic is "drop of the horns" or, better, lack of drop. Most buffalo nuts agree that one of the most impressive characteristics of a "good" Cape buffalo bull is horns that drop down, spread outward, and then curve up. If the only thing that you are measuring is spread, then the curve means nothing. On the other

These are classic Nile buffalo bulls from Aswa-Lolim in western Uganda, north of Murchison Falls. The horns have defined bosses, but there is very little drop. At least theoretically, a Nile buffalo's horns will never drop below the jaw.

hand, if you're using the SCI measurement around the total curve, then the drop of the horns becomes really important. Just like with wild sheep, you want the bottom of the curl to be below the jawline. Nile buffalo bulls almost never have this characteristic.

Nile buffaloes may or may not have classic bosses and they may be wide or narrow, but their horns will almost always be fairly "flat." According to the SCI record book, a Nile buffalo's horns will *never* curve below the jawline, and the horns of most will not drop below the eyes. As to where to draw the line, I'll leave that to the folks who like to make the rules. My opinion is that buffaloes in northeastern Uganda are tainted. After all, depending on the time of year, there is free movement across the Kenya border.

Karamoja has produced some big, beautiful, and incredibly wide buffalo bulls that are way too big to be classic Nile buffaloes. My buddy Mike Adams got one when we were in camp together in 2017, a gorgeous bull with big bosses and about forty-seven inches wide. (*Jeez!*) I took a very nice forty-inch bull a few days later. Bulls like these are extremely unlikely on the other side of the country toward Sudan. However, even these exceptionally wide bulls don't have much drop, and by SCI measurement, the scores won't compare with southern bulls that have the same width but with a typical curve.

With Sudan completely closed and Ethiopia's small buffalo harvest now reclassified, I'm perfectly happy to keep it simple and surrender

This is a classic, mature Nile buffalo bull. Although most herds will have red or brown cows or calves, all of the bulls I've observed have had black bodies.

Uganda to the Nile buffalo (or vice versa). I do think South Sudan may reopen, and outfitters I know are nosing around. There's a lot of game in East Equatoria, including a half-dozen races and subspecies not hunted since 1983. The great prizes are probably Nile lechwe and white-eared kob. Both are certainly present in huntable numbers, and there are lots of buffaloes! If Sudan should reopen, you'd need to get into some of the Nile's big swamps to find lechwe—remember the very name "Sudan" comes from the Great Sudd, a monstrous swamp. Buffaloes would be there, too, and some of Sudan's famous heavy tusked elephants might have found refuge in the deepest swamps. For sure it would be different Nile buffalo hunting than currently exists!

At this writing, the hunt for Nile buffalo isn't unique in any way, except that, as I wrote in the preceding chapter, the Karamoja district offers some of the most open country in which I've ever hunted buffalo. I thought buffalo hunting in the Karamoja was totally crazy and very enjoyable, in part because the area is absolutely gorgeous, and in part because, in forty years, I have never seen mature buffalo bulls in such concentrations. Whether morning or evening we could look over bull after bull, purely spot-and-stalk, no tracking required. It was just a matter of time before we found really good ones. In terms of spread, Mike Adams's wide bull was fantastic, and Steve Hornady's bull was exceptional with its unusually big bosses and more drop—and, thus, more length in the curve—than is normal for Nile buffalo.

I was with him when he and Chris Weth stalked this bull, and as we got close, Steve raised his eyebrows, asking what I thought. Well, this was a great bull and I thought he ought to be shooting it, but I don't like to get into such discussions. I just sort of shrugged and nodded, not wanting to be a wet blanket, but also not wanting to be too insistent. Good thing he shot it because, by SCI score, it was the best bull of the 2017 season. This is meaningful because Weth's annual quota, then twenty-some buffalo bulls, is by far the largest number of Nile buffaloes taken since Sudan wound down thirty-five years ago.

The "other" Nile buffalo hunting is on the west side, sort of above and below Murchison Falls National Park. These are totally pure Nile buffaloes, with no southern Cape buffalo influence, and the Murchison Falls Park must be one of the very best places to observe and photograph this race of buffaloes. There are giants dying of old age every year! I hunted along the northern edge in 2011 and again briefly in 2017. I'll be honest, this is a pure—and purely frustrating—park boundary hunt, pretty much rolling tires until something comes out. That said, they do come out, and it was obvious to me in 2017 that more buffaloes were spilling out of the park than had been the case six years earlier. Then, again, from the aspect of hunting, wildlife, and conservation, *everything* in Uganda had improved in six years! It now has more areas, more wildlife, and better camps; from a fairly rough start Uganda has grown into a very mature, successful, and well-polished destination.

In 2011, I had a remarkable, and personally memorable, Nile buffalo hunt north of Murchison Falls National Park in Uganda. While I honestly think the majority of the buffaloes taken along that park boundary are probably spotted and stalked, this particular bull was tracked, absolutely fair and square. It was already fairly late in the morning when a villager came into camp to tell us he'd found the fresh tracks of a big bull headed north. Direction was important because the bull was already more than a mile off the boundary, and since he was headed north, it was extremely unlikely he had turned around and gone back to the park.

The tracks led us up a tall ridge, and then wound along a shaded plateau on top. The bull had bedded three times before moving on to

I took this very good Nile buffalo bull—with a spread of forty inches—in March 2017 with Christian Weth of Uganda Wildlife Safaris in the Karamoja district of northeastern Uganda.

find better shade. It was very hot that morning—so hot that I could feel the heat pounding on me and searing deep into my lungs. We found the buffalo in his fourth bed, a fine old bull and a very classic Nile buffalo. He stood, and at my shot he went no farther, falling down in his bed on the crest of the ridge. It was right there, at that moment, with the old bull breathing his last, that I had my heart attack. The ground came up to meet me, and for a few moments I was down and out beside the buffalo.

I mostly crawled into some shade and lay there for a while, having absolutely no clue what was wrong with me. They poured water on me, and while I didn't know what was happening, I was fairly certain I wasn't going to be staying on that ridge. So, after a little while, I crawled back over to the buffalo where we took some stills and shot some footage for television. He was far short of my best-ever Nile buffalo but, at that time, I figured that he would probably be my only Nile bull.

Without a doubt, my 2017 Uganda hunt was a whole lot better in all ways!

Savanna Buffalo

Chapter 11

All the buffalo races have transition zones, and none care exactly what we call them as they can move back and forth across our manmade boundaries. Naming buffaloes found west of the Nile and north of the little dwarf buffalo used to be quite simple: We called them all "northwestern buffalo."

To the south of the former northwestern buffaloes and current savanna buffaloes, we find the dwarf forest buffalo, *Syncerus caffer nanus*. This is the smallest subspecies of the African buffalo, which is also called "Congo buffalo" and, very incorrectly, "forest buffalo." It is the only subspecies that occurs mainly in the rainforests of Central and West Africa, with an annual rainfall around 1,500mm. *S. c. nanus* is a much smaller buffalo. Cape buffalo weigh anywhere from 400 to 800 kg (880–1,760 lbs), whereas the true dwarf forest buffaloes weigh just 250 to 320 kg (550–705 lbs).

This size difference is distinct, but *nanus* also varies markedly in appearance: This subspecies has a reddish-brown hide, often shading to mahogany or black, and is darker in the facial area and front quarters. The shape and size of the horns also distinguish the dwarf forest buffalo, for they are much smaller and are rarely joined. Cape, Nile, and savanna buffalo bulls have much larger horns. Cape and Nile buffaloes have horns that are joined or fused together at the bases, forming the distinctive bosses. This is almost never seen with true dwarf forest buffaloes, and is increasingly rare as you move from east to west and north of the forest zone.

So, our "savanna buffaloes," formerly "northwestern buffaloes," occur as a natural transition from east to west, with these buffaloes

This is a herd of West African savanna buffaloes in Benin. That's an exceptional bull on the left with his head down. (Photo courtesy of Christophe Morio)

getting smaller in body, being less black, and having smaller horns that are increasingly divided at the bases. We now call those buffaloes found west of Sudan and across the C.A.R. and northern Cameroon "Central African savanna buffaloes." Those found farther west and above the forest zone, are now called "West African savanna buffaloes." I'm totally OK with that. These buffaloes are all some mixture of browns and reds within the herds, and while mature bulls *still* seem to be mostly black, lighter-colored mature bulls do occur, and probably in greater frequency as you get farther west. The major justification for splitting the old northwestern buffalo into two was that bulls from Benin and Burkina Faso were smaller and couldn't compete with bulls from Cameroon and C.A.R.

There is also now a third "savanna buffalo": Ethiopian buffaloes are now categorized as "East African savanna buffalo." I'm OK with that, too, so long as we all understand that "savanna" is very much a misnomer! Properly, a "savanna" is an open grassland. There are savannas all over Africa. Implied is, if not a treeless plain, at least it's a partially open area. Across both Central and West Africa numerous countries have genuine climax forest in the south and belts of sub-Saharan thornbush to the north. How open the vegetation is depends a lot on how close you are to the true desert, the Sahara, but the term "savanna" is often used not to correctly describe the area but rather to juxtapose it from the genuine forest to the south.

The country in northern Cameroon and northern C.A.R. where I've hunted the Central African savanna buffalo—and species such as Derby eland, western roan, etc.—is often referred to as "savanna" by local hunters and outfitters because it sure isn't the climax forest where bongos are hunted. However, it is technically Terminalia forest, the northwestern equivalent of southern Africa's mopane and *miombo* forests found in Zambia, Mozambique, and Tanzania. Density varies, but a lot of it is pretty darned thick, as thick or thicker than anything you'll find in Zimbabwe. So, when they talk about these "savanna buffaloes," don't be misguided into thinking the country is so open that you'll simply be glassing and stalking for a bull. I'd call Uganda's Karamoja region a savanna, although technically it's acacia forest, and we hunted it accordingly.

All my buffalo hunting in both Cameroon and the C.A.R. has been by tracking, sometimes easy, sometimes not so easy—but usually in really thick vegetation at least some of the time. I also hunted just to the north in Chad, on the north side of the Aouk River that separates

My old friend Bruno Scherrer took this Central African savanna buffalo in the C.A.R. This is an extremely unusual specimen of this buffalo: The red color isn't uncommon, but it's very unusual for these buffaloes to have such a well-defined boss, rather like Nile or Cape buffaloes.

the C.A.R. and Chad. We hoped to find buffaloes there and did not, although a couple of parks hold good numbers. Southern Chad does have some thick thornbush, but it's definitely more sub-Saharan, and you can see the country starting to open up.

Farther west there's a major enclave of wildlife in northern Benin and eastern Burkina Faso. These are the most likely places to hunt the West African savanna buffalo, although this buffalo still occurs discontinuously all the way west to Senegal. This region, technically the sub-Saharan Sahel, could also be called "savanna" because for sure it isn't true forest! I found it not as thick as the northern C.A.R. and Cameroon and much like southern Chad. However you wish to characterize it, this is country where you might well run into buffaloes, make a quick stalk, and get a shot. That said, most buffaloes will be taken by tracking.

Interestingly, according to both Jason Roussos and Peter Flack, the newly designated East African savanna buffaloes of southwestern Ethiopia are also generally not found in savanna but are mostly hunted in big swamps! So perhaps this is another option for the swamp buffalo hunting I've come to love. For sure it doesn't sound like savanna buffalo hunting.

Lying to the northeast of the Nile buffalo, these Ethiopian buffaloes are an anomaly. The Central and West African savanna buffaloes continue the African buffalo's western transition, growing lighter in color and smaller. Most of us have taken at least a few black southern Cape bulls; thus, the opportunity to take a "red buffalo" holds special appeal. The problem is it's a bit like deciding whether to shoot black bears for color or size. In my experience, most mature bulls are very dark—if not black, then dark brown—all the way to Benin and Burkina Faso. I'm told it's the same in the parks in Senegal, a country with beaches on the Atlantic.

So, if you want a red buffalo, your selection is limited, but they do occur. My old friend Bruno Scherrer took a huge, almost blond buffalo in the C.A.R. some years ago, and I took a bull in northern Cameroon that was extremely red. Both were absolutely mature. I think many of these western buffaloes start out pale as calves and turn dark with age, but for sure there are some mature bulls in all sorts of colors. In Burkina Faso, adjacent to the Arly Park, we tracked three bulls that turned out

As you move farther west, you see more shades of red and brown in buffalo herds. Even so, all the way to the Atlantic the majority of savanna buffalo bulls seem to be black, with lighter colors more common among females and young. (Photo courtesy of Christophe Morio)

to be five bulls when we closed. Two were dark and three were light, but I went for size rather than color: The biggest bull, and a very good bull, was pretty much black.

With both Central and West African buffaloes, the downward transition in body size is much more noticeable, and probably easier to define. Nile buffaloes might be 10 percent smaller than southern Cape buffaloes. Between the C.A.R. and Cameroon you're probably dropping another 10 percent, and yet another 10 percent when you go west to Benin and Burkina Faso. So now we're down 30 percent from the southern Cape buffalo, meaning our fifteen-hundred-pound bulls are closer to a thousand to eleven hundred pounds.

Interestingly, in Burkina Faso the game department goes to huge pains to recover game whole when possible. Weights and measurements are recorded, so they have a pretty good database for their West African species, at least in their part of West Africa. Donna's buffalo was bigger than mine, but we were unable to recover it whole. Mine was in flat ground. The folks there described it as a normal "big bull," and on the scale it weighed 471.7 kilograms. That's 1,040 pounds, and while still a big animal, it clearly was a whole lot smaller than a southern Cape buffalo bull.

I've never seen buffalo bulls from either Cameroon or the C.A.R. actually weighed, but just to my eye, the West African savanna

In Burkina Faso they go to great lengths to recover animals whole, with weight and measurements recorded. This big West African savanna buffalo weighed 471.6 kilograms, or 1,037.5 pounds, about a third less than the average Cape buffalo bull.

buffaloes certainly look smaller. As the books say, 1,200 pounds is probably close to the actual weight of Central African buffaloes, and that's 20 percent smaller than southern Cape buffaloes.

Horns can vary tremendously between Central African and West African buffaloes. Especially in the C.A.R., the buffaloes are continuing a slow transition from the southern type, often with bosses and horns that spread outward. Some, but not all, C.A.R. buffaloes have well-defined bosses and, like Nile buffaloes, tend to have flat horns that can achieve very respectable spreads.

I was hunting with Rudy Lubin in the C.A.R. in 1992—my first time there—when we got onto a herd that had such a bull. I can still see him and wish I'd shot him, but I was on a "Derby-eland-or-nothing" mission. I didn't get the eland that trip, but I had chances at most of the other game and pretty much wound up with nothing. Single-minded dedication is good, but sometimes it's best to accept what Africa offers!

Remember I said that the old outfitters in Sudan—you'll find this in older books—used to talk about distinct types of buffaloes. You will definitely find this in the C.A.R. Some buffalo bulls are very much like Nile bulls, sometimes with good bosses but flat horns, and never with significant drop. Many others, especially as you get west toward Cameroon, have horns that are more of the "forest type"—separated on the skull without defined bosses and curving upward. Now, these buffaloes and their horns are much too large to be true dwarf forest buffalo, yet they sure don't look like Nile buffaloes.

In the early 1990s Sudanese poaching gangs got into the area where I was hunting in the eastern C.A.R., so on subsequent trips buffaloes were scarce. The only buffalo I ever shot in the C.A.R. was definitely of the "forest type." He was an old bull with just one eye, and his "devil horns" curved out and up, with a significant gap between. He was coal black, but many of the buffaloes I saw in that area were red, brown, or tan.

West African savanna buffaloes almost complete the transition. This race has bosses like Cape buffaloes, most horns are of the forest type, and it's mostly unheard of to find horns like those of the Nile buffalo. By the time you get to northern Cameroon, I think the transition from Nile buffalo-type horns is pretty much complete. I haven't seen any buffalo bulls from there—or even photographs—that show well-defined bosses, though occasionally I've seen bulls with decent horn spreads. The majority, however, have the "forest-type" horns that are well-separated on the skull, curve out and then up, and sometimes turn back in. These are sort of triangular in cross-section rather than round and are, to me, more reminiscent of water buffalo or bison horns than Cape buffalo horns.

The SCI minimum for southern Cape buffalo is 100 points or inches, a high mark to meet. To keep it simple, all African buffaloes are measured the same way, even though the bosses are not always as defined, and the forehead gap may be larger. No matter, it's an understandable measurement, and as you progress through the smaller races, the minimums go down, I think fairly, in accordance with size:

Nile buffalo	70
Central African savanna buffalo	65
West African savanna buffalo	55

This is clearly a stair step of normal horn size, with the initial minimum for Ethiopia's "new" East African savanna buffalo set at 65. This was Jason Roussos' recommendation, not only as an experienced

Ethiopian outfitter but also as a degreed wildlife biologist. Jason based the minimum on the surprisingly high percentage of Ethiopian buffaloes taken that were unable to meet the 70-inch minimum for Nile buffaloes. For completeness, the minimum for the much smaller dwarf forest buffalo is 40 points or inches, but beyond identifying it as we have, we are *not* discussing that buffalo in this chapter!

I don't see much difference in hunting methodology between any of the savanna buffaloes and the southern Cape buffalo. Difficulty in hunting them depends on the thickness of vegetation, which varies. I have taken a couple of these buffaloes by spotting, sometimes from one hill to another, or from a vantage point down onto a flat, but even then I've never strolled up and actually shot a buffalo; sightings have turned into tracking jobs, and sometimes *long* tracking jobs. So, I don't think hunting the various savanna buffaloes in the several countries they inhabit is either more or less difficult than hunting the southern Cape buffalo. Locally, it always depends on the relative density of the buffaloes and the general density of the cover. Possibly the most important factor of all is how much pressure the buffaloes have been subjected to—whether from safari hunters, poachers, or lions.

Some of the most difficult buffalo hunting I have personally ever done was in the C.A.R. during and after the times when the Sudanese poaching gangs were decimating the area. These poachers invaded the eastern C.A.R. in big camel and donkey caravans. First, they poached all the hippos in the rivers. Then they turned to the herd animals, not so much the Derby eland because this antelope is too nomadic and, consequently, not easy prey. While I'm not certain they greatly impacted buffalo numbers, at least not when I was there, the buffaloes developed paranoid schizophrenia. We could track them, and we did—but they were almost impossible to approach.

I think this was an abnormal situation and the result of heavy poaching. Generally, it has seemed to me that these Central and West African buffaloes are just buffaloes, and any difficulty in hunting them varied with the conditions, which change by the day. It is often said that these buffaloes are more aggressive than Cape or Nile buffaloes. I do not buy into this at all. However, despite the term "savanna," my experience is that the proximity of an *average* encounter with a

I took this very good West African savanna buffalo in Burkina Faso with Arly Safaris using a Montana Rifles .375 H&H. These are typical horns, curving out and up.

Central or West African buffalo is closer than what one will find in Southern or East Africa. The closer the initial encounter, the more likely you are to get into trouble.

It also depends on your perspective. In May 2018 I hunted in the Congo with Christophe Morio, a very experienced Central African hunter who also hunts in Benin. When I was in camp, he told me the story of how he got run over by a savanna buffalo, his throat slashed and windpipe opened in the encounter. Yep, he's lucky to be alive. Christophe doesn't necessarily support the theory that western buffaloes are more dangerous; he thinks it always depends on the cover. The idea, always, is to shoot straight the first time and avoid close encounters. However, a lot of serious encounters with southern buffaloes end with damage from the boss or even the buffalo's nose—but the carnage does not include horn tip wounds. The western buffaloes usually don't have a pronounced boss to smash with, but their horns often have needle-sharp tips that are much closer together than with Cape buffaloes. I have no desire to be on the receiving end!

You can't really hunt the savanna buffaloes for color phases; mature bulls that are red are fairly uncommon, but this is an excellent bull and very red, with the darker neck reminiscent of the dwarf forest buffalo. It was taken in northern Cameroon in 2004.

What's the best caliber rifle for hunting a savanna buffalo? Purely on a hypothetical basis, I suppose we could theorize that a buffalo bull weighing a third less could be taken effectively with a third less powerful cartridge, right? Maybe. Through Central and West Africa, we often find fewer formal rules. Stated minimums, whether 9.3mm or .375 caliber, are not as common as in East and Southern Africa. However, shooting is often very close, and in most of these countries logistics are complex. Camps can be great distances from arrival airports, meaning either poor roads or charter aircraft or both. These factors drive one to bring just one rifle for all game to be hunted. Across the entire range of the (now three) "savanna buffaloes," there is almost no elephant hunting today, but there is a marvelous variety of plains game. So, even though buffalo encounters may be close, add in the plains game, and a scoped rifle is the most sensible, with 9.3mm or .375 the odds-on choices.

Forest Buffalo

Chapter 12

Throughout Africa there are buffaloes that can be found in forest habitat, but the dwarf forest buffalo is Africa's only genuine "forest buffalo." To avoid confusion (and save a few words), we'll refer to him as "DFB." These DFBs occupy a large range in Central and West Africa—but not so large as is often believed. There are broad transition zones between the DFB and the savanna buffalo to his north and Nile buffalo to his east . . . and probably between him and the southern Cape buffalo to the south.

Confusion is easy because, in many transition zones, the hybrid buffaloes carry the typical curved "devil horns" of the DFB—but they're just too big to be from a DFB. The dwarf forest buffalo is a small animal. At perhaps six hundred pounds for a big bull, the true DFB is less than half the size of a southern Cape buffalo and at least a third smaller than the West African savanna buffalo.

A DFB is not found in Sudan and occupies only a small corner of the extreme southwest of the C.A.R. This means that the buffaloes of the northeastern Democratic Republic of Congo (D.R.C., former Zaire) are not the real deal. However, true DFBs are widespread in both the Republic of the Congo and much of D.R.C. Like the C.A.R. and the D.R.C., Cameroon holds two races of buffaloes, with the division fairly simple: Central African savanna buffaloes are found in the north (in Derby eland country); the DFB is found in the southern forests (in bongo country). The DFB may be most plentiful in Gabon. From there he extends westward across the bulge of Africa, following the forest zone. For sure he is found in the Ivory Coast, Liberia, Sierra

The forest buffaloes we tracked often wound their way in and out of streams, like this clear, running stream in the Congo forest.

Leone, and Guinea, although he is not common anywhere in West Africa. South of the Congo he extends into northern Angola.

My friend and hero George Parker shot a fine bull in northern Angola in 1952, the year I was born. That must have been one helluva safari; on the same trip George became one of just a small handful of Americans to take a giant sable. In George Parker's day the DFB was often referred to as a "bush cow" to differentiate from larger buffaloes.

The DFB is so different from the other African buffaloes that modern biologists are not in agreement as to whether he is a subspecies (*Syncerus caffer nanus*) or whether he deserves classification as a full species, *Syncerus nanus*. It isn't just the size. Many bulls have dark highlights on their necks and forequarters, shading from red to black—and some mature bulls are very dark. However, the majority of DFBs are red—they vary from tan to brown—not black. When I eventually took one, mine appeared black in shadows, but up close his hindquarters and back were covered in golden hair flecked with black, shading into pure black on its chest and head. Few people have seen a whole lot of genuine DFBs, but my theory is that younger animals are generally red . . . and that at least some bulls darken with age.

Their habits, too, are different. Clearly, the relative density and availability of food has much to do with this, but even under ideal conditions DFBs do not congregate in large herds. In this they are more like Asiatic water buffaloes that usually form in small family groups of a half-dozen. Even ten is unusual. Christophe Morio said he saw a herd of thirty in Congo's Odzala National Park, which is ideal habitat, but no matter the conditions, you won't find DFBs in herds of hundreds like you will with other African buffaloes. One of our trackers in central Cameroon reported that he'd recently seen "a very large herd" that he estimated as possibly fifty animals—but this must be an unusual gathering.

The DFB seems more nocturnal than other buffaloes. Like all buffaloes, he must go to water, graze, and ruminate. A dense, well-watered forest is his sanctuary, but there isn't much grass in dark forest . . . so he seems to venture out to graze more at night than do other buffaloes. This, too, could be a matter of habitat, but it could also be the result of frequent pressure from meat poachers.

These buffaloes love swampy areas, but not necessarily more than his other African cousins. Grazing is critical, so he's more plentiful—and he'll probably form into larger groups—in transitional forests where there are small meadows than in climax forests where grass is sparse. He shares the forest with the bongo, but I've often groused that there must be ten bongos for every buffalo. This is based on nothing and might not be true, but in much of the forest there are many more bongos than buffaloes . . . and in terms of relative density as well as difficulty, there are probably many more buffaloes than sitatungas!

Throughout its range, the DFB (and all buffaloes that live in a forest habitat) have a reputation for being more aggressive. Publisher Ludo Wurfbain's African mentor, the late Peter Beaujean, shot a *lot* of buffaloes throughout West Africa. He swore that they were more aggressive, and this is a common belief. Ludo himself, hunting mostly *chasse libre* (do-it-yourself), has taken more DFBs than anyone I know. He has not seen obvious aggression, even with wounded buffaloes.

I haven't seen it, either, although in the effort to take just one, I've had many close encounters in really thick vegetation.

In March 2019 I hunted in the Likini area of central Cameroon. In that neighborhood three hunters had been killed by buffaloes in recent years, two local hunters and a French concession owner. This seems a lot of mayhem for one area, but I'll hold to my theory that it's not the buffalo but the close cover that's the problem: Visibility is poor and encounters are close. It's easy to stumble within the "fight or flight" radius of a buffalo.

Regardless of how many there are and how aggressive they are, the DFB is the devil to hunt! This I know to be true because, despite extreme effort, about sixty days of specifically hunting DFB in the forests of four African countries, I have taken exactly one. This was not for lack of effort! As I said, our publisher and my friend, Ludo Wurfbain, has taken several on do-it-yourself safaris into remote corners of Africa, each representing weeks of effort in inhospitable places. Ludo figures the DFB to be one of the most difficult animals on the African continent that you can hunt on purpose—as opposed to relying on the eventual chance encounter. I echo this, but it still takes a bit of luck.

I was hunting in Mayo Oldiri's area with Guav Johnson on a safari in southern Cameroon, and we really concentrated on buffalo. We had fresh tracks to follow seven days out of fourteen. Luck determines exactly where the buffaloes are when you catch them. Several times we heard them moving in front of us, and a couple of times we saw the bushes moving from their passage—but we never saw even a small patch of hide. The forest was just so thick! On three different days we tracked the same bull. Each time, with the spoor getting fresher, he led us to a fast-flowing stream. We could see his oozing tracks on the far side, which was a park boundary where we could not follow.

Honest, while hard, it's not impossible to get a DFB. Relatively few among even serious African nuts have a DFB, but several are taken every year. My friend Mark Hampton, the great handgun hunter, took a bull in southern Cameroon in 2017. Often the chance comes when a bull or a small group is tracked into a *bai*, one of the low, swampy meadows that dot the forest; or they are caught crossing a stream. The

Over the course of four C.A.R. safaris, this is the only buffalo I ever shot there. I caught him at a waterhole as we were returning from tracking bongos. This was an old bull, blind in one eye, and obviously with horns of the forest type.

best odds are always to follow a single bull. When following groups, the challenge in that thick foliage is determining which is the bull. The horns are small, and the color and body size of the animals are often much the same. Note that a clear view is unlikely.

Sometimes dogs are used, as when hunting bongo. This can work, but it's more difficult for the dogs to hold (or delay) a buffalo than a bongo. The hunt can also quickly turn dangerous—a wild melee in thick vegetation. It's also much more difficult to be selective. It is simple fact that, of the relatively few DFBs taken annually, even fewer are mature bulls.

There's no shame in this; it's so darned thick that getting any shot at all is difficult, and properly sorting the bull can be nearly impossible. Over the years I had a couple of chances to take "any buffalo," but I managed to hold out, waiting for a chance at a grownup bull. That said, sometimes the buffalo makes the choice and forces the shot, so even with the purest of intentions, you can wind up with the wrong buffalo!

These fresh dwarf forest buffalo tracks are from the northern part of the Republic of the Congo. Buffaloes were not scarce; we had fresh tracks to follow most days, but the climax forest was so uniformly thick that we were unable to close.

Until spring of 2019 I had not taken a DFB . . . but I have taken a few buffaloes *in the forest.* Regardless of race or subspecies, it's exciting stuff and it's always at close quarters. The one buffalo I took in the C.A.R. was during a bongo hunt in the forest, a tracking hunt without dogs. Jacques Lemaux and I followed a big bongo track away from a salt lick. That's slow going, and after a couple of hours we lost the track. Although much of this area was very thick, it wasn't uniform climax growth, but "finger forest" where strands of forest were interspersed with small savannas. We circled back and picked up the tracks of a small buffalo herd.

We caught them in thick green growth at the edge of the same clearing we'd started from, so thick that, when we sorted the bull, I had to stand on tippy-toes to shoot over some underbrush and under and through other branches. Any one of several DFB hunts could have gone like this. That was twenty-some years ago, in a time when awareness wasn't what it is today. A buffalo like that, from the forests of the C.A.R., could easily find its way into the listings as a DFB, and some have. Except it was too big and I was in the *southeast* of the C.A.R., far from the nearest genuine DFB!

I mentioned in chapter 8 that swamp hunting in coastal Mozambique is so different from the surrounding forest that we refer to the buffaloes as "swamp buffaloes" and "forest buffaloes," as if they're different creatures. They are not, but forest hunting is so different and so much more difficult that some hunters forsake the swamps, insisting on trying for a "forest buffalo." I mentioned this in a story, and a reader chided me sternly, asserting that these were *not* DFBs. *Duh*, of course they aren't; they're just buffaloes that happen to live in the forest. The forest they live in isn't usually quite as thick as a true forest, but you still have similar factors to contend with: poor visibility with a crunchy carpet of leaf litter and notoriously unstable midday eddies.

I've followed buffaloes in these forests many times. Usually after wind shifts have spooked them three or four times, we give up, but several times we've gotten a good enough look to be fairly certain there were no "shooters" in the bunch. It's telling that I hunted in this area annually for ten years before I got a shot at a "forest buffalo."

On my first day hunting with Ben Rautenbach in 2017, we weren't an hour from camp when we crossed fresh tracks. The wind was still strong and steady, so we gave it a whirl. We got on them fairly quickly and got a glimpse of what appeared to be a good bull, but the vegetation was too thick for a shot. They moved off naturally, and then we got totally lucky; the herd skirted a fresh burn that allowed us to walk quietly. A few hundred yards farther—we were in the burn and the buffaloes in thick stuff beyond—Ben set up the sticks and I got my first "Mozambique forest buffalo." Nothing there is as thick as the normal conditions you will find in a true African forest, but when I heard the bull's death bellow, it was still a major triumph!

An increasingly famous forest buffalo hunt is on the thick slopes of Masailand's isolated volcanic mountains. My first buffalo hunting experience was under very similar conditions far up on the slopes of Mount Kenya. It was thick and difficult and, quite honestly, way back then I wasn't mentally prepared. Since then I've hunted buffaloes up on Tanzania's mountains several times. It's still thick and difficult, but I'm better at close-cover work today than when I was twenty-five. It is different up there, thick, close, and dangerous. A few PHs have made semicareers out of hunting these buffaloes.

Just like we call our Mozambique "forest buffaloes," they call theirs "mountain buffaloes" to emphasize the difference in hunting them—and it is different. There is one wrinkle: Some biologists postulate another race of buffalo, *S. c. mathewsi*, the mountain buffalo or Virunga buffalo, after the Virunga Mountains running from northern Congo through Rwanda and into Uganda. Many biologists don't validate this race, but if it exists, it doesn't occur in Tanzania.

So, there are buffaloes in forests and buffaloes in mountains but the dwarf forest buffalo—aka bush cow or my DFB—is very real, and I've tried hard to get one. Part of several safaris in southern Cameroon and southwest C.A.R. were spent hunting them, tracking and waiting over a *bai*. On both my safaris in Liberia I had hopes of getting one. While Liberia is primarily a destination for small, localized forest duikers and the water chevrotain, the dwarf forest buffalo occurs in Liberia and is on license. My second Liberia safari, with partner Mike Adams, was a fourteen-day hunt. I was hoping that a few extra days might give us a chance at a buffalo and pigs. We were fantastically successful on the little guys, but although we saw buffalo tracks, we had no chance.

In years gone by, Gabon was "the" place for a DFB. Limited hunting reopened in 2018, but initially only for duikers and other small game. Southern Cameroon is actually pretty good, but while bongo hunting is fairly certain, getting a buffalo is "iffy." Jason Hornady and I had been shopping for a forest hunt, and our research suggested the Congo as the place to try. That's "Congo-Brazzaville," as opposed to former Zaire. The Congo has also been on-again, off-again, but it's open now. Without question it's a superb destination for bongo, and the buffalo population is considered larger than southern Cameroon.

So, in May 2018, Jason and I headed for a long-planned two-week hunt in Democratic Republic of the Congo, bongo as his primary quest, the DFB for me. We hunted with Christophe Morio and Jean-Luc Damy of Congo Forest Safaris. There have been horror stories about the Congo with its red tape, road blocks, extortion, and worse. We saw none of this. On the way in, a short commercial flight took us from Brazzaville to Ouesso in the far north, and in a couple of hours we were in a clean, pleasant, and well-appointed camp, looking across the Sangha River to Cameroon. At the end we drove back to Brazzaville. It was an all-day journey, but the roads were good, and the few roadblocks posed no problems. It was a smooth and trouble-free forest safari.

By their second year in the area, Christophe and Jean-Luc had developed their area well, with their focus primarily on hunting bongos. Roads were a work in progress, but they had located (or created) dozens of mineral licks, irresistible to most forest species, and they'd done their homework with trail cameras as well as instituting effective anti-poaching policies. Finding the tracks of big bongo bulls was not difficult, and, indeed, there were plenty of DFBs leaving tracks we could follow. From the start, however, we had our work cut out. Their concession was primarily climax forest with few swampy meadows. Not too far to the south, along the edges of the huge Odzala National Park, the forest starts to thin and conditions are much better for buffalo hunting, but in 2018 these more open areas were not available.

Jason had to cut his hunt short, which is risky on a forest hunt. Hunting with young PH Yannick Exalto, he got a fine bongo on the

PH Yannick Exalto poses with a truly exceptional dwarf forest buffalo taken in 2018, a few weeks after my hunt. I am assured this is not one of the several bulls we tracked!

Dwarf forest buffaloes are usually found in small family groups. The darker bull is a very good specimen, with typical dark forequarters and lighter flanks. (Photo courtesy of Christophe Morio)

fourth day, so, with a shortened hunt, he beat the odds. Christophe and I focused mainly on buffalo. From my notes we tracked buffalo nine of my thirteen hunting days. Just past the midpoint, we had a perfect morning after a big rain. There were no fresh buffalo tracks; instead, we found a huge and very fresh bongo track that I couldn't resist. Our excellent Pygmies took the track with their dogs, and at 7:05 A.M. on May 25th I shot a fantastic bongo, long and wide, horns polished smooth all through the curve, ivory tips starting to wear, with bases I couldn't get both hands around. This bongo was not what I was there for, but he's probably my very best African animal . . . this tale shows that it's wise to take what the forest offers.

In the Congo, I was impressed by the numbers of buffaloes. There were times when we came very close, like the day when we caught three cows with a big-footed bull crossing a small river. After several hours of tracking, we found ourselves about seventy yards downstream, which is a huge distance in the forest. I could see them clearly and had the Aimpoint on them. I could easily have shot any of the cows, but the bull stayed hidden by the third cow, so I couldn't shoot, and then they all spooked and crashed away. At other times we heard them break ahead of us (and around us), and a couple of times we heard them feeding just ahead, but it was too thick to see them clearly.

The Pygmies and their dogs do very well on bongo. Having hunted bongo with and without dogs, I have no ethical issues about using dogs. You simply must see how dense the forest is to understand. With dogs, you can see the horns and judge the animal; without them, you will shoot a spot of red hide and hope for the best. When I saw this bongo, I knew it was a giant! The buffalo is a different deal. Once in a while a buffalo will hold for dogs, but usually not. Sometimes the buffalo will try to kill the dogs, and a smart dog might run back to the hunters with the buffalo right behind. This is a preferred (*gulp!*) result, but it didn't happen for me.

We tried tracking with and without dogs, and our Pygmies had no trouble holding the tracks. The problem was that we couldn't close for a shot—meaning, mostly, that we never got lucky enough to catch up in a spot where a shot would be possible. So, the Congo forest didn't yield me the DFB I wanted so badly. Adding insult to injury, on the drive back to Brazzaville we saw three fine bulls standing on the edge of the highway; they were along the edge of the Odzala Park, really south of the true forest. There are plenty of buffaloes in the Congo!

Bongo hunting is exceptional, and there were plenty of tracks of most other forest species. Christophe Morio and Jean-Luc are exploring for country with more openings to increase their chances for buffalo. I'd like to hunt in the Congo again!

However, despite our best effort, this book, certainly my last on this subject, was nearing completion and I *still* hadn't taken a DFB—for some years at the top of my dwindling African bucket list. At the 2019 Safari Club convention I was tending my booth when two friends cruised by. First came Chris Kinsey, one of the most experienced African hunters alive. Next came Adam Biondich, a great young guy and one of the luckiest hunters I know. Each delivered the same message: "Boddington, if you really want a dwarf forest buffalo, you need to go talk to Philippe and J. P. Bernon at Club Faune. They've got an area in Cameroon *north* of the forest where they've had tremendous success with your DFB."

Christophe Lemée's trail cam caught this herd of DFBs at a waterhole just at daylight. This is an "OK" bull, a bit younger and with smaller horns than the one we got.

Honestly, I had neither time nor finances to mount another forest safari right then . . . and it sounded much too good to be true! I did not go talk to them, but my buddy Adam was relentless, so I made contact. The area is Likini, north of Yaoundé, Block 41, the *only* allocated hunting block in central Cameroon. The area is a bit like the "finger forest" where I hunted in the southeastern C.A.R., so there were dense strands of true forest following watercourses and interspersed with wooded flats and ridges. In March and April when the grass is greening up, they focus on buffalo; in May and June, when rains have made the grass long, they concentrate on bongo. I was thinking about saving my pennies and going in 2020, but they had a cancellation for late March 2019 at an awesome discount. Donna and I talked it over, and soon I was on my way for yet one more try for a DFB.

All my other Cameroon hunts have originated in Douala on the coast. Yaoundé is the capital; it is up-country and reachable by Air France from Paris. Getting to Likini was just too easy, an eight-hour drive, including waiting for the ferry to cross the Sanaga River. Christophe Lemée, another veteran Central African hunter, was there to meet me when I arrived at camp. It's an excellent camp, sited atop a ridge to catch the breezes. The lounge/dining area was decorated with *nanus* skulls and horns, and someone had come up with a clever idea I'd never seen before: The generator-fed lights were *red*, thus ensuring almost no bugs!

This is an interesting area. Christophe said that, before the rains, few bongos show up on his trail cameras, and, indeed, while checking salt licks, we saw almost no bongo tracks. In 2018 from April onward, however, the area produced *eight* bongos. When bongo hunting is good, buffalo hunting is almost impossible because the grass gets so tall. So, in late March and early April, when grass is still short, the buffaloes come out of the forest to graze. It's still thick, but so long as you catch them before they retreat into the real forest, they can be tracked and hunted just like "real buffaloes."

Lord, it almost happened on the first morning! Our trackers spotted two bulls from the road, so there was a quick stalk, we put up sticks . . . and then they spooked and galloped off. We followed, but the forest edge was close-by and we let them go. Honestly, on the first morning I don't think anyone was too keen on shooting, but these were DFBs, so I didn't know exactly what to think: Would there be another chance?

Using a "camp gun," a very good Sako .375 with a Leica scope, I'd had my crosshairs on one of them. It was a very tan bull, but I judged him young and Christophe agreed. He broke first, and then I caught just a glimpse of the second bull, bigger in the body and dark. This one made me kick myself, but I had no real chance of a clear shot.

The game here was a mix of forest and savanna. Up on the ridges there were lots of kobs, waterbucks, harnessed bushbucks, and red-

In the Likini area of central Cameroon, we picked up this massive old DFB on a trail camera. He was frequenting a salt lick deep in the forest in the wee hours and we couldn't figure out how to hunt him. Horns are short and worn, an awesome DFB.

I took my dwarf forest buffalo—at last!—in central Cameroon in March 2019. The small body size is striking—just note how huge the rifle appears! This is a fully mature bull with long horns and a dark but obviously reddish body color.

fronted duikers. The forests held bongos, sitatungas, forest duikers, and buffaloes wandering back and forth. My sense was there are not a lot of buffaloes—Christophe agreed, perhaps a few hundred—but as DFBs go, this is a huge number. Even better . . . they were huntable!

We followed several tracks but were unable to close—the same old story. We were monitoring some salt licks and trail cameras with an eye toward sitting in *machans* late in the hunt if we needed to, but it didn't come to that. However, we didn't actually *see* any more buffaloes until the halfway point of my safari. I try to be optimistic, but after so many attempts, fatalism creeps in. I wasn't sure this was gonna happen, although, logically, the signs were good.

One day shortly thereafter, we were cruising down the main track about an hour from camp, just after full light, when I got a partial view of a large red animal about seventy yards away. Bushbuck? Right color, too big. Kob? Too red and also too big. A quarter-second later my brain clicked, and I was just starting to motion when the trackers also saw the buffalo. It was a replay of the first morning, except this time the buffalo I'd seen had walked off to the left and vanished. Although we'd seen only one, the tracks showed there had been four. Two had gone straight downhill to the forest, but two, probably both bulls, had kept to the edge.

They were walking fast—not good—but at least they weren't headed into the forest. We could surely track them there, but closing for a shot would be unlikely. We followed, already sweating despite the morning cool. We hadn't gone far, maybe a thousand yards and certainly not an hour, yet the two bulls kept walking. They

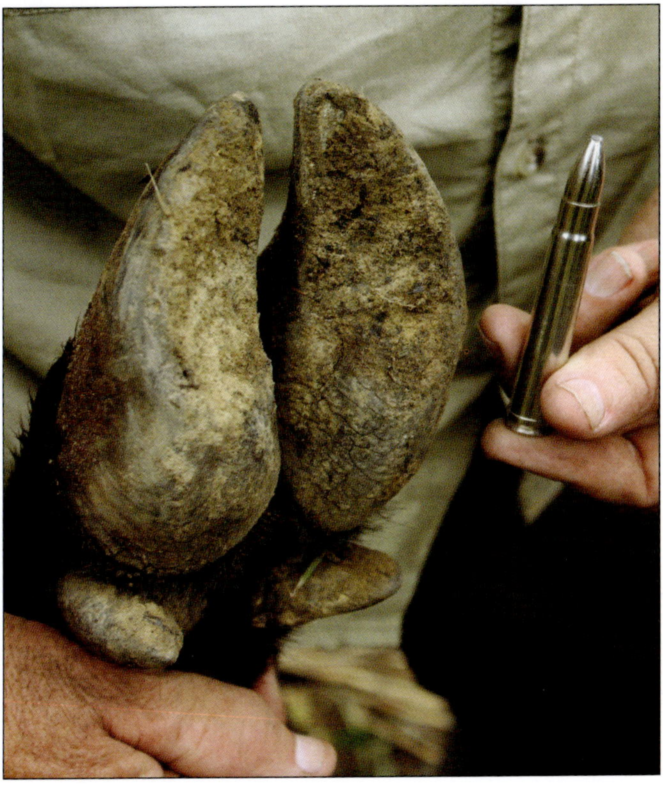

Christophe Lemée compares the front hoof of my DFB to a .375 cartridge. As with everything else, the feet are very small . . . as are the tracks!

never ran, so we continued even though our footing was terrible. A seasonal worm causes dirt clods, and these threatened our stability—if we weren't careful, we could turn an ankle with every step. I stayed close behind the trackers until Christophe tapped me, indicating a boot lace had come loose. I stopped to fix it, and, of course, that's when the trackers, now five yards ahead, motioned. Boot lace, *later*!

The trackers were on a small mound, setting up the sticks. Off to the right, forty yards away, stood a red buffalo. I could see the horns and I realized he was a bull—I could see the penis sheath—but he probably was a young bull. I had him in the scope for an instant, and then he stepped out of my window. Horrified, I'd forgotten the second bull, but my team had him. He was standing in deep shade to my left front, a bit farther away and quartering to me. He was very dark, and he had longer and heavier horns. I think Christophe said something unnecessary like "Shoot the black one." Tracker Louis was trying to move the sticks, also unnecessary as well as risky.

I got the crosshairs on the point of the shoulder; the buffalo took the bullet hard, and then he ran to the right. I was milliseconds slow with a right-hand bolt, so the second shot flew behind him and I knew it . . . but I also knew the first shot was good. We found lung tissue sprayed behind where he'd stood and lots of blood along his tracks. In less than a hundred yards, Louis pointed to a dark form lying ahead. I saw an ear move, and this time I needed the sticks because my hands were shaking!

We'd seen an older bull on a trail camera, but this bull was fully mature with long horns and good bases (for a *nanus*). At long last I had my first dwarf forest buffalo!

Cape versus Water Buffalo

Chapter 13

Looking at a picture of an African buffalo, he, she, or *they* exclaim, "Water buffalo!" To me, that response is like fingernails on a blackboard! As we've seen, not all African buffaloes are the southern Cape buffalo. Honestly, with their shorter, curved horns and often absent the signature boss, the savanna buffaloes of West Africa actually do resemble the Asiatic water buffalo, but they are still African buffaloes. Obviously, they're related since they're large bovines all and similar in many ways.

They are also different in many ways. Different enough that biologists place them in separate genera: The African buffalo's genus is *Syncerus* while the water buffalo's is *Bubalus*. These are not the only genera that, whether technically correct or not, we might refer to as "buffalo." Genus *Bos* includes the gaur, the world's largest wild ox; it also includes the much smaller banteng and the aurochs, the extinct European wild ox. The American bison, so often called "buffalo," is the genus *Bison*, as is the similar European bison or wisent. Other relatives in family *Bovidae* include the muskox and takin.

In the little known and extremely messy—and messed up—jungles of Southeast Asia, we read old accounts about variations that may or may not have been real and may or may not still exist. These include the almost mythical bovines such as the kouprey, mithan, and seladang. The mithan is a cross between gaur and domestic cattle, while the seladang is probably a subspecies of the widespread gaur. The kouprey is or was a distinct large bovine, properly identified by science as *Bos sauveli* in northern Cambodia in 1937. Unfortunately, it was last seen in 1988.

Danny Deshotels (center) took this awesome water buffalo bull with his Blaser double .470. Robert (left) and Danny Deshotels and outfitter Greg Pennicott are on the floodplains south of Elcho Island in Australia's Northern Territory.

My old friend Charlie Askins wrote briefly about these in his *Asian Jungle, African Bush*. Long before our major involvement in Vietnam, Askins spent a long tour as chief marksmanship instructor for the South Vietnamese army. Now, Colonel Charlie wasn't beyond stretching a story—especially a *good* story!—but he didn't claim to have seen any of these bovines. In his ramblings across pre-1960 Vietnam, he talked to a lot of local hunters, so his second or third-hand knowledge of these strange "buffaloes" still beats anything I know about them.

The gaur is very real and still with us. Sometimes called "Indian bison," the gaur is the world's largest *extant* bovine. This is a tall, imposing creature, and a big bull can exceed 3,000 pounds. As an admitted buffalo freak, I view hunting a native-range, free-range gaur to be the ultimate quest, but there is very little likelihood of that happening. This is odd because the gaur occupies a huge range, from southeastern India across Burma (now Myanmar) to Thailand and into Southeast Asia. Although certainly threatened and extirpated in many areas, the gaur exists in huntable numbers across much of its range. Unfortunately, nowhere does organized and legalized hunting for the gaur exist. I do know a few folks who have hunted them in years gone by. Like me, Jack Lott, of the .458 Lott fame, considered the gaur as the ultimate bovine. Using local contacts, he made a couple of attempts—never mind where—saw fresh tracks, but never got a shot.

The banteng is also real, with wild populations in Indonesia, Malaysia, Java, and Borneo. The banteng, *Bos javanicus*, is a colorful bovine; mature males can be almost black with pale underparts. Weighing perhaps eight hundred pounds, in appearance and build banteng are sort of a miniature gaur but with cylindrical horns. Said to be an ancestor to domestic cattle, there is no opportunity to hunt native-range banteng, but they can be hunted free range in Australia's Northern Territory northeast of Darwin. Introduced on the Cobourg Peninsula as a meat source in 1849, they were once more or less confined to Cobourg by a fence across the peninsula's neck, which was, theoretically, put there to prevent the spread of bovine disease. The fence has long since been in disrepair, and in recent decades bantengs have spread well to the south through trackless marsh country. They are also found on privately owned stations fairly close to Darwin.

Cobourg proper is a park—Garig Gunak Barlu National Park—with permits tightly controlled. Open ground to the south is aboriginal land where the banteng is not protected, but landowner permission is required to hunt them. While the feral water buffalo occupies a huge slice of Australia's "Top End," the banteng's range is much more limited, and access to them is problematic and hotly contested among Australian outfitters. The result is that hunting the banteng is more limited and costlier than hunting water buffalo in Australia. This is regrettable because I think the banteng, although much smaller, is the more interesting of the two.

A banteng bull is an extremely attractive animal. Bantengs live in heavy cover, so by nature they are almost a jungle creature, and although my experience is limited, I have found them warier than the water buffalo. By reputation they are more aggressive. I don't have enough experience with them to confirm this, but the Australians I've hunted with all attest to exercising a lot more caution with banteng than with water buffaloes.

The water buffalo is much larger than the banteng, and it is actually considerably larger than any African buffalo. As I've written so many times, the description of a Cape buffalo as "a ton of black fury" is hogwash. It's not impossible for an outsized Cape buffalo bull to exceed two thousand pounds, especially with some of today's "game-ranch" conditions—but such size is rare and, in the wild, highly unlikely. The *normal* mature water buffalo bull, on the other hand, will weigh about a ton—and maybe a couple hundred pounds more.

I have hunted free-range water buffalo in Australia, Argentina, and the Philippines. I also shot one on Joey O'Bannon's place in Florida, and I've been an observer on a couple of water buffalo hunts in Texas. It seems to me the size is fairly consistent; a water buffalo bull is *big*. Without accurate scales and plenty of logistical support, "estimated" weights are always questionable, but the water buffalo bulls I've taken are all noticeably bigger than any African buffaloes I've seen. Its coloration is generally uniformly black, often with a white throat patch; however, individuals that are tan to reddish do occur. This seems less common for water buffaloes in Australia than I've seen elsewhere.

The water buffalo has been domesticated for about five thousand years, and domestic water buffaloes are, literally, found all over the world. Thus, clearly there are several distinct gene pools of water buffaloes. The total world population of domesticated water buffaloes is about 130 million, with more people dependent on water buffaloes than any other livestock. In much of Asia the water buffalo remains in common use as a tractor, as well as for milk and meat. Much more interesting for hunters is the fact that there are a few genuinely wild populations of water buffalo remaining in Southeast Asia.

The various breeds probably relate somewhat to color, but for sure genetics relates to horn size and configuration. The old pictures of water buffaloes taken in India show wide, sweeping horns. The bulls we took in the Philippines were similar. Australia's water buffaloes have a similar shape, but neither area seems to produce horns with the incredible length of some of the old Indian records. However, Australian water buffalo horns seem to me to have more mass with their thicker horns with heavier bases.

Brazil's Marajo Island water buffaloes, unlike most South American animals, have those wide, sweeping horns. Although no

Although much smaller than the water buffalo, the colorful and cover-loving banteng offers an excellent hunt. Prime bulls are often nearly black but fade to brown with age. Donna Boddington's banteng had long horns but was very brown.

longer hunted, Marajo Island has a large water buffalo population. Introduced as a meat source and to make "buffalo mozzarella," water buffaloes are widespread in Argentina, both free range and estate, but the horns are entirely different. They are very thick and impressive, curving out and up like overgrown bison horns, except they are triangular in cross section. The water buffaloes I've seen elsewhere, as farm animals in Central Asia and in the United States, seem generally to have smaller horns that may grow out and around into almost complete curls.

The Philippines has its own native wild bovine, the tamaraw (*Bubalus mindorensis*) on the island of Mindoro. The tamaraw, with a dwindling and protected population, is essentially a dwarf water buffalo, weighing up to possibly seven hundred pounds. Slightly smaller are the mountain and lowland anoa of Indonesia, respectively *B. quarlessi* and *B. depressicornis*. Weighing about fifty pounds less than the tamaraw, they are the smallest of the world's wild bovines.

American ex-pat Jay Carlson is the only guy who figured out how to break through the cultural and bureaucratic barriers and operate in

The native wild bovine of the Philippines is the tamaraw, a species of water buffalo. Considered endangered, they now exist only on Mindoro. The water buffaloes we hunted were feral water buffaloes. (Shutterstock image)

the Philippines. He hunted first on Mindoro, and his last few seasons on Luzon. The water buffaloes we hunted in northern Luzon were definitely not tamaraws! Domestic water buffaloes are legion throughout the Philippines; theoretically the buffaloes we hunted were feral water buffaloes. I knew Jay for years before the hunt, but, unfortunately, and much too young, he succumbed shortly after my hunt, probably from an accumulation of tropical diseases. Jay conducted maybe a half-dozen *shikars* per year for more than a decade. It was hot and uncomfortable, always with the shadow of security issues flitting around.

The domestic water buffalo is called *carabao* in the Philippines, and it is their national animal. The Philippines is a huge archipelago of over 7,600 islands, and Luzon is the largest. Most of the domestic water buffaloes I saw in fields and villages on Luzon had small, circular horns. The bulls we shot had wide, impressive "sweeping" horns. I can't explain this, but photos of "*carabao*" sometimes show the wide, sweeping horns. So that gene pool exists, and since water buffaloes have been present for many centuries, it is almost inevitable that there are feral populations in more remote areas. We hunted on private land, adjacent to a park of heavy jungle with low mountains, and according to Jay, "wild water buffaloes" would wander in from the park, usually bulls hoping to mate with domestic females.

So far so good. The only thing is, when we needed a water buffalo, one would sort of appear, and it would be a good bull. I'm not a suspicious guy, but it seemed almost too good to be true. In any case, we located and stalked our water buffaloes in very thick cover in horrible heat and humidity. Another factor made hunting there interesting: You simply cannot bring firearms into the Philippines, so, we went to the local gendarmery and checked out a well-worn M14. We got a partial belt of corroded 7.62x51 NATO machine gun ammo, so we left the tracers and stripped out the ball cartridges!

I was hunting with my buddy Saso "Gaspar" Ivanov from Macedonia. Gaspar had been an officer in the Yugoslav army, so he knew the AK, but he'd never seen an M14. After a quick practice and sight-in session, we were ready to rock and roll. We had just the one rifle, so the designated shooter would take the M14 since the .308 Winchester with 155-grain nonexpanding military bullets is not my idea of a buffalo gun. For backup, the other hunter would take a pump 12-gauge loaded with slugs. It was thick enough that our shots were at a matter of feet, no more than ten or fifteen yards.

We shot two buffaloes each and had no problems at all, but I noted that when we got close, our local trackers found trees and weren't shy about shinnying up them! Fortunately, that old M14 functioned perfectly and we had plenty of ammo. How real the danger was, I can't say, but it's worth noting that Carlson himself had been badly gored by an unwounded buffalo a few years earlier. He suffered for nearly a day before he got medical help, and it's amazing he survived; I suspect internal injuries contributed to his early demise.

With Carlson gone, the window to hunt in the Philippines is closed. There has been a little bit of hunting in Vietnam, including for water buffalo, which I assume are feral. There have been a few other opportunities here and there, including in the United States, but throughout the world the two primary opportunities to hunt water buffalo have been and are in Australia and Argentina.

Water buffaloes were first released into Australia at the mouth of the Mary River in 1841. The population expanded and became huge, then was reduced because of bovine disease. Inevitably, helicopter gunning became unaffordable, and in the last few decades water buffaloes have rebounded significantly. The Top End is a very big place, but there are lots of buffaloes. Sometimes you catch them in a eucalyptus forest or along some riverine cover, but often you catch them on wide-open floodplains. With plenty of buffaloes and the outcome relatively certain, it's a fun place to use a big double, but it's really not open-sight country.

I figure the average, normal shot on a water buffalo is a bit beyond a hundred yards, possible with iron sights but pushing it hard. One year I was hunting with CZ's Jason Morton, who brought a .338 Lapua. We had a lot of fun shooting buffaloes at four hundred yards or so. I would never try that with an African buffalo, but this doesn't speak to any difference between the two. Rather, we were hunting in Greg Pennicott's area, a huge, open floodplain. There was no cover for miles, thus little likelihood of losing a buffalo if something went wrong.

Argentina is different. I think I've shot four or five water buffaloes down there and have seen more taken. The buffaloes are not so much in the open hills of Patagonia where a lot of red stag hunting is done; instead, they're more in La Pampa and points north that feature rolling plains with trees, which is excellent country for stalking. My Argentinian buffaloes have all been close, mostly sixty to one hundred yards.

I shot one bull with a 7x57. That choice does not reflect a lack of respect for the water buffalo but rather an awareness of situation. I loaded up some 175-grain solids, just like Walter Bell, except I used a Barnes homogenous alloy "Super Solid," not the Kynoch steel-jacketed solids Bell used. Marcelo Sodiro and I found a group bedded, so we crawled in close, and I shot a huge bull at the base of his ear from about thirty yards. I probably wouldn't try something silly like that on the open floodplains of northern Australia. There are few situations where I would attempt such a stunt on an African buffalo—or where it would be legal!

Due to the open floodplains, extremely close shots are less likely in Australia. So, I guess Australian buffalo hunting leans more toward shooting while Argentinian water buffaloes are more about stalking. However, my intent was not to compare the hunts, which are both good, but to compare the water buffalo to the African buffalo. At the shows I'm asked this a lot: Is the water buffalo worth hunting? Is he as tough as an African buffalo? As dangerous? And so forth. Sometimes

Saso Ivanov, my buddy from Macedonia, took this excellent water buffalo on Luzon in the Philippines using a borrowed M14 with 7.62x51mm NATO ammo. This was a very old bull and obviously in poor body condition.

this comes from hunters who have already hunted the African buffalo and are looking for a different experience. Other times, quite honestly, they're shopping. In my view an African buffalo hunt is worth every penny, but it costs more pennies than it used to. Water buffalo hunts have also escalated in cost, but are less expensive than Cape buffalo hunts; moreover, in some circumstances, there are opportunities for culls at a reduced rate.

I've already given my opinion on banteng. Our universe of hunting big bovines is very limited these days. Whether in Europe or North America, the bison may be called a buffalo, but is not a buffalo; there are good reasons why the bison almost exited into extinction so easily. I'm glad both the American and European bison are still with us, but there's little challenge in hunting them. So, how do our two most available buffaloes, the African buffalo and the water buffalo, stack up against each other?

Although locally threatened, the gaur is not endangered and still occupies a huge range from India to Southeast Asia; this large herd was photographed in Thailand. Hunting a wild gaur would be the ultimate bovine adventure, but no organized or legal opportunities currently exist. (Shutterstock image)

The water buffalo is bigger, and from the standpoint of sheer size, it deserves respect. The African buffalo is legendary for toughness, but I've never had reason to think the water buffalo was less tough. With both species, most bulls succumb readily to a well-placed bullet of adequate caliber. However, with both species, backup shots are important and can save the day, so don't avoid taking that extra precaution. I'm not certain that the water buffalo is as tenacious of life as the African buffalo. It seems to me that, most of the time, water buffaloes go down more readily to a really proper hit.

There's always an exception. I was hunting water buffalo with Greg Pennicott in Australia, and there was this one bull that just wouldn't go down and wouldn't give up. The African buffalo is legendary for taking punishment, but this water buffalo gave me pause. We were hunting on a big floodplain south of Elcho Island, and the bull was on the edge of a mangrove swamp. We saw him at distance, got the wind right, and stalked along the edge for several hundred yards. The first shot, with a .375, looked really good, but the bull immediately headed into thick cover. We caught up with him quickly—postmortem showed the first hit was just fine—but it took another half-dozen shots to get him down. Although the bull was in a perfect situation to defend himself, he never became aggressive . . . he just wouldn't give up.

The Australian outfitters I've worked with, primarily Bob Penfold and Greg Pennicott, have shot hundreds of water buffaloes. I have not and don't claim extensive experience. My Aussie friends who have that experience are not unduly concerned about them, but they are also not casual; they seem to exercise much the same degree of caution that experienced African professional hunters use around Cape buffaloes. The big difference, again, is water buffalo country is generally more open, where point-blank encounters are rare.

Despite the legend, in my personal experience, charges with African buffaloes are rare. I've seen them, but not many. I have never seen a water buffalo charge, but, as I said, I have much less experience with them than I do with African buffaloes. In both Argentina and Australia, hunters I know have been charged by water buffaloes.

I mentioned that Philippine outfitter Jay Carlson got badly hammered by a water buffalo. Given the small number of water buffaloes Jay had available, it's unlikely he saw fifty shot—and yet he was nearly killed by an unwounded animal that came out of nowhere. He had also been on the receiving end of charges when out with clients. Because he hunted in a jungle, most encounters were very close. This adds greatly to the danger factor and increases the likelihood of a charge. Also, considering the impossibility of bringing firearms into the Philippines, *all* of Jay's buffaloes were taken with marginal weapons, either 7.62x51mm military ammo or shotgun slugs!

Possibly the water buffalo is not as tenacious as the African buffalo, but I'll leave the jury out on that. They are enough bigger that they should be considered as tough and should be approached with the same powerful cartridges and certainly the same deep-penetrating bullets. I'm pretty sure that if you hit them poorly, their instincts will take over and you can have the same level of problem on your hands. Just because I haven't personally seen a water buffalo become aggressive, whether wounded or not, doesn't mean they won't.

Of one thing I am certain: The water buffalo is not as naturally wary as the African buffalo. I'm sure my Australian friends who make their living hunting water buffaloes don't want to hear this, but I have found this consistent wherever I have hunted this species. It isn't that you can walk up and brain them with a baseball bat. You have to keep the wind right and not all approaches are going to work, but they seem a lot more trusting, and you can take more liberties while getting within range for a shot.

Perhaps this is simply the nature of the beast, but there may be two other factors at play. First, with the possible exception of the remnant populations of native-range, wild water buffaloes in Southeast Asia, most water buffaloes and *all* populations currently hunted have lived without tigers for umpteen bovine generations. Almost all free-range African buffaloes deal with lions at least occasionally, many on a constant basis. Lions keep African buffaloes on their toes.

Second, we shouldn't forget that water buffaloes have been domesticated for thousands of years. In South Africa they are successfully ranching the Cape buffalo, but to my knowledge the African buffalo has never been effectively domesticated as livestock. Even the folks who are ranching buffaloes regard them as unpredictable and dangerous. My old friend Raymond Theron was gored through the heart while closing a gate, checking on a disease-free breeding herd in the Northern Cape. Come to think of it, in the United States domestic cattle are a leading cause of animal-related human injury and death, and the Cape buffalo is a lot more unpredictable than an Angus steer! I just don't know enough to be able to state with certainty if the water buffalo's long history of being domesticated has changed and "softened" its genetic programming or if it is naturally not as wary as some other bovines, especially the African buffalo.

I remain certain that the water buffalo is not as suspicious as the African buffalo and is also not as attuned to sensing danger by sight, hearing, and smell. This does not mean that the water buffalo isn't a worthy adversary. A good water buffalo bull is huge and magnificent, and hunting him is interesting and exciting. His pursuit is very much not the same as hunting the African buffalo, but in today's world with our shrinking opportunity to pursue the great bovines, I'm glad we still have plenty of opportunity to hunt the water buffalo.

The Best Country

Chapter 14

"So," I'm often asked, "where is the best place to hunt buffalo?" Here's the good news: There are lots of great places! I certainly haven't hunted in them all, but I've hunted the African buffalo in a lot of different areas. To some extent "best" depends on what you're looking for. Is it success, horn size, overall experience, or the most reasonable cost? Africa is a big place, and all of these things have changed, not just over time, but during my time in Africa. Countries have opened, closed, and reopened. Game management has changed, sometimes for the better. Today Mozambique, Namibia, South Africa, and Uganda are solid destinations if you want to hunt buffalo even though none was considered a good "buffalo country" in the 1980s and 1990s.

Africa consists of a mosaic of countries where the only constant is change. Unfortunately for wildlife, change is rarely for the better. Human encroachment is the biggest issue. Much wildlife habitat has been lost to villages, farms, and cattle. Tanzania and Zambia still have some fantastic areas with great buffalo hunting, but many former blocks have been settled or heavily poached and are no longer viable. In the 1980s Botswana was the land of buffalo. We rarely tracked because we could expect to run into herds almost on a daily basis. Safari hunting on Botswana's government lands is currently closed, so there's no buffalo hunting at all. I expect some form of reopening, but things will be different if and when hunting resumes.

Botswana is now home to a fast-growing and overpopulated herd of a quarter-million elephants, at least a third and possibly a half of the continent's total. The entire Chobe region in the north looks like a nuclear blast zone because of the damage from elephants. I hunted in Botswana in 2007 and 2008, just before the current suspension. We saw buffaloes, but nowhere near the numbers we saw in the 1980s. Northern Namibia's Caprivi Strip (now Zambezi Region) is long and narrow. There are resident buffaloes, but the operators up there rely on movement from Botswana. There are big herds and they come across, but Botswana isn't the land of buffalo that it once was. There are just too many elephants.

In Zimbabwe, predator management can be an issue. I've hunted in Zimbabwe's Lower Zambezi, eastward from Mana Pools, and it is one of few areas I've seen in Africa where there are just too many lions! The outfitters saw it coming: Clear back in 2008, the lack of calves in the herds was obvious. This is not from poaching or safari hunting. It's from lions. For a few seasons the operators were able to resume a lioness quota. In time this would have helped, but the concept of hunting female lions became too politically sensitive, so the quota was removed.

Human habitation is another factor that will reduce the population of buffaloes or, for that matter, any game. To counter this, there are Designated Safari Areas (DSAs) in Zimbabwe where human habitation is not allowed: Chewore North and South, Dande North and South, and Sapi. In the early 2000s there were lots of buffaloes and lots of groups of bachelor bulls, and we rarely had trouble finding bull tracks to follow. Today there are still lots of buffaloes, but there are now many fewer *dagga* bulls, and fewer herds contain mature bulls. At every convention I hear that poaching is a factor, but these are still remote areas, and while elephant poaching has spiked, I don't think there's much meat poaching and certainly not for buffalo.

When wildlife populations change dramatically, there's usually more than one factor involved. I think it could be argued that buffalo quotas were too high, but in the Lower Zambezi, lion predation has been a major factor. Zimbabwe's Zambezi Valley remains a classic hunting area, awesome for elephant, leopard, and lion. It's still an area where buffalo hunting remains a classic tracking experience in

A nice herd of buffaloes is grazing in an open meadow in the Rungwa area of central Tanzania. This was fantastic buffalo country, where we daily encountered herds.

thick bush, and there are still a lot of buffaloes and some good bulls. However, buffalo hunting isn't what it was just a decade ago.

In buffalo hunting there really is no "better or best." It's all good, and there are many choices. My favorite areas have certainly changed, and buffalo hunting has changed and will continue to change. Change is a constant in African hunting, so anything said in 2019 will inevitably change. So, if you are reading this in the 2020s, take my conclusions with heavy doses of salt, and do your research based on what is happening when you are planning your safari. Since my crystal ball seems defective, I can't predict what the future will bring, but let me try to evaluate buffalo hunting in 2019 based on the criteria of cost, success, horn quality, and overall experience.

Cost is a huge factor for many if not most of us. It is important to get your money's worth and to have a good and memorable experience, but there's really no "bad" buffalo hunting. There are bad hunts, and there are unsuccessful hunts. To avoid them you need to do your homework. Some areas are better than others, but in terms of raw cost, the various competing operators in any given area tend to have fairly similar prices. Now, a buffalo safari is not going to be as inexpensive as a plains game safari, but a buffalo hunt should cost less than a safari for other members of the Big Five, and, in today's crazy world, and in North American terms, it should be less than an outfitted hunt for moose, grizzly, or Dall sheep.

Ron Bird took this magnificent buffalo in Tanzania's Rungwa while hunting with Michel Mantheakis.

For many years Zimbabwe offered the least costly buffalo hunting. When Mozambique became a destination for buffalo hunters, prices were about the same and remain similar—but prices have crept up in both countries. In order to be competitive, South African game ranchers began breeding buffaloes and have done a great job. As I said in chapter 4, I missed this sea change! Just a decade or so back, when available buffalo bulls were far fewer in South Africa, prices were high, maybe half again the cost of a buffalo hunt in Zimbabwe or Mozambique. In the last decade, with more and more mature buffalo bulls available, prices have dropped dramatically.

Today, without question, South Africa offers the least costly buffalo hunting on the continent. Operating costs are lower, so daily rates are lower, and it's just a matter of adding the trophy fee for a buffalo. This is somewhat negotiable because most available buffaloes today are on private land. At recent conventions I've seen South African buffalo hunts for less than ten thousand dollars, sometimes quite a bit less.

This is no longer possible in Zimbabwe or Mozambique. In 2019 you need to add a couple thousand bucks to hunt buffaloes there.

Other factors that affect the cost of a hunt will be logistics and the number of days you will need to hunt in any particular area. Because of good road networks, costly air charters are rarely required in South Africa. Also, due to the private land situation, success on a seven-day buffalo hunt is fairly reliable in South Africa. There are some places, such as northern Namibia or Tanzania's Selous Reserve, where I'd have no qualms about doing a seven-day buffalo hunt and would expect to be successful, but in most of wild Africa, ten-day buffalo hunts are the norm. In general, I don't recommend buffalo hunts of less than ten days. Obviously hunting days increase costs, and at some level, for all of us today, time equals money. So, in terms of raw cost and nothing but cost, South Africa now offers the most affordable buffalo hunting.

There are offbeat options. Both Benin and Burkina Faso offer extremely good and surprisingly affordable hunting for the smaller West African savanna buffalo. In Burkina Faso the government trophy fee for a buffalo, at least recently, was 486 euros, the cheapest buffalo on the continent. Daily rates are higher than in South Africa, but the total is about the same.

So, let's look at success. Yeah, I know, it's all about the experience, but if we're spending ten "k" or more, it's nice to have a buffalo in the skinning shed when the hunt ends. Mind you, there are no guarantees, but if you do your homework, give the hunt adequate time, and concentrate on securing a buffalo, you will probably be successful. On the one hand, it's a numbers game. In wild Africa your chances are better in areas with lots of buffaloes.

South Africa, again because of the private land situation, is an exception. As we've seen, these are ranch buffaloes, their general whereabouts known on finite acreage. This does not make them easy to stalk and shoot, but most South African buffalo hunts will be successful. In wild Africa other factors come into play: rainfall, grazing, movement in and out of parks, predators, and poaching. Mind you, we're talking primarily about the large southern Cape buffalo now.

As I said, Burkina Faso and Benin have proven to be highly successful hunting destinations for the West African savanna buffalo.

Northern Cameroon offers very successful hunting for Central African savanna buffalo, and Uganda is awesome for Nile buffalo. There are no "sure things" in hunting dwarf forest buffaloes!

There are lots of places to hunt the southern Cape variety. Tanzania, Zambia, and Zimbabwe are marvelous. But I didn't get a buffalo on my first Zambia hunt clear back in 1983. It was May, so we were early, and the herds were in the Luangwa Park and weren't coming out. I've generally had good success on buffalo in Tanzania. Often, I've concentrated on other game, but with three buffaloes on license, they've always hovered in my subconscious. I always expect to take one or two and usually have, but of seven Tanzanian hunts there were three when I never had a chance at a buffalo. This happened in southern and western Tanzania, and in Masailand. So, it's a matter of not just picking your area, but picking the right time *for that area* . . . and hoping for some cooperation from the rains. I've also failed to get buffalo on hunts in Zimbabwe. There is no sure thing in hunting!

However, in considering areas and outfitters that I would recommend to my friends, I can think of several places where I would be extremely surprised if hunters came home buffalo-less. Coastal Mozambique is certainly one of them. With one of the greatest concentrations of buffaloes currently on the continent, success is routine. Northern Namibia has a small quota of lightly hunted buffaloes. The areas where Namibia has buffaloes, she has plenty! Again, success is fairly routine. Zimbabwe is trickier, but the large conservancies are extremely well managed; Save Valley, Bubye (former Lemco), and the newer Nuanetsi Conservancy are all excellent. Zimbabwe rarely offers the easiest buffalo hunting, but success is very high.

Tanzania is still trickier since a lot of the great hunting blocks are bordered by parks. Depending on the rains and available grass, buffaloes may not be moving out of their sanctuaries, and if that's the case, you're stuck! If a buffalo is the primary goal on a Tanzanian safari, then the Selous Reserve is probably the best, but the Rungwa area is very good and so is the Kilombero Valley southwest of Selous. Zambia is also very good, with both the Luangwa Valley and the Kafue regions offering very successful buffalo hunting, but, as with

In Namibia, buffalo habitat is limited to the north. The overall quota is small, but where they occur, buffaloes are plentiful and genetics are excellent. I took this beautiful bull in Caprivi with Dawid Muller of Daggaboy Safaris; that's a Krieghoff double .500.

Tanzania, do your homework and be there at the right time, which is often a bit later in the season. Because of its unique private land situation, South Africa must be added to this list, and while success isn't a given, it is expected.

As for horn quality, big bulls can turn up anywhere buffaloes are hunted. Zambia is not known for big bulls, but while I've taken few buffaloes there, Zambia produced two of my very best trophies. Tanzania's Masailand is famous for big buffaloes. My personal best bull was taken there in 1988. However, Masailand is tricky, and while the northern parks have huge bulls, success is not high. The Selous is not known for big bulls, but I've taken and seen others take several great bulls there. Again, to some extent it's a numbers game. When the timing is right, you can get into a lot of buffaloes in the Selous, and the more buffaloes you can sort through, the better your chances for finding a big one.

Zimbabwe is also not known for big bulls, but I've seen some spectacular bulls there. In part I think this is simply because the

South Africa has superb buffalo genetics, and, with numbers up, right now they are the most affordable buffalo bulls on the continent. That's a beautiful old bull in the Limpopo province . . . just wait until he steps out from behind the tree.

generally thick bush makes it more difficult to sort the herds. Big bulls are definitely there; today they are taking awesome buffaloes on the big conservancies. Northern Namibia has fantastic buffalo genetics. They don't take a lot of buffaloes, but the bulls are good and solid, and there are some dandies, so my advice is: Do not overlook Namibia for big buffalo bulls! Our swamp buffaloes in Mozambique on average are a bit smaller, but as the numbers come up, I see them getting better every year. The coutadas around Marromeu are probably not the place to look for a heavy bossed bull in the "upper forties," but I've seen them, and I've taken several great bulls with spreads over forty. They're there, but it's hard to sort them from those big herds.

And then, once again, for horn quality South Africa cannot be overlooked. South African buffaloes have big bodies with excellent horns, and part of their great success in breeding disease-free buffaloes has included selective breeding. There are many truly spectacular "breeding bulls," and they're passing their genes along. Now, let's accept that South African hunting is very much a market economy. They certainly have very big bulls, but the biggest bulls often command a premium price. Today, at the lowest prices, you can and will get a good, solid bull that might exceed forty inches . . . but the biggest bulls may be priced separately.

At the conventions I'm often asked where to go for a really big buffalo, meaning upper forties, with hard bosses and good shape. To have a decent chance, you'll probably need to go to a costlier area, and perhaps you should think about devoting at least two weeks so that you can look at a lot of bulls. The best odds are probably conservancies in southern Zimbabwe, northern Namibia, or just pay the money for a really special bull in South Africa. Or, just keep hunting buffaloes in good places until you find what you really want. Really big bulls are scarce everywhere, so the search is a matter of time, persistence, and luck. In wild Africa it may not happen!

My primary goal in continuing to hunt buffalo is to get the best overall hunting experience. I will probably never take a bigger bull than I already have, and I really don't look very hard anymore. I won't mount another buffalo, so great bulls are best left to hunters who will take them home and enjoy them. I look for older bulls, and I still love the experience of getting close and sorting through the herds.

My two buffalo hunts in Caprivi were spectacular. It's a beautiful and scenic area, and my safaris there were almost idyllic. Except there's one aspect to the experience that you cannot control: It's a park-boundary hunt, and you simply must be patient and wait for the buffaloes to come out. They will, but the waiting isn't all that exciting.

This is common to many areas. Uganda's Nile buffaloes are park-boundary hunts. A whole lot of hunting in Tanzania is park-boundary hunting, so are some in Zambia. Given a choice I prefer big country where you can look for tracks and follow tracks almost endlessly. Regrettably, these situations are increasingly rare in today's Africa. Almost all areas have some limits or boundaries. Obviously, South Africa's private-land buffalo hunting is on restricted acreage. That's about the only negative to the situation. Only rarely will you actually see a fence and its existence has little effect on tracking and stalking.

However, if you want to hunt buffalo in big, wild country, the Zambezi Valley is still there, as are the big conservancies. Some of the blocks in Tanzania are huge, and the Selous Reserve is the size of Switzerland. These areas all offer tracking hunts, which is a

Marromeu, with its 25,000 buffaloes, has one of the greatest concentrations of buffaloes in Africa; this is a nice herd in a freshly burned-off area near the Marromeu Reserve in coastal Mozambique.

wonderful way to hunt buffalo. The swamp buffalo hunting we do in Mozambique is so different that it's almost impossible to compare. I love tracking buffalo, but the Mozambique swamps are limitless, horizon to horizon, and there's no experience quite like crawling into one of those big herds. It's a situation unlike anything I've seen anywhere else.

So, you want a buffalo? Consider all the factors and weigh them. There's really no right or wrong answer. Expect to have a marvelous experience, and whatever your decision, chances are you'll want to do it again. Buffalo hunting is all good, but just remember that it's not all the same!

Bulletproof Buffaloes

Chapter 15

The African buffalo is big and powerful, and although I don't know that there's any way to scientifically verify this, I think it's true that, when injured, it receives an unusual surge of adrenaline. I do not agree that the buffalo has the almost supernatural powers often attributed to it in our sporting literature. The African buffalo is not by nature "a ton of black fury," nor does he weigh a ton! Nor is he bulletproof. One of Ernest Hemingway's better exaggerations is found in *The Short, Happy Life of Francis Macomber*. When Macomber finds his courage and, in his final seconds, faces the buffalo charge, he is blazing away with his .30-06 and 220-grain solids, his bullets deflecting off the buffalo's boss to no effect.

It is poor manners to critique a literary masterpiece, but we should be impressed that Macomber was fast enough to work his bolt so many times during a charge! We might also argue that he might have chosen a bit more gun. We concede that, as part of the story, Macomber was not an experienced hunter, so we need to forgive him for not knowing that the hard boss of the buffalo's horn was, perhaps, not the ideal aiming point. However, in the almost forgotten world of nonexpanding solid bullets, even Walter Bell concluded that almost nothing penetrates as well as the long, heavy 220-grain, .30-caliber solid. Though always inadvertently—meaning that's not where the bullet was intended to go—I have seen enough expanding bullets penetrate a buffalo's hard horn from various angles to suspect that Macomber's bullets should have done more than send chips flying.

Bill Jones (left) with PH Craigh Hamman and a buffalo Bill killed cleanly with a single 156-grain solid from a 6.5x53R. This was in Mozambique, which had no caliber minimum at the time. The rifle was built for Frederick Selous by Holland and Holland in 1898.

Had Macomber lived another day, he might have been taken aside and gently counseled on his choice of cartridge. Also, he would have been reminded, perhaps, to have aimed *between* the bosses or, if the buffalo's head was up, a few inches lower. Or, at the very last, it would have been pointed out to him that when the head drops so that the buffalo can use its horns, he should shoot *behind* the centerline of the bosses and down into the middle of the neck. Had he lived, he would have been advised that if he waited that long, he was probably going to get hit.

We'll come back to the rather important subject of shot placement, but let's return to just how bulletproof the African buffalo is . . . or isn't. Robert Ruark had plenty of respect for the African buffalo, as do I. Ruark's comment that he'd taken buffalo cleanly with a .30-06 "like a cow in a pasture" is absolutely correct. *Sometimes*. It's also correct that if the first bullet is misdirected or doesn't take immediate effect, then the next several bullets might not seem to do much. I don't have much experience taking buffaloes with light calibers, and I really don't want more. Play with fire, and sooner or later you're going to get burned.

Because situations are different and not because I believe the animals to be so much different, I have taken several water buffaloes with good, heavy-for-caliber 7mm and .30-caliber bullets. I was with Bill Jones when he used a Holland & Holland single shot in 6.5x53R to take a Cape buffalo in Mozambique. At the time Mozambique didn't have any caliber minimums, so this was perfectly legal, although I understand new game laws now incorporate minimums.

This was a historic journey of sorts. Jones's rifle had been built for Frederick Selous in 1898, and Jones used a 156-grain solid, much like Selous or Stigand or Bell might have used. He hit the bull centrally, tight behind the shoulder. The immediate effect was not impressive; in fact, there was no reaction at all except that we all saw dust from the bullet's impact. The stricken bull was immediately lost in the press and went off with the herd.

Typical in those swamps, the herd ran a hundred yards, stopped, bunched up, and faced us. PH Craigh Hamman thought he saw blood on the nose of one buffalo, but we lost sight of the bull as it milled with the others. That made another shot impossible. We waited a few minutes, studying the group to see if we could spot the wounded animal. We could not, but after a while, the herd drifted off, leaving one buffalo behind, a dark lump in the grass, stone dead. The bullet, placed centrally through both lungs, had exited. I was impressed enough that, for the first time, I gave full credence to all the old reports about the efficacy of the early 6.5mms. Even so, it's not a stunt I'd want to make a habit of!

My old friend and mentor, Geoff Broom, was a teenager when he took his first buffalo with a .303 using a military 215-grain solid. He recalled that there was no visible impact, but a couple minutes later he and his father heard the death bellow. Untold thousands of buffaloes were taken with early 6.5mms and 7x57s—and both the French 8mm Lebel and the German 8mm Mauser—all using heavy-for-caliber military solids. Because of its widespread use, the .303 British probably accounted for more than all the rest, but history doesn't record how many buffaloes were wounded or how many hunters and their companions were injured as a result.

In 1933 Hemingway preferred his .30-06 over his .470 because of the double's heavy trigger, but the only buffalo he describes taking was wounded and lost. By that time the early small-bore versus big-bore debate was nearly over; in the postwar era, caliber recommendations were much as they are today. That's true except in the British sphere. Dictated by the East African Professional Hunters' Association, a .40-caliber minimum was enacted for thick-skinned dangerous game. Through the 1950s until 1977 when the EAPHA was dissolved, this meant that the .375 was illegal for buffaloes, elephants, and rhinos. This has much to do with Winchester's introduction of the .458 Winchester Magnum in 1956 and why Roy Weatherby followed with his .460 a year later: Neither the Weatherby .375 nor the .378 Weatherby Magnums remained legal in the most common African destinations of the day.

Few hunters alive today have significant experience with rhinos. There are still a few hunters who shot elephants into the hundreds—and thousands—back when there was a lot of control work and culling. Many used .375s, and a guy I met who did problem elephant work in northern Namibia swore by the .338 with 300-grain solids, which, if you think about it, have sectional density far superior to the .375's standard 300-grain solid. From my own experience, however, I am convinced that the .375s are marginal for elephant, especially in the thicker cover where most elephant hunting is done today. I will never be convinced that the .375s are in any way marginal or inadequate for buffalo, and, with today's awesome expanding bullets, the .375s are far better today than they were with 1912-vintage bullets.

No matter what you are using, the placement of that first shot is critical—and it must penetrate deeply into the vitals and do serious damage. These days we mostly use expanding bullets. Even at the beginning of my African hunting career, softpoints were widely distrusted. In those days I think that was correct. Bonded-core bullets didn't exist; the Nosler Partition was pretty much the only "premium" bullet; and the .375 Partition was discontinued and unavailable for years. I am convinced that, provided it penetrates adequately into and

Veteran Zimbabwe PH Owain Lewis was killed by a wounded buffalo in the Zambezi Valley on the third day it was tracked. Although shot only once in the first encounter, by eyewitness accounts it was shot seventeen or eighteen times before it succumbed. That's the most I've ever heard of.

through the heart/lung area, an expanding bullet does more damage and results in the buffalo going down more quickly and more reliably than with a nonexpanding solid.

Today most professional hunters recommend expanding bullets, at least for the first shot on a buffalo, but caution must be used. A solid will usually penetrate and exit and so will many softpoints on "behind-the-shoulder" shots, but if you stay on the heavy shoulder, preferably *both* shoulders, most expanding bullets will not exit. This is mandatory in herds. In Mozambique we're almost always working herds and we don't use solids because the risks of a bullet passing through and hitting a second buffalo are simply too great. When I did a "professional hunter survey" for *Safari Rifles II*, a lot of PHs recognized this in the "bullet choices" section, recommending expanding bullets in herds but solids for bachelor bulls.

Regardless of bullet or caliber, placing that first shot well is essential. Buffaloes are not especially impressed by foot-pounds of

This water buffalo was an animal that just wouldn't give up; although hit properly in the vitals several times, it refused to go down. Every animal is different and you just never know.

energy. A first bullet that is *truly* in the right place and does its job will usually turn the trick. On the other hand, I'm convinced that if that first shot isn't in the right place, it really doesn't matter much what cartridge or caliber you're shooting. Anything short of an antitank rifle and you're in for a long day. That surge of adrenaline kicks in, and it can take a lot more shooting to clean up the mess.

Reasonably, there is some margin, but not much. A bullet from an extremely large and powerful caliber that's slightly off *may* result in a shorter tracking job than a similar shot from, say, a .375—but even this isn't certain. The only buffalo I've personally seen shot with the mighty .505 Gibbs was wounded and lost. The hit was too far back, and obviously the 6,000-plus foot-pounds didn't impress *that* buffalo.

Let's look at the converse: I've seen many one-shot kills with .375s, and since I've probably shot more buffaloes with various .375s than anything else, I've seen more one-shot kills on my own buffaloes with .375s than anything else. However, "pure" one-shot kills are relatively rare. When they happen, you can assume that first bullet was placed exactly right. If it wasn't placed right, that first bullet will not be enough. Neither its caliber nor its weight really matter—nor how fast it was going, nor how many foot-pounds it was carrying. Misplace that first bullet, and things are likely to get *interesting*, and anything can happen.

Clear back in the 1950s, on an early safari with John Kingsley-Heath, Jack O'Connor wrote about a Tanganyika bull that took *fourteen* shots from rifles of adequate caliber before succumbing. As I recall, most were from a .458 Watts, forerunner to the .458 Lott, and a .416 Rigby. We can probably assume that the first bullet wasn't placed perfectly—and probably some that followed. However, since we're talking sixty-five years ago, it's possible that bullet performance wasn't at the same standard as modern bullets. Also, in that era, some (or all!) shots were probably with solids. In exactly the right place, a solid will kill a buffalo nicely . . . and, when an outgoing and already hit buffalo is running for cover, a solid up the tail pipe can save the day. On that day, however, the chase went on for some time because this buffalo just wouldn't give up.

I thought that was the record. *Fourteen* shots are a whole bunch, and until recently the most I'd ever heard of. In 2012 veteran Zimbabwe PH Owain Lewis was killed by a buffalo. It was hit just once in the initial encounter, and, yes, we can conclude that bullet (from a .375) was not placed exactly right. In fact, the hit was a bit far back, but postmortem results suggested that the initial bullet damaged the liver, so it's amazing the buffalo kept going as long as it did. They tracked it for three days, also unusual and a testament to determination and great tracking. The buffalo was ultimately found lying down. In the tragic melee that ensued it is not entirely clear how many shots were fired or, among the several hunters involved, exactly how many shots each fired. When the buffalo rose and charged, it is clear that Owain put himself in front of the buffalo and was killed instantly. The buffalo, by now hit several more times, refused to go down. By all accounts the buffalo took *seventeen* hits before succumbing; other witnesses believe it might have been *eighteen*. All were with adequate cartridges, .375 and upward.

We can assume that not all hits were vital, but without question some were. Let's also make sure we understand: Not all shots are always perfect, especially in a situation like this where terrible things are happening fast. But *seventeen* shots? *Eighteen*? I have never seen anything like that, and I don't want to.

The buffalo isn't the only animal that is hard to put down. Big bears are notorious for being tough, and the bigger the bear the tougher. I was in a valley in southeastern Alaska when a hunter in the next valley started shooting, same outfitter, different guide. I counted twelve shots. It was a very big bear and he wouldn't go down.

I got a big Arctic grizzly up on the Noatak River out of Kotzebue. We caught him on a moose kill in a frozen valley where there was no cover and the ravens above him were acting as sentries. Snow was blowing hard and there was no way to range the distance, but it must have been 250 yards, pushing the envelope for a bear of this size. Holding a bit for the wind, I hit him well but he wouldn't stop; moreover, he kept moving slowly toward a strand of thick timber where I didn't want him to be. It was a horrible situation, but I continued shooting until he gave up. That experience aside, I've seen big bears go down and stay down with one well-placed shot.

Buffaloes are much the same. All are big and strong and potentially tough, but some give up more easily than others. There is no real average, and you never know what's going to happen when you face off against a bull. The one thing you do know, however, is that once you open the ball game, it's essential to finish it. Late in a hunt in the Binga area of the Zambezi Valley in 1992, Russ Broom and I got onto a fine bull in a small group. This bull had medium bosses but wide horns. I was shooting a double .470, and the shot was quartering slightly away. Plenty of gun, acceptable angle, and the bull was close, maybe sixty yards away. He took the bullet hard and ran with the group.

After the initial shot, and if there's no immediate chance for a follow-up shot, some hunters prefer to wait and assess while others try to keep the animal in sight as long as possible. There's really no right or wrong. It's purely situational, and snap judgments are made based on the cover, on where that first shot might have hit, and on the fitness of the hunter. Russ and I were both much younger and in good shape, so we ran like mad, with me reloading the fired barrel as we ran.

This time it worked. We dashed through scrub mopane, and in a hundred yards the bull, distinctive and wide, though not noticeably injured, pulled up broadside on a slight rise. This time I gave him both barrels. That should have done it and I suppose eventually would have, but this scenario was repeated once more. When we came on the bull for the third time, he was down but his head was still up. I lost count, but I think I shot him eight times. That's a lot of foot pounds of energy.

This is not pretty stuff, and honest, it doesn't happen often. Genuine, pure one-shot kills are rare, and are usually more or less unintentional. Of course, you *want* the first shot to do the trick, but only an idiot consciously withholds a good follow-up shot. More on that later, but to me a lack of follow-up shots usually means circumstances were such that a second shot was impossible—other buffaloes in the way, uncertainty about which buffalo was hit, or vegetation that's too thick.

Situations where buffaloes require a whole lot of shooting are also rare. Implied is that the first shot either wasn't quite right or wasn't as good as it looked, which surely can happen. I'm not sure there's any real average, but two or three shots is common and normal. Anything approaching double digits is very unusual, but it happens, so be sure to carry plenty of ammo.

While we want to be prepared for any eventuality, carrying extra ammo means physically hauling around extra weight. This becomes a much bigger hassle with large-caliber cartridges than with the deer/elk cartridges. There's an equally big difference between .375 cartridges and the long, heavy, large-caliber Nitro Express rounds. Often, I wear a "culling belt" with cartridge loops, not just because they look sexy but because they're practical. Alternately, I might put a single cartridge in each of several empty pockets and also take a cartridge slide that carries five or six rounds. If you use pockets, it's essential that cartridges not rattle in your pockets!

While this savanna buffalo isn't charging, he has his head up as a buffalo usually does during a charge. It should be obvious that any shot into the horns or between the horns is much too high. Between the eyes will work, as will a solid into the buffalo's right nostril. (Photo courtesy of Christophe Morio)

I don't have a set number, but I like to carry about a dozen rounds. This is generally plenty, but remember, as the perennial hunting client, I rarely carry the only rifle in the party. Andrew Dawson, who puts on his Jeffrey .470 like the rest of us put on trousers, always carries a full box of twenty rounds—a few in his belt and the balance in his tracker's pack. Almost nothing is worse than running out of ammunition when a job is unfinished! Twice I've had situations where hunters had wounded animals and ran out of ammo. You never know what you might run into, so prepare for the worst.

The worst case I've ever seen was not with a Cape buffalo but that big water buffalo bull I mentioned earlier. Indications were a good initial hit on the shoulder with a .375 and a good bullet, but the bull's butt vanished into thick mangroves. We followed, quickly found it standing, and shot it again . . . and then again. The mangroves, fortunately not flooded, were thick and dark, but I expected a charge at any moment. It never happened. Just as with the African buffalo, some do and some don't. In that awful vegetation, shot placement was no longer an issue; it was just a matter of hitting the bull again until it went down. Eventually the bull moved out of the mangroves and back onto the floodplain . . . and it still took more shots before it went down. There were certainly not fourteen or eighteen shots, but this is the only one I've seen that might have gone double digits.

It wasn't possible to determine exactly what happened with the first shot. It looked perfect, but even the very best bullets might turn on a shoulder. Perhaps more likely, shots that appear more or less broadside usually aren't. Black animals deceive the eye, and a few degrees of quartering angle can make a big difference, especially with very large animals. A buffalo is a big animal, and no rifle one can carry and fire from the shoulder is a really big gun.

So, briefly, let's review shot placement one more time. On any side-on shot, that big, black shoulder is always the key. As I've written before, divide the animal into horizontal thirds and come up the center of the foreleg one-third to no more than one-half the body depth above the brisket-belly line.

When making a classic shoulder shot, the biggest aiming error is usually to shoot too high, above that halfway point. This is all too easy to do. I think it's because the buffalo is so big that you can't just shoot at that massive shoulder; you must concentrate on the center and avoid that noncritical upper half. This is compounded by the fact that low grass will often obscure the belly line, so you must envision what is really there, not necessarily what you think you see. Again, black animals seem to distort one's perception, perhaps because we lose the black crosshairs against the black hide. Lighted reticles or red-dot sights greatly simplify aiming and especially on dark animals.

I have written that it's equally good to come up the *backline* of the on-foreleg, again one-third to one-half up into the body. This is a central lung shot, which, if executed correctly, is as effective as the classic shoulder shot. This is the shot Bill Jones used with his little 6.5x53R, an absolutely (though not immediately) fatal double-lung shot. *However*, the problem with this shot lies in being certain you are properly visualizing how the buffalo is standing. Again, perfect broadside shots often aren't! Dark animals, shadows, and low brush obscuring the legs complicate this. If, instead of being genuinely

This bull is quartering slightly away, so a shoulder shot may be a bit too far forward. I would "divide the light" showing between the forelegs and come one-third up into the body. That will be perfect right now, but the greater risk is that the buffalo may turn farther, offering a bad-angle raking shot. (Photo courtesy of Christophe Morio)

broadside, the buffalo is quartering slightly away, then shooting tight in the crease behind the shoulder is perfect. Instead, if the animal is quartering slightly to you, then you have very little leeway; just a bit of angle and you may only catch one lung, which is not enough. So, with a behind-the-shoulder shot, it is essential to be absolutely certain the buffalo is really broadside.

All things considered, on a side-on shot it is generally best to work on that big, black shoulder, and remember: One-third up is perfect, but between one-third and one-half will work just fine. Odd things happen, but if you execute this shot with anything from a 9.3x62mm on up while using a good, tough, modern, expanding bullet, you should not be faced with a bulletproof buffalo.

Quartering shots can be fine, provided you can visualize the angle and adjust the hold. Slight quartering away angles are excellent, and this is the shot that bow hunters seek. As written before, and as Andrew Dawson taught me, if the animal is more-or-less broadside, you can see only one foreleg. The center of the shoulder—one-third to one-half up—is the safest aiming point. If you can see both forelegs, then the animal is quartering. If the "off" foreleg appears *behind* the "on" foreleg, the animal is quartering away. If the "off" foreleg appears in front of the "on" foreleg, the animal is quartering-to. Either way, provided there isn't brush in the way, you should see a triangle of light between the forelegs, apex pointed upward. The apex of that triangle *always* points toward the chest cavity. "Divide the light" and come one-third up into the body to make your shot.

This is a good rule of thumb, but there are limitations. Slight quartering-away angles are great, but don't take strong quartering-away angles. Elmer Keith's "raking shot" must be avoided on buffalo because there's no assurance that any bullet of any construction and of any diameter, weight, and velocity can reliably get through the rumen and into the vitals. You may have the "line" perfectly correct, but your bullet may not penetrate.

As I've written before, the rumen is like a thirty-gallon drum full of packed grass and can stop almost anything. As veterinarian Kevin "Doctari" Robertson points out, a left-side presentation is worse than a right-side one because the buffalo's stomach lies more on the left side. On quartering-away shots, if the path to the vitals lies forward of the ribs, in other words tight behind the shoulder, you're fine, but if you must aim farther back, you must wait for a better opportunity.

Quartering-to shots are a bit trickier because you must not only visualize where the vitals lie—divide the light between the forelegs—but you must also find the point of the shoulder, which can be easily lost in that big black mass. All quartering-to angles are acceptable shots because the vitals are accessible to a bullet, *but* you must be able to properly visualize the angle for the shot to work. The correct aiming point may be inside the on-shoulder, which is basically where the neck joins the body, or it may be on the point of the on-shoulder. Too far outside, and a bullet can skitter between the shoulder and the body and do little damage; too far inside, and you will only catch the brisket and the bullet will exit behind the off-shoulder, again doing little damage. Both results are aiming errors and poor shots. The whole secret is to take your time and be steady and sure.

Facing shots are excellent provided the buffalo is really facing you and not slightly quartering. With a facing shot, you have a huge target about the size of a basketball and with no heavy bone in the way. You can see the legs, and instead of a triangle of light between them, you have an up-and-down rectangle. One-third up above the brisket will take out the major vessels on top of the heart. Chances are the buffalo will lurch a few steps toward you, but he won't go very far. The only tricky part about a facing shot is that you must be steady and certain. Flub it right or left, and you have one of those horrible inside the shoulder "skittering" shots. Do that and you can expect a long and unpleasant day.

While we are working the big herds in coastal Mozambique, we get a lot of quartering-to and facing shots. Often, we work within range of a herd and then study them for many minutes—occasionally an hour—in order to locate a suitable bull. Even when bedded, buffaloes will mill and shift, and remember that bulls will usually work to the edge . . . eventually. I would even say that quartering-to and facing shots are more common than broadside shots. I like them because it is virtually certain that a lead-core expanding bullet will stay inside the animal. We don't use solids and we avoid homogenous alloy expanding bullets; they penetrate wonderfully, but in these situations the last thing you want is an exit wound. In the press of black bodies and in bright light, visualizing exactly how the buffalo is standing is more difficult than it sounds. Take your time and do it right, and your bull will not be bulletproof!

Keep Shooting!

Chapter 16

It's unusual to get into trouble with a healthy, uninjured buffalo. Sure, it can happen. Get between a cow and her calf or surprise a buffalo at very close range, within the "fight-or-flight" radius, and you'll see what kind of trouble a buffalo can produce. Also, there are too many buffaloes out there carrying AK-47 bullets, dragging a snare, or carrying wounds from another buffalo's horns or a lion's claws. So, it isn't just wounded buffaloes that are dangerous. However, human injuries, though horrific and sometimes tragic, are rare. The most common result of a poorly placed shot is *that* buffalo will never be seen again. The subject of wounded and lost animals is something we don't talk about much. Unspoken or not, it happens, and because the African buffalo is so big and strong, it happens more frequently than with many species. We will devote the next chapter to that touchy subject, but this chapter is devoted to preventive measures.

The best way to avoid problems is to shoot the buffalo with a good bullet from an adequate cartridge and place that first shot where it needs to go. The vital zone of a buffalo is not a small target. If that first shot is placed well and *if* the bullet does its work, the buffalo should be found within two hundred yards. Realistically, not all shots are perfect—yours, mine, or anyone's. The bullets we're using today are much better than what we had forty years ago, but bullets can still fail. Of course, if an animal is lost, we can never know exactly what went wrong. Human nature being as it is, we're more likely to blame the bullet than our poor shooting.

This is the first buffalo I took for the Boddington on Buffalo *DVD in 2004. I shot the buffalo four times with a Dakota .375 then switched to a double for the follow-up. I was criticized in some quarters for continuing to shoot. Perhaps it wasn't necessary, but how do you know?*

Let me give you another stark statistic: I have lost buffaloes, and I've seen many others wounded and lost. I have a pretty good idea how many buffaloes I've taken, but I have no idea how many I've seen shot, certainly deep into the hundreds. *I have never seen a buffalo lost that was hit more than once in the initial encounter!* That doesn't mean the buffalo was found dead or that the follow-up was simple. Anything can still happen, but I want to say that again as a foot-stomping point: *I have never seen a buffalo lost that was hit more than once!*

If the first shot was placed well, additional shots were probably unnecessary . . . but you often don't *know* what that first shot did or didn't do until you start tracking. Realistically, the best opportunity is probably the first shot. After that things happen fast since the buffalo is usually moving and the presentation isn't likely to get better. Although my lifetime experience with this isn't scientific, it does suggest that an additional bullet (or two) will do more damage and leave a better trail to follow. So, all things equal, I strongly believe in continuing to shoot as long as a buffalo is still on its feet *and* the target is clear.

Many of you have seen the video from the first time I hunted in the Zambezi Valley with Andrew Dawson. This was in 2004. We got into a big herd at a remote spring up in the hills. Most had passed, and we let some bulls—both old and young—in the rear of the herd go past. Then, to our right, well off the path of the main herd, a nice bull came out of nowhere. He was walking straight to us, and I doubt he was fifteen yards away when I shot him in the center of the chest. As they often do with a frontal shot, he took a couple of steps toward us, then floated in a half circle to our left.

I was shooting a left-hand Dakota M76 in .375 H&H with 300-grain Swift A-Frames. Working the bolt fast, I think I shot him three more times. The last shot was quartering-away, but none was from more than a distance of twenty-five yards. I suppose the first shot would have done the job, certainly aided by the second. I make no excuses: The bull wasn't slowing; he was *accelerating!* So, I kept shooting. We lost sight of him just after the last shot, and a few seconds later we heard his death bellow. I think he went maybe fifty yards. Experienced PHs whom I respect immensely gave me grief for continuing to shoot and for leaving the additional shots in the video.

We can argue as to exactly how many shots were necessary. There's no way to know. After the first shot, there was certainly no danger, but this was an unusual situation. There have been many times when I've been able to fire a second shot, especially with a double rifle, but I haven't seen many buffalo bulls stay completely clear for that many seconds with no visible signs of slowing. I can agree that I didn't have to keep shooting, but I don't feel bad about it, and if another buffalo presented me with a similar situation, I'd do the same thing. I'd keep shooting. It's unlikely, however, that I'll ever see anything quite like that again.

Usually the brush is too thick or other buffaloes get in the way. I believe in following up that first shot, but only if additional shots are clear and you're certain you're still on the correct bull. After that first shot, things happen fast and you must be very quick—but you also must be absolutely certain. So, while my purpose here is to stress that you should keep shooting if you can, in my experience it hasn't been possible anywhere near 50 percent of the time.

The more buffaloes there are, the less likely you will be given the chance of a follow-up shot. A bull in a small bachelor group is one thing, but a bull in a herd of several hundred presents a whole different situation. Typically, when a shot is fired, the herd will stampede. A stricken animal will try to stay with the herd, but if it is hit well, it will quickly drop to the rear, and when that happens, it can be positively identified. That's what you and your PH are looking for, and if the herd is still close enough, you may have a chance for another shot within a few seconds. However, once past the first encounter, it's unwise to shoot again unless you and your PH can absolutely agree on the correct animal.

My advice is to prepare for multiple shots. Practice off sticks with a full magazine and learn to work the bolt fast or learn to immediately find the second trigger on a double. Practice unsupported, too. When you're really close, the extra movement required to set up sticks can mess things up, so at very close range, you should be prepared to stand up and shoot. Practicing multiple shots can enable you to follow up your first shot, and an additional shot can save the day if that first shot is off a bit. Just don't expect that's the way it's going to happen. Even lone bulls can vanish into brush while you're still in recoil, and when there are other buffaloes around, the complexity is greatly increased.

Nothing is faster than a double rifle for the second shot. I use doubles a lot, and I'm fast with the second barrel, but there have been more times when I was unable to fire the second barrel than when I've managed a fast "one-two" punch. I think it's good when you can shoot again, but you have to be sure you're shooting at the right animal. The only thing worse than a wounded buffalo is to have *two* wounded buffaloes to trail and find. Oh, yeah, I've seen that happen, so you better be sure!

A few years ago, Mark Haldane and I were on a medium-size herd of a couple hundred animals. A nice bull stepped out on the right side,

The first shot is gone, but have you instantly worked the bolt and prepared to fire again if possible? A second shot often isn't possible, but time on the range should be spent practicing repeat shots with a full magazine . . . or finding the second trigger on your double.

quartering slightly to me. I shot him with a McMillan .404 Jeffery. Mark had his binocular on the bull at impact, the shot felt good to me, and the reaction looked good to both of us. The bull was immediately swallowed by the herd, so there was no chance for a second shot. They ran just a few yards and then bunched in a short-grass savanna. Now the only thing to do was wait, and, as the herd milled about, keep studying and hope the stricken bull would reveal itself. Obviously, you'll be watching for a bull of similar horn configuration. This won't be definitive, so you'll need to see blood on the shiny nose or on the body, or you'll need to observe a visible limp.

That day, after the shot we saw nothing for a long time except a press of black bodies. Sooner or later we knew they would move off.

There's a water buffalo in the thick vegetation just to right of center and he's very close. This is in the Philippines, so I'm using an M14 that I borrowed from the local military. It functioned perfectly, and you bet I kept shooting until the bull was down!

In a perfect world your bull will be down and dead and left behind; in a slightly imperfect world he will trail as the herd moves off, show adequate evidence of being hit, and offer another shot. In our situation nothing happened for long minutes, and then a single bull detached itself from the herd and walked across about forty yards of open space to the edge of a big patch of sawgrass. One buffalo separating for no apparent reason is not normal behavior, so our combined experience told us that this was our bull. The problem was that there was no visible sign of injury. The light was bright and harsh, and the shot had been on the opposite, hidden side, of the bull. No blood was visible on the body, and none was on the nose. The bull walked at a slow, measured, but steady pace. He was not limping, so the opposite shoulder was not broken.

In recalling the shot presentation, we could speculate that the bullet struck inside the opposite shoulder. That shoulder shouldn't be broken, but with a 400-grain, .423-inch bullet, the bull should be dead. Maybe he was, which meant he might be lying unseen in the press of black bodies. Maybe he wasn't, which meant that this was probably our buffalo. The problem was that we weren't certain enough to shoot, so we watched in frustrated agony while the bull walked slowly to the tall sawgrass, stepped into the first row, and vanished completely. The herd was now bunched directly in front of us and about a hundred and fifty yards away. We watched for a while longer, saw nothing, so we advanced slowly toward the herd. They didn't stampede, just moved off to the left. No inert black mounds were left in their wake, and although a couple of bulls trailed the herd, neither showed signs of being wounded nor did they have similar horns.

If necessary, we would check their trail for blood spoor, but first we had to check that deadly sawgrass. *Not fun!* Mark and I and our trackers had all marked the spot where that single bull had vanished. We would search for blood, but first we needed to take a quick look. Rifles at high port, we advanced toward the forbidding sawgrass. That stuff grows almost like a row crop with lines and furrows and is as thick as standing sugar cane. I doubt we were three steps from the edge when a buffalo suddenly materialized from behind the first green barrier. He went from being invisible to formidably looming. Immediately, he turned to us. At a distance of ten feet, Mark's .470 fired before the bull had fully gained his feet; my .404 boomed just behind Mark's. The combined impact drove the bull down, back into the first furrow where he had been bedded. End of story and, in this case, danger quickly avoided.

The postmortem showed the first shot seemingly well placed, just inside the point of the on-shoulder. Other impacts were on the opposite side. I've seen many buffaloes succumb properly to a first shot similarly placed. This one didn't, who knows why except that, for whatever reason, the bullet apparently slid between body and shoulder without fully entering the chest cavity. A safe second shot might have saved the day, but it was simply not possible. There was no chance to "keep shooting," and that's going to happen, perhaps more often than otherwise.

Although I've done it many times—and probably will again—nobody *wants* to go into sawgrass after a buffalo. We were just lucky that the bull, probably hit harder than it appeared, simply walked past the first row and lay down. When it jumped up almost under our feet, there was no choice but to shoot—and "keep shooting"—until the buffalo was down to stay.

Wielding his double .470 like a 20-gauge, Haldane beat me to the punch by a quarter-second. Although the first time in many years, this was certainly not the only time that a PH has chimed in for me, and probably won't be the last. In this case it was a no-brainer: This buffalo was too close and needed to be put away quickly. Of course, I would always prefer that a PH not shoot at any of my animals, dangerous or not. On the other hand, I don't have any ego about it. Once the ball game is opened and an animal is hit, it becomes a judgment call. I expect my PH to use sound judgment, which always includes shooting in case of immediate danger. It may also include shooting to prevent the escape of a wounded animal.

As I said, it should *always* be a no-brainer for a PH to shoot first or as an immediate follow-up in a dangerous situation. One of the best displays of coolness under pressure I've seen on the part of a PH was when Chad Allen and I were hunting in Chewore North with Mike Payne. We took a completely unprovoked charge from a bull that, as it turned out, had been badly mauled by a lion in a very sensitive area. I guess you could say the bull was provoked, but we didn't do the provoking.

We were walking up out of a sand river, thinking a herd was a short distance ahead. We had no idea a buffalo was nearby. The bull of this story rose from his bed in dark shade twenty-five yards ahead, shook his head once, and came in a full-out charge. I was fourth in line, and thus very safe, with a tracker in the lead and followed by Mike and Chad. Unarmed, the tracker did an agile and sensible "exit, stage right." Mike took a half step right and Chad stepped forward to his left shoulder,

I was hunting in the Zambezi Valley with Andrew Dawson when we saw this bull in deep shade near the opposite bank of the Chewore River. I got steady on the sticks (top), and then I shot him several times in an effort to keep him from gaining the bank and the thick stuff beyond. I failed to stop him, but he died right on top of the riverbank.

Mark Haldane and I walked to the edge of the sawgrass and this wounded bull stood up when we were about ten feet away. We both shot . . . and I wouldn't have it any other way.

both setting their feet to meet the charge. With the buffalo closing ground fast, Mike Payne had the presence of mind to say, very clearly and quite calmly, "Take him, Chad, take him now!"

Mike didn't give Chad time for a second shot. Perhaps it wasn't wise for Mike to let Chad take that first shot, but, to his credit, Mike let his client have the first shot, and to Chad's credit, he got his double up and got in the first shot. Mike followed instantly, his first barrel and Chad's second sounding as one. Regardless of who shoots first, the important thing is to stop the charge. In this case, the buffalo was coming full steam and was going to run over *somebody*. So, obviously, this was a situation in which the PH should be shooting. I have no patience with PHs who are itching to shoot, who will strive to beat you to the punch if things are a bit hairy, and who will automatically follow up your shot.

Again, a charge must be stopped, and it shouldn't matter too much who does the shooting so long as it's fast and straight. Absent imminent danger, it's a judgment call as to whether the PH should shoot. The decision must be based on experience and a split-second assessment of where the first bullet went. Then, often, the PH will hesitate, giving you a chance to fire again. Good PHs will help with a calm, "Hit him again!" or they will try to clarify the correct animal, but this is no more always possible than is a second shot. Finally, there needs to be an understanding between the client and the PH as to when or *if* the PH is expected to fire.

The strictest credo of the profession is that "it's the client's animal" —let the chips fall where they may. Any PH worthy of the license will follow a wounded animal into the deepest thorn and try to clean up the mess, ignoring all risks. Maybe, just maybe, a scary and possibly unsuccessful follow-up might have been averted if the PH had chimed in. That said, I have a lot more time and respect for a PH who avoids shooting under almost all circumstances than I do for the trigger-happy idiots, but I think a fine balance is better.

My friend Ian Gibson, killed by an elephant in the Lower Zambezi that he loved, was one of the guys who avoided shooting if at all possible. Stationed in the Zambezi Valley during the Rhodesian War, he essentially never left, and for some thirty-five years, he was the "resident PH" in Chewore North. He guided clients to countless buffaloes, hippos, elephants, and leopards, and in most seasons personally guided the full quota of lions. I have described him as Zimbabwe's most experienced dangerous-game PH. This is impossible to measure, and in the hero worship we develop for our favorite PHs, many of us might propose other candidates.

At least, I can say that I had no hero worship for "Gibbo!" He was taciturn, could be difficult, and suffered fools poorly. Many clients loved him; others didn't. I had huge respect for him, and I *never* saw him shoot on a client's animal. I saw a few wounded-

and-lost buffaloes that might have been recovered had Ian joined in, but that wasn't his thing. Regrettably, his reluctance to shoot is at least partly responsible for his death. I can see what happened to him in my mind's eye: As the elephant bore down, he waved and shouted until the last second. Then Murphy's Law took over. His frontal brain shot failed to stop the bull. Maybe there was time for a second shot, maybe not, but his bolt-action jammed, and that was the end.

I am not going to make a recommendation as to the guidelines you should give your PH for when—or whether—he should use his rifle. This is a very personal thing, and it depends on your experience, competence, and confidence. I hope it does not depend on the size of your ego! Some have proposed that it's a good idea to ask your PH to back you up on your first buffalo. I neither agree nor disagree. Clearly your first experience with a seriously dangerous animal will be different from your friend's or from anyone else's. While there will be lots of excitement and healthy fear, if things go set-piece perfectly—and sometimes they do—then I think it's silly to have any kind of inflexible plan. This could mean that your PH *will* shoot, or it may mean that, no matter what, he *will not* shoot. The former does little harm but isn't necessary; the latter can have serious consequences, including a lost buffalo or much worse. Also, as with military operations, all plans go to hell when the first shot is fired!

When I hunted buffalo with Diekie Muller in 2017, I was using a .460 S&W handgun, and I think that was the first time in my life that I *implored* a PH to back me up. I wasn't concerned about the *power*, but I was totally uncertain of the bullet's performance. I asked Diekie to shoot right after me if he possibly could. Like most good PHs, he prefers not to shoot, but I thought I had him convinced. Maybe I did, maybe not, but in the event he couldn't get a shot off. I wish he had.

While my bullet's performance was fine, my shot placement was not, and we had a long, scary follow-up that ended in a charge. So, just like you can't count on being able to back up your own shot, you really shouldn't count on your PH being able to. Rather than any firm plan, I simply tell my PHs to use their judgment. If one should fire and it appears to have been unnecessary, we can argue about it later, but that's not an argument I've ever had.

My final thoughts on expending multiple bullets should be a discussion on whether to fire "insurance shot(s)." The scenario now assumes the buffalo is down, and you have a visual on the animal. The problem is you don't know for sure if the buffalo is dead. A Ruark adage, attributed to Harry Selby, is, "It's the dead ones that get up and kill you." This is absolutely untrue and obviously impossible, but the "almost-dead ones" certainly can!

After you've hit a buffalo and think you've hit it well, but you've lost sight of him, often you'll wait a couple of minutes in anticipation of hearing that deep, guttural death bellow. If you hear it, chances are very good the buffalo is down and will not get up, but even this is not definitive. I have personally never seen a buffalo get up after that bellow, but Berit Aagaard, Finn's widow, told me she saw a buffalo bull get up after bellowing. I consider Berit an irrefutable source, so even the bellow isn't definitive. Given this, my advice is: When you walk up to a downed buffalo, you can't be certain it's dead. The safe money is to pay the insurance!

Exactly how and if you should do that depends entirely on the situation. Under no circumstances should you approach closely until you're very sure, and you should never approach a downed buffalo from the front where you might make eye contact. If the buffalo has enough strength left, this can trigger a charge. While this looks great on video, not all charges can be stopped. If the buffalo is able to get up, the first few feet will almost always be straight ahead, the way the buffalo is facing, and for sure you don't want to be in his path!

Ideally, I like to circle so that I can place a finishing shot either into the chest between the front legs or through the spine down into the chest. In thick cover this isn't always possible. Rather than get too close, I've paid some insurance shots from the rear. A solid is good for this if you have one, and most of the time I still carry a few solids specifically for follow-up shots. One thing for sure: Once you fire the insurance shot, you will know instantly if the buffalo is down for the count. If he jumps up, my initial premise rules: Just keep shooting! Finally, remember our theory about "bulletproof buffaloes": Shot placement is also essential. If a downed bull gets up, what you will see is pure adrenaline at work, and you've got trouble on your hands.

Paying the insurance is a good rule of thumb, but it's not always essential. Attitude is important. If a buffalo is down with the back of its horns flat to the ground and its nose straight up in the air, he's almost certainly finished. Rather than waste a bullet, you can throw a couple of sticks or rocks to see if there's any response. The standard test with most big-game animals is to check for eye movement, but I don't recommend this for buffalo, at least not initially. This puts you too close to those deadly horns. Stick with the rear, throw a stick, and give the buffalo a healthy push with your boot. Have your rifle ready so that you can keep shooting if necessary. *Then* check the eye for any response. If there's no response, you can finally relax, clear your chamber, and enjoy the moment.

Wounded and Lost

Chapter 17

My old friend Bill Bynum likes to say "We need more hunters writing . . . and fewer writers hunting." Which is another way of putting a very sad truth: Most hunting writers shoot better with their word processors than their rifles. To fully update that thought, between camera angles and the cutting-room floor, most of today's outdoor TV "celebrities" appear to shoot better on camera than they actually do with their rifles. Although he wrote beautifully, Robert Ruark probably wasn't the perfect role model to follow, given his shooting and considering that he died of acute alcoholism at just forty-nine. He was, however, extremely honest about his shooting—and possibly to a fault. He wrote about misses and foibles so often—and always well—that my guess is he was a far better marksman with a rifle than he let on. A few of my colleagues follow his example by writing honestly and including their mess-ups, but most do not.

If you read hunting and shooting magazines and watch outdoor TV shows, you might get the idea that hunting is routinely successful and all shots are perfect. I think it's regrettable that we have created this "unreality" because it leads to false expectations . . . and it just isn't true. Not all hunts are successful. If you check the harvest data from a handful of states for almost any species and compare that against licenses or tags sold, you would quickly understand that failure—as defined by not taking game—is more routine than success. We don't always win. The corollary to this is that not all shots are perfect, and it doesn't matter who you are.

This Zambian buffalo took us on the longest spoor I remember that ended with a dead buffalo…probably not a quarter mile! After following for a short distance, one should accept that you're no longer looking for a dead buffalo but following a wounded one.

I have always tried to write honestly, the bad with the good. Perhaps I've done this to a fault. Every time I write about the poor shots I've made, I'm almost certain to draw a few letters from hunters who insist they have never, ever missed a shot or wounded a game animal. I used to think these guys either had very limited experience or extremely selective memories. Eventually I realized there was another option. Playing a pure numbers game, a large percentage of my readers must be among America's ten million whitetail hunters. Relatively few are *buffalo hunters*! I can understand that hunters who harvest their venison annually from favorite deer stands at known distances might hunt for decades without a misstep. Regardless of the game, to hunt in big country and shoot at varying distances from myriad field positions changes the nature of the hunt. You've never missed? Stick around! Not all shots are perfect.

A hunt for a buffalo changes the game again. The animal is big and strong, and when the moment comes, there's a lot of excitement and a bit of palm-sweating terror. If these elements are lacking, well, you may have a malfunctioning adrenal gland or a serious lack of imagination. If that's the case, you should consider another pastime, perhaps shuffleboard. Not all shots on buffaloes are going to be perfect, and, although it isn't easy, it is not impossible to miss an entire buffalo. I've done it! Three times I've had bullets diverted by unseen sticks. Note that this is more likely with open sights than with a scope. Twice this resulted in clean misses. Then there was the time that I flattened a buffalo. That happened when the .470 solid centered on the neck side-on and about eighteen inches left of where I was aiming! The big problem with less-than-perfect shots on buffaloes is that mostly they don't miss altogether.

The vital areas of a buffalo are plenty large enough that we really should be able to get a bullet in there. If you don't think you can make the shot, you should not take it. Even so, and always with the very best intentions, sometimes we fail. As big as the vital zones are, a buffalo has large areas of nonvital mass. Hit a buffalo in the wrong place or on the edge of the right places, and you have a wounded buffalo. You're going to do some serious tracking, and that means from the very start the outcome is uncertain.

Let's define what I mean by a "wounded buffalo." What I mean is a buffalo that, wherever hit, is not going to immediately succumb, and when you come up on him, if you do, he will be alive and ambulatory. Ruark in *Horn of the Hunter* described a well-hit buffalo going a great distance before being found dead. I have heard other accounts of following a buffalo for a half-mile and more and then finding him dead. Maybe, but when you're following the blood spoor of a dangerous animal, every step seems like three, and I suspect these distances are often exaggerated.

Anything *can* happen, but I have never tracked such distances after a *dead* buffalo. The longest track I have ever been on that led me to a *dead buffalo* was in Zambia in 1984. Back then I had taken few buffaloes and I'd already lost one. My feelings were natural horror combined with "here we go again!" The bull had been in a small *dambo* when I shot him. He exited the clearing at a dead run, so we picked up the spoor where the *miombo* forest began. It *seemed* like a very long distance, but I doubt the bull had gone much more than two hundred yards before we found him stretched out and still in a thick patch. Russ Broom's trackers threw some sticks at him before we moved in, but the bull never twitched. He was dead.

Regardless of where all witnesses think the bullet hit and whatever reaction they observed—and even if the death bellow is heard—once a hit buffalo is out of sight, the hunters need to follow a blood spoor with extreme seriousness. At first, unless all indications are positive, they take the track with careful optimism in hopes they're tracking a deceased buffalo. Again, there are anomalies, but after a couple hundred yards, a frank assessment must be made that the buffalo is likely still alive. He could be miles away, or he

The game changes when you find blood, for now you must concentrate ahead and to the sides. Soon the spoor will tell you if you're looking for a downed bull or following one that might be waiting for you. Mukasa is focused on the spoor.

might be lying in wait just a few yards ahead. By now the spoor has probably yielded some clues. If it's frothy lung blood, that is good. Remember on a buffalo, however, one lung isn't enough. If the blood contains stomach matter, that's not good. Or you may find just red muscle blood, which means that you'll not have a clue as to the location of the wound. The tracks should reveal if a limb is dragging.

So, you have clues, but after a few hundred yards, you must face the reality that you're no longer looking for a dead buffalo. You are following a wounded buffalo. The tension increases, the pace slows, and you have no idea what lies ahead. With a solid hit that's not immediately fatal, some buffaloes will stop within a relatively short distance. This is the scenario where a charge is most likely; however, more likely than a charge, you'll get a chance to finish the job. Unfortunately, let me give you the bad news: If the blood spoor leads you more than a few hundred yards, the most likely result is that *you'll never see that particular buffalo* again.

Because you can't be sure of the outcome, you will follow as long as you can, but the blood spoor will diminish, and the tracks will mix with other tracks. Sometimes African trackers are like magicians, but they don't have supernatural powers. There are exceptions. In an amazing but tragic piece of tracking, the buffalo that killed Owain Lewis was tracked for three days. This buffalo was hit only once in the first encounter. It was a shot into the liver that must, eventually, be mortal, but this buffalo, an older bull, suffered for three days before wreaking his vengeance. Also in the Zambezi Valley, hunting with Ian Gibson, my friend Randall Pence, long a mainstay at Ruger, recovered a buffalo on the third day after it was hit. The hunters finished the bull without drama, but to be able to hold a spoor for that long is a testament to great determination as well as awesome tracking expertise.

Sometimes, after a few days, vultures will show you a buffalo's final resting place, but most of the time you simply follow as long as you possibly can. It isn't over when the spoor is lost because in the course of a normal tracking job, it will be lost several times, relocated, and then lost again. All too often, regrettably, there comes a time when

Scuff marks from a hard-hit buffalo. We hadn't found blood yet, but the bull was already struggling to keep his feet. After another fifty yards, we found him down.

the spoor is utterly and completely lost. Repeated casts in various directions reveal no trace, and the only sensible decision is to call it a (bad) day.

When we were doing a lot of filming in the Lower Zambezi, Chifuti Safaris controlled several of the Designated Safari Areas with a total buffalo quota exceeding a hundred bulls per season. It seemed to me that we were losing about one buffalo in ten. Yes, that seems high, but the ground is very hard, so tracking is difficult. Roads are few, so there are no shortcuts. At the same time, it seems to me we were only getting a couple of serious charges. Both of these are very informal "statistics" that reflect the efforts of at least a half-dozen PHs in the field. Combine these, and I'm very confident in stating that, in a normal encounter when only one shot is fired, if that one shot wasn't properly placed, the loss of a wounded buffalo is about four or five times more likely than a charge.

The last dozen years I've been hunting annually in coastal Mozambique, mostly with Zambeze Delta Safaris. These days their harvest is also about a hundred buffaloes per season, but they seem to lose only a partial handful per year. This has nothing to do with relative competence; it's just that the hunting situations are different. In the swamps there's more open ground, and although there are no roads at all, they have swamp vehicles, so if a trail is lost, they can plow into the sawgrass or papyrus. Sawgrass is bad, papyrus is worse, and if a stricken bull gets into that stuff, recovery is very difficult, and chances aren't good.

Ultimately, dead is dead. A buffalo hit through both lungs, through the heart, or through the great vessels above the heart, is dead. Except for brain or spine shots, there are other points of impact that may cause the buffalo a long, lingering death, which it doesn't deserve. The immediate result is a wounded buffalo that must be followed . . . and may or may not be recovered. Other than my own, I'm not going to name any names here, but I've participated in the tracking of a substantial number of buffaloes that were never seen again. The obvious preventive is to place the first shot well—and don't shoot unless you're quite certain of the shot. Secondarily, my experience is that a second follow-up shot, when possible, will usually save the day. Additional shots, however, aren't always possible, practical, or safe.

I guess it's dumb to discuss poor shot placement; for sure we don't want to practice bad shooting! However, it seems to me that a buffalo with significant damage to one limb or with a hit that's too far back—in the viscera, for example—is fairly likely to be recovered. Regrettably, there's still a lot of nonvital buffalo areas that can be hit. Hitting a bull too far forward, through the brisket, is bad. Going too low, under the heart, is also very bad. Hitting the bull too high, in that "no man's land" between the bottom of the spine and the top of the lungs, is very, very bad. Of the buffalo bulls I have wounded and lost in the past forty-three years, I'm fairly certain I have committed all three errors, but since I didn't recover these buffaloes, it's impossible to be certain.

I think shooting too high on the shoulder is one of the most common deadly sins. This is because we train ourselves to zero in on that big, black shoulder, but in doing so, we really need to ignore the top half of the shoulder. The bottom third is really the proper

This forest buffalo is standing at a very odd angle with its head low. Can you properly visualize where the vitals lie and where the aiming point should be?

focus, but we've now reduced a huge target to just a generous one. Once again, you have that odd distortion caused by a big, black animal, and sometimes the critical bottom third is obscured by low brush. Provided you don't slip too low, anywhere on the shoulder or just behind the shoulder—no more than halfway up from the brisket—should work. When you get above the halfway point, you're playing with fire. Yet again, when a hit buffalo is lost, it is nearly impossible to determine exactly where the hit was and what went wrong. However, it seems to me that with a lot of these wasteful tragedies, the hit was too high.

For the record, I think I've shot about ten buffaloes that required tracking. Most were recovered within a few hours. Two went well into the next day after very long and restless nights. None of these was hale and hearty when we finally encountered them, but they were alive and, one way or another, offered chances to terminate them. In my case, of these wounded buffaloes, hitting a bit far back was probably my most common error, but there were a couple of one-lung hits, taken either at an angle I shouldn't have taken or I didn't visualize properly. All the rest of my buffaloes have either been down in sight or within a couple hundred yards. So, I guess I've shot reasonably well most of the time. Based on what I've observed, although any losses at all are too many, my lifetime loss rate probably isn't unusual. That said, these buffaloes still haunt me.

As I've written and don't need to repeat, I lost the first buffalo I ever shot at, in Kenya in 1977. I did not receive a copyright for losing my first buffalo because, unfortunately, it happens to all too many first-time buffalo hunters. Please remember that and be careful! Having relived the shot ever since, I'm pretty sure I hit the animal too far forward. Another lost buffalo could have been a bit high, but the truth on that one is that I just don't know: The shot felt good, but the spoor wasn't definitive, and we couldn't follow it very far. After my one shot, this buffalo made a beeline for the boundary of a nearby park. We were not allowed to follow, so I just can't say what happened. Boundary hunts are always tricky, so, again, be careful. That buffalo was shot with a good expanding bullet from a .416 Rigby. It should have been dead and perhaps it was, but I will never know. Like all wounded-and-lost animals, the only real answer is simply, "I don't know."

On a third wounded bull, I can say this: "Pride goeth before a fall!" Otherwise, I have no idea what happened. I was using my Krieghoff double .500 and the distance was sixty or seventy yards, so there was obviously plenty of gun and we were close enough. The bull was broadside in shadow, but totally clear. The shot felt good and was an obvious hit. We followed sparse and diminishing blood for a couple of miles and then there was nothing, just undulating grassy hills to the horizon. The trail suggested the hit might have been low. That's bad news, but at the time I pressed the front trigger, I'd have given that shot 99 percent odds for a proper hit. The truth is, however, that I was just starting to lose my ability to properly resolve iron sights, but I hadn't yet accepted that my time to use express sights was diminishing. I've since taken other buffaloes with open sights and with that rifle, but I've learned that I have to shorten my distances and be more cognizant of the light. This was a loss based entirely on ego and overconfidence, a great tragedy for the buffalo and a huge comeuppance for me!

Once done, a shot cannot be undone. Such events are a waste and a shame, but they happen. With an animal as big and tough as a buffalo, they can happen to anyone and on any outing. There's really nothing for it but to accept that infrequent losses are a sad part of hunting, and, in my experience, an infrequent but unavoidable part of buffalo hunting. Be as careful as you can with the first shot. Follow it up if you can, or be grateful if your PH was able to. Just understand that animals can be hit and not be recovered. A point may be reached when the trail is lost, and you want to shout or rant and rave, but all you can really do is reach down deep and take it. You can't do anything to help the buffalo or even yourself. I hope I never have to again, but when it happens to me, I apologize to the rest of the party for my poor shooting—and make a vow to do better next time.

Just One Shot

Chapter 18

Safari Club International, God bless 'em, is the largest organization of its type in the world, but it's certainly not the first or only group of hunters interested in international or African hunting. The famous Shikar-Safari International is older, but there were a number of "sort-of local" groups that predate SCI: the San Francisco-based Mzuri Safari Club ("*M'Zuri*" means "good" in Swahili), Houston Safari Club, the Safari Club of Southern Florida, and the Southern California Safari Club.

SCI's founder, C. J. McElroy, broke away from the Southern California Safari Club to found Safari Club International in 1973. The Southern California organization eventually withered away, but in the 1970s it was a vibrant organization. One of its "subsets" was a group called the "African One-Shotters," organized by L.A. raconteur and hunter Dick Griffin. For some years he'd organize a group safari along the lines the Lander One-Shot Antelope Hunt, except they'd give prizes for taking African game with just one shot. I never participated; this was all just a bit before my time, but I knew a lot of the "One-Shotters"—many of whom would remain active in hunting circles for decades to come.

It was all in fun, and, at the time, I thought it quite harmless and admirable. When nondangerous game is considered, it probably is admirable *and* harmless. The essence of ethical hunting is always to make that one perfect shot to dispatch the animal cleanly, humanely, with minimal fuss, and no suffering. This applies to all game at all times, but there is a slightly different spin with dangerous game. Only

When hunting with a single-shot rifle, there will probably be just one shot. That knowledge tends to make one very careful, which is not altogether a bad thing. I took this bull with a Dakota M10 in .375 Dakota.

a fool would withhold an additional shot and risk a lost animal in order for a few seconds of recognition, and only a crazy fool would withhold a necessary bullet on a potentially dangerous beast and risk endangering everyone in the party.

Hunters have come a long way since we used clubs and spears. We revere the one-shot kill—and we should—but with dangerous game it's more important to revere the clean, *safe* kill. With the buffalo, a genuine, pure one-shot kill with no follow-up, backup, or insurance shot(s) fired is usually an unintentional accident.

It is most unusual for a buffalo to "drop to the shot." Hey, it happens. Obviously, a brain or central-spine shot will drop a buffalo and anything else, and the animal will stay down. I don't like these shots because the target is small and the risk of wounding the animal too great. The "high-shoulder/spine" shot, high in the shoulder where the curving spine drops down from the neck, is a "lights out" deadly shot. It's also very tricky! There's great margin for error, and you'll have trouble on your hands if you flub it.

Realistically, I think an awful lot of neck/spine shots are because of hunter error: The shot was intended elsewhere, but the shooter got lucky! The brain shot is a very small target and is difficult; however, you can't ignore it because there are times, such as during the final moments of a charge, when the brain shot may be the best option. Whether intentional or completely accidental, when the passage of a bullet scrambles the brain or severs the spine at or forward of the shoulders, the buffalo is down and the game is over.

Most normal shots, such as the classic "heart/lung" shot, will not drop a buffalo in its tracks. It does happen, and I've seen it. It occurs most often when you combine near-perfect shot placement with an exceptionally—and perhaps unnecessarily—powerful rifle. Even on buffalo, kinetic energy does matter . . . especially when it's delivered in copious quantity. You can see it with extra-powerful .45-caliber cartridges such as the .458 Lott, .450 Rigby Rimless, and .460 Weatherby. You'll see it even more with monsters like the .500 Jeffery and .505 Gibbs, and, of course, old-timers like the .577-3". Such really big cartridges do have the capability of knocking a buffalo down or dropping it to the shot. If placement is good, the buffalo will stay down. That does not mean extra-large cartridges are the answer because they are much more difficult to shoot well, and if you shoot poorly, there isn't much difference in the result: You're still going to have a long day.

I do believe adequate cartridges are essential, along with good bullets. We'll take these two as a given: There are dozens of "adequate" buffalo cartridges, starting with the 9.3mms and .375s, and there are many great bullets. Some are better than others, but today's hunting bullets are so good that it's hard to make a "bad" choice. Year in and year out I have probably seen more "pure" one-shot kills with .375s than anything else. This suggests—as if there's any argument—that the .375 is adequate. However, in fairness, I have probably seen more buffaloes shot with .375s than with everything else put together. So that doesn't mean the .375 is the final word, just that I've seen it work over and over.

In 1996 I was hunting in Zambia with Bob Petersen, Ken Elliott, Gary Williams, and artist Doug Van Howd. "Pete" had just sold Petersen

Publishing Company, so he bundled us all up in his Gulfstream so he could spend his seventieth birthday on safari. Uh, yeah, it was quite a trip! One day I was out with Gary Williams, Pete's ranch manager, and we got onto a big herd of buffaloes. Gary was shooting a .375 H&H with Winchester 270-grain Fail Safe bullets. Do you remember that long-discontinued bullet? It was almost a homogenous alloy but had a small lead core, very much a "penetrating" design.

Hunting with PH Austin Wienand, we circled ahead of part of the group, and, as they passed, Gary shot a very nice bull toward the end of the herd. They bunched up immediately, and although Gary would have shot again if he could have, there were just too many buffaloes for a clear shot. The herd thundered off, taking Gary's hard-hit bull with them. We waited a few minutes and then followed in their wake. Had it not been for a little rise, Gary's bull would have fallen in sight. We followed over the rise, and there was Gary's bull, down and still, back of his horns flat to the ground, nose straight up in the air, bright blood shining on the nose. This buffalo was *done*.

At this moment there is a choice: Pay the insurance any way you wish or approach with reasonable prudence and accept congratulations for pulling off a "pure" one-shot kill on an African buffalo. A one-shot kill ain't that easy, and it ain't that common. This was, however, an extremely classic situation. The buffalo was in a herd. In this case we all thought Gary's 270-grain slug might be a bit light, but, no matter what, had it been possible Gary would have followed up. It wasn't possible, so we waited until the herd was out of sight, followed barely a hundred yards, and there was Gary's bull. No one would have blamed him for maneuvering slightly and firing an insurance shot. He chose not to, and no one can blame him for that, either. The ground was hard-baked and open, the buffalo was not just down, but completely still, and there is no recovery from that obviously unnatural nose-up attitude.

Most of my own "pure" one-shot kills have been similar. Honest, they are always pretty much accidental in that I would have fired additional shot(s) had it been possible, but other buffaloes got in the way or things happened too fast. Then, when the dust settled,

I was sitting over sticks with a steady perch (bottom), watching a bedded group of bulls with Mark Haldane coaching when a good bull stood and offered a shot. There was no second shot, but we watched him tip over, horns flat to the ground, nose up. The rifle is a new Rigby Big Game in .416 Rigby with 2–7X Leupold.

the buffalo was down and in safe enough circumstances that there was no imperative for an insurance shot. Mind you, there's nothing wrong with firing that insurance shot. Complacency can be deadly when dealing with buffaloes. I'll admit that I'm somewhat less likely to automatically fire the insurance shot than I used to be. I hope that means I am not less careful in approaching a downed buffalo!

There is no right or wrong answer here. When a buffalo is on its feet and you're certain you're still on the right animal, I absolutely believe one should keep shooting. I also absolutely believe in paying the insurance if there is any uncertainty whatsoever . . . and that includes even if you aren't certain whether or not there is uncertainty!

Let's look at the following scenario: Supposing you concentrate hard and place your shot well in the first encounter, and that's the only shot fired. For whatever reason you lose sight of your bull, but a few minutes later you find him down, completely immobile. You fire the insurance shot, and there is no reaction whatsoever. This buffalo was *dead.* The insurance shot was clearly unnecessary. Should you give yourself credit, a little private pat on the back, for a one-shot kill? That's between you and your conscience or, since this is mathematics, you and your calculator. But, yes, I think it's probably appropriate to consider this very common two-shot scenario as a "one-shot kill." Available evidence suggests that the first shot killed the buffalo; the second shot was purely a matter of prudence. I'm pretty sure the buffalo doesn't care, and from a safety perspective it's always a good thing to have fired that second shot, whether it appears to have been needed or not.

What you don't want is to mess up your head with too many congratulations—self or otherwise—over one-shot kills. All too often I hear hunters describe their hunt results with comments such as "I took seven animals with eight shots." That's great and it's definitely fine shooting, but I doubt there were three buffaloes in that mix. If there were, I suspect the math would be different. The important thing is to get the job done, preferably with the least number of shots, sure, but *getting it done safely* is more important.

I've written about this before, but Americans have a really bad habit of "admiring" their shots: We set up and get as steady as we can,

I took this bull with a LAW .375 H&H and a single 300-grain DGX bullet. After the shot, he was covered by other buffaloes, so there was no possibility of a second shot. We watched him go down in the group and stay down as the herd moved off. Most "pure" one-shot kills are a bit like that: accidental and unintentional.

we place that first shot as well as possible, and then we stand there, watching for results. I suppose it's as if we're expecting magic to occur. Once fired, that first shot is no longer of immediate importance. More important is to make ready to fire again, assess, and take additional shots as needed.

Europeans are generally much better at this than Americans, especially at the moderate ranges at which buffaloes are typically shot. This is because shooting running game in the "driven hunt" is a huge part of their culture and experience. Also, this being the case, most European ranges have running-game targets to train on; this is often boar and sometimes moose or red deer. They thus have much more opportunity to practice working their actions and firing multiple shots. Our European cousins usually don't stand around waiting to see what happened with that first shot; they just keep shooting if they possibly can.

Please understand, however, that this is always with the *caveat* that you have to be very, very sure. A couple of years ago, hunting with Mark Haldane, we got into a medium-size herd bedded tightly on the far side of a small, short-grass savanna. It was midafternoon, meaning our Cinderella clock was ticking, and we had, maybe, a couple hours before we needed to head out of the swamp. It isn't that we turn into dust at midnight or anything like that; however, at dusk the mosquitoes, relatively placid all day, threaten to carry you away, and, equally aggressive, hippos become active in the channels. Perhaps most important, in case of a breakdown, we try to reach the floodplain by dark.

On this day I was carrying a Rigby Big Game .416, blessedly scoped. We had good cover behind sawgrass at one edge of the savanna, but these buffaloes were already out of reach for iron sights. At the moment we didn't have a bull picked out, but we knew there should be bulls in a herd this size, so Mark spread the shooting sticks low for a steady sitting position and we started studying the group. We found several bulls, and it was just getting to the time of day when the herd should get up to start feeding. We waited, studying them and ticking them off. In a while a very nice bull got up, but he was standing on the back side of the herd. Distance was one hundred and eighty yards. That's a *very* long shot on a buffalo, probably my longest ever, even mitigated by a scoped rifle and a very steady position.

I decided to take it anyway. When the shot broke, most of the herd was still lying down. The shot ended recess with black bodies everywhere and dust coming up fast. In the split seconds before panic ensued, we thought the first shot looked good, but we lost our bull in the melee as the herd stampeded to the right. We were lucky in that we'd identified this bull lying down; he was obviously shootable, and we were pretty sure he was the best bull in the group. When he got up we just stayed on him, waiting for him to stand clear and offer a good presentation. Often it isn't that easy. Usually we identify bulls by mud patches, scars, bald spots, even bird droppings, and, of course, by horn shape. We had none of that with this guy—he was just a very nice mature buffalo—and we'd only just marked him when he got up, so it wasn't like we'd been studying him.

Now, with the herd running in a tight pack to the right, we had to find him again. There was a similar bull running behind the herd. Still on the low sticks, I'd swiveled my butt around to the left to stay with them. This bull was running alone, seemed dead last in the group, and although he showed no sign of injury, I felt this almost had to be our boy. I was on him, ready to shoot. It's probably a good thing I'm not a PH. Either Mark or the tracker said something, I don't know what. I glanced back left, just in time to see *our bull* tip over, amazingly almost obscured by drifting dust.

We approached him on the short-grass savanna, which was much like a putting green. The bull was on his side, neck twisted so the back of the horns was flat to the ground and the nose straight up. We checked him carefully as we approached. On open ground, herd long gone, I certainly could have paid the insurance, but there was simply no reason to shoot again.

Whether I fired again or not, that first 400-grain Swift A-Frame had done the job. As you perhaps know, I am a writer by trade; thus, although I try not to get too fixated on semantics, I am obligated to be mindful that words matter. In a situation like this where only one shot is fired, period, no additional shot(s) whether superfluous or not, I like to call a "*pure* one-shot kill." If you see that reference in my writing, this is what I'm talking about—no insurance, no additional shots at all.

At that particular moment I had a nice string of these going. Obviously not on the same hunt, or even with the same rifle, but over a two-year period I'd had three "pure one-shot kills" with Hornady DGXs, and now I had another with this bull using a .416 and Swift A-Frame. As always, these were all totally unintentional. If there'd been a chance for a second shot, you can bet it would have been fired. All these bulls, now four in a row, went down to one shot and stayed down, with no incidents.

With a string like that, an unsolicited and very dangerous thought popped into my head: "Hey, Boddington, after all these years you've finally got this buffalo thing figured out!" I suppose the thought was unavoidable, but, of course, I hadn't figured out anything; it was just random chance. My next three buffaloes took two, three, and four shots.

None of this is important. It's OK to count shots, and you probably should. Just don't get wrapped up in it. Shoot your buffalo as well and as carefully as you can, and if you need to, shoot him again. What's important is to get him down without drama. When you accomplish that, it's a good buffalo hunt, regardless of the number of cartridges expended.

The Charge

Chapter 19

Just before attacking, the African buffalo will often shake his head once, utter a short, deep snort, swing the massive horns toward the intended target, and then launch himself at you. Perhaps the shaking and snorting allows the buffalo to get his bearing and decide on direction and target. If you are foolish enough to approach frontally and make eye contact, the buffalo will eliminate these preparatory moves. If bedded, the buffalo will rise and attack in one motion; if standing, he will come straight in.

The buffalo attacks directly with head up, keeping his eyes on his target, and then, at the very last moment, his head drops to hook you with the tips of his horns or to smash you with his boss. Like most horned animals, the buffalo knows exactly where his horn tips are, but, from a decade of fighting and defending himself against lions, I assume the buffalo recognizes he has a choice of whether to smash or toss. I can't know this because I've never been able to ask a buffalo, but I know (or knew) people who were hammered by a boss and others who were hooked by the horns. Sometimes both.

Niki Atcheson, wife of Keith and sister-in-law of Jack Jr., all old friends, is among few female hunters to be injured while hunting Africa's dangerous game. She was smashed, then severely gored, and literally flattened when the buffalo was finally killed and fell with his full weight on top of her. She was lucky to survive.

Tossing, by the way, doesn't necessarily involve the horn tips. Buffaloes are extremely adept with their horns. Remember that they come in low. My two friends who were killed by buffaloes were

A buffalo attacks with its head up until the last. At this distance you can kill him with a frontal chest shot, but it will not stop him. A bit closer and you must hit the brain or spine. A shot between the eyes is about right. (Photo courtesy of Ivan Carter)

apparently struck frontally, below their centers of gravity, and tossed, not on the tips but by the boss, frontal surface, or *nose*, a mere flick of the giant neck. They were then met again on the way down with hard horn. Both, according to witnesses, were killed instantly. Only then did the buffalo use its sharp tips, continuing to wreak vengeance.

Few people have a lot of experience with buffalo charges, and I can't imagine anyone who would want the distinction. Harry Selby, an acquaintance, and Franz Coupé, a friend, have the rare distinctions of doing fifty full seasons as professional hunters. Harry, regrettably, is gone. Franz, an amazing man, is still hunting at eighty and still guides forest safaris! I was just with him in Coutada 11 in Mozambique in October of 2018. I asked him how many buffalo charges he had seen. His answer was immediate: "Forty or fifty," he said. Neither Harry nor Franz were ever injured, nor was anyone in their parties injured by a buffalo.

When hunting elephants, you evade charging cows on a daily basis, but with buffaloes, charges are not normal, and human injuries or death unusual. I never thought to ask Harry how many buffalo charges he'd seen—I wish I had—but for sure he saw quite a few. Franz's forty or fifty sounds like a huge number, but that's not even one per year over his long career. Keep in mind, he did a lot of hunting back in the days when several buffaloes were commonly on license. Also, while buffalo cartridges haven't changed much, the bullets we use today are a great deal better than what we had prior to the 1980s.

Also, where we hunt our buffaloes makes a difference. Franz commented to me that "Serengeti buffaloes" were especially aggressive. He attributed this to, in those days, a high population of lions that kept the buffaloes constantly on edge. I haven't seen this personally in terms of frequency of charges, and I will never attain that level of experience. What I have seen is that in areas where lions are numerous, buffaloes are much more nervous and difficult to approach. I saw this in the Lower Zambezi in the early 2000s where, at least at that time, I think lions were genuinely overpopulated.

There were lots of buffaloes, enough that eventual success was relatively certain, but the buffaloes were always on edge and extremely wary. In contrast, the calmest buffaloes I've hunted are in Mozambique's Zambezi Delta, where lions have been almost absent since the civil war ended and hunting resumed around 1990. I've also found the buffaloes in Namibia's Caprivi (now Zambezi Region) and Uganda's Karamoja province to be amazingly calm. Lions are present in both areas, but there aren't very many.

South Africa's privatized buffaloes are a seeming anomaly. Excepting for park buffaloes, South Africa's disease-free buffaloes on private lands haven't seen a lion in many bovine generations, but I found them surprisingly wary and difficult to close with. Today's availability of buffalo in South Africa is a relatively new thing. Most PHs there didn't grow up hunting buffaloes, and few have a lot of buffalo experience—but as numbers and availability increase, they're learning fast. Some of the guys who are hunting them a lot are experiencing two or three charges per season, which would greatly exceed Franz Koupe's average of about one per year. One explanation is that, although there are no lions and actual hunting pressure is light, these buffaloes are frequently bumped by plains-game hunters,

These were the exact positions of Diekie Muller and my wounded buffalo when Diekie stopped the charge. The bull went down six steps from Diekie's bootlaces. The first barrel from Diekie's .470 Krieghoff hit the bull between the eyes, a perfect shot.

so they have become naturally edgier than buffaloes in unrestricted wild areas with a low lion population.

Another obvious factor is the thickness of the cover. As mentioned, western and forest buffaloes have local reputations for being extremely aggressive. I haven't really seen this, but I have much less experience in Central and West Africa than I have in southern countries. However, regardless of region, "close-cover" buffaloes are consistently locally regarded as more aggressive. This applies to buffaloes in the dense cover of Masailand's hills and mountains and buffaloes encountered in the thick *jesse* bush of Zambia and Zimbabwe. It should apply to buffalo hunting in the uniformly thick mopane of the Limpopo Valley, and for sure to the incredibly thick Addo thornbush in the Eastern Cape, where hunting privatized buffaloes is also becoming commonplace today.

However, no matter where you hunt them, not every buffalo is going to charge. For sure charges happen, sometimes a matter of luck or circumstance, sometimes from error. Bumping any buffalo at very close range increases the danger. Shooting poorly the first time increases it even more, but then there's the random chance of running into a buffalo that's nursing wounds from a lion or poacher, that's dragging a snare, or that simply has a bad attitude. After studying these things for years, I'm pretty well convinced that fickle chance is involved. Even with the very best effort and intent on your part, not all buffaloes go peacefully, and when things turn bad, not all charges can be stopped. It depends on distance and angle, and, like people, buffaloes are individuals. Some give up more easily than others.

Peter Hathaway Capstick was a friend and great storyteller, and his books are worth reading. After his passing, "debunking" Capstick became common sport. I won't indulge, in part because it's in bad taste . . . and my turn may come when I'm gone! More importantly, however, Peter Capstick introduced a whole generation to the excitement and adventure of Africa. He brought a lot of people to the party, and every African professional hunter blessed with paying clients should toast him frequently. I will say only that Capstick's work created a false impression that hair-raising close calls are so commonplace that some hunters come away disappointed if they don't get charged at least every other day.

Such things do not happen frequently in the real world of the African safari, but they do happen. Just the other day I was talking to Texan Clay Johnson. Clay is an outfitter and owns the 5J Ranch in Texas; I'd call him a very experienced hunter. He and his son, William, then twelve, were on their first Cape buffalo hunt in 2018. The first shot looked so good that when they heard the bull's death bellow, they assumed their belief in the shot to be justified. Then the buffalo got up and charged. This, by the way, was the *second* time I've heard of a buffalo getting up after that "final" bellow. In camp in Mozambique in October 2018 Mark Haldane added a third instance, so obviously this happens.

In a wild melee that followed, the buffalo got to his feet and started for Clay. The surrounding cover was too close for a safe shot, so the bull managed to run over Clay and knock him down. Then, while Clay watched in horror from ground level, the bull overtook his young son and flattened him from behind. By that time someone was able to get a shot in and finish the bull. Amazingly, although both were badly bruised and shaken, the buffalo didn't use his horns to hook either Clay or his son, so neither was seriously injured. A postmortem examination showed the first shot should have been fatal, and all present had heard the "death bellow." The bull should have been dead, yet there seemed very little wrong with his mobility or the velocity of his charge. One would have suspected that the initial shot was placed well enough to prevent serious injury, yet somehow it wasn't. That was some first buffalo hunt!

Strange things happen. I've heard of other instances where hunters have been hit by a buffalo and walked away with minimal injury. In our camp in Botswana in 1986, my stepson's PH was knocked down from behind, and then, as is most common, the buffalo proceeded to hook him. He didn't exactly walk away but, courtesy of a land mine in Angola, the buffalo hooked him in his prosthesis. It took him a while to find all the springs and pieces to put his leg back together but, thanks to the soft mud he was pressed into, he was bruised by the impact but otherwise unhurt.

Joe Bishop and I are smiling now, but we had just had a bad moment. This Mozambique buffalo was down in long grass and seemingly dead, but it jumped up and tried to attack just as Joe fired an insurance shot. Fortunately, we were all ready and the bull went nowhere.

Considering a buffalo outweighs a puny human by a factor of nine or ten, minor injuries are not the most common result. I have no desire to test my luck! However, the only real way to avoid danger is to stay completely away from buffaloes and all other potentially hazardous situations. Considering actual statistics, that means avoiding cars, public conveyances, and even bathtubs. That doesn't sound like much of a life. Danger from buffalo is best avoided by following these three suggestions: First, shoot straight in the first encounter; second, pay attention; and, third, *stop* the charge if one occurs.

We've briefly discussed shot placement, and certainly not for the first time. The first shot is always critical. Repeat shots, when possible, can be equally important. However, on that first shot it's also a matter of taking your time and waiting for the right presentation. Charges from wounded buffaloes are usually the result of imperfect placement of that all-important first shot. Often this is not exactly a matter of poor shooting. Taking a shot with questionable presentation causes many wounded buffaloes, and that, in turn, causes a lot of charges.

Unusually, this savanna buffalo ran straight toward me after receiving the first bullet. It's impossible to say if it was a real charge or if the bull just took that line, but I couldn't ask him. An Aimpoint on the .375 made stopping the bull very simple.

I'm not throwing stones; I've taken shots I should have passed, but the worse the angle, especially quartering-away shots, the more you're asking the bullet to do.

After three days of increasingly hopeless tracking, the buffalo that killed Owain Lewis was lying down when finally encountered, and a tragic and protracted firefight reignited. For a hunter it's always a great victory to get the drop on a bedded animal, but it's a risky shot, and the bigger the animal, the riskier it is because it becomes increasingly difficult to visualize exactly where the vitals lie. As Andrew Dawson said perfectly in his clipped speech in our first buffalo DVD, "The lying down shot—I don't like it."

I don't either. In fact, over all the years, I've only employed it once on an unwounded buffalo. This was the "nontypical" bull I recounted earlier when I was hunting with Roger Whittall in the newly formed Save Valley Conservancy. When we finally crawled into the bedded herd, it was a blistering hot midday, and the baked red soil was burning our hands and knees. The bull was lying down on his haunches and knees, with his head to the right. His good horn was up, and the weird horn looked as though it was grounded for support.

That was twenty-odd years ago. Today I might be more patient and wait for him to get up, but the herd was comfortable and in no hurry, so we lay and sweated for ages while I tried to make sure I could properly visualize the shoulder. I was shooting a Dakota Model 10 in .375 Dakota with a 300-grain Swift A-Frame, plenty of gun and a great bullet, and I was lying prone with a tight sling. I was reasonably certain I could see and hit the aiming point that was right over the top of a forked stick.

The bull was probably sixty yards away, and there were lots of reasons in favor of taking the shot, but I don't think I should have, especially since with the single-shot there would be no second shot. Anyway, hindsight is crystal clear vision. I took the shot, lots of commotion ensued, and we found the bull stone-dead just a short distance away. It worked, but if I'd waited, he'd have gotten up sooner or later and *probably* would have offered a more certain shot. Since then I've waited, sometimes hours, for other bulls to get up. I still think this is the better option, but it depends on distance, how the buffalo is lying, and how certain you are that you can properly visualize the shot. There's also a chance that you may wait endlessly, other buffaloes may get in the way, or there may not be the possibility of a shot at all.

Wounded buffaloes that are lying down are a different deal. When the hunters approached the Owain Lewis bull, I can't assess what was in their minds except for the obvious: After three days of tracking, let's get this finished! I actually don't know if they were sure the buffalo was still alive. I've fired insurance shots into a number of buffaloes that had been shot, tracked, and were found lying down, but I've rarely been certain whether it was alive or dead. Generally, it was just that, an insurance shot into the chest or spine from the side, if possible; and if that was not possible, from the rear, preferably with a solid. Reaction, or lack thereof, tells you if additional shooting is needed.

I recall a buffalo Joe Bishop shot in Mozambique. The first shot was facing, and Joe knew the shot was slightly off to the right. We tracked a considerable distance, and when we found his bull, it was down and still, just a dark mound in yellow grass. Joe approached and fired an insurance shot. I don't remember where he placed it, and at the moment it didn't really matter because we all thought the bull was stone dead.

We were disabused of that idea when the bull lurched to its feet, very much alive and turning to us as it rose. J. P. Kleinhans shot his .470, I shot with my .416 Taylor, and Joe shot again with his .375. The buffalo went nowhere, but things could have ended differently.

When hunting buffaloes—or when hunting any potentially dangerous animal—one should be on full alert all the time. This is patently impossible, for there will be moments when attention lapses. Perhaps something extraneous catches our eye, or maybe we just get tired and bored. This is when Mr. Murphy lies in wait for the unwary and unready and pounces to enact his law. I'm sure most of us have seen Mark Sullivan's amazing videos filled with close-range charges. I do not agree with the ethics of purposefully inciting charges, and for sure I don't want to hunt with PHs who orchestrate situations so they can shoot. However, the evidence from the video makes it pretty clear that Sullivan has stood more charges than most modern hunters, and also that he shoots extremely well and has very large *cojones*. These things I give him.

However, in any film clip all one can really know is what's on the screen. We can't know exactly what planning or maneuvering went into causing the charge, and we aren't shown other rifles that might be covering off-camera. In many instances it's clear that the approach is made frontally, allowing eye contact and essentially taunting the animal to attack if it's able. In my view these are ethical "no-nos." There is one advantage to actively provoking a charge and that is the hunter can choose the ground and prepare himself. It's a bit like walking in on a staunch gun dog pointing a quail. You know more or less where the bird is (because the dog is telling you), so you walk in with shotgun at high port, physically and mentally ready. Peripherally you study the ground ahead so you can plant your feet solidly without stumbling, your eyes watching not where the bird is, but where it will be when you raise the shotgun, slip the safety, and take the shot.

The analogy holds when you have no pointing dog but you're walking along, perhaps tired, gun not quite ready, and a cackling rooster pheasant or a covey of bobwhites get up unexpectedly at your feet. This is a whole different deal! You still have to set your feet, perhaps turn your body, and get a proper grip on the gun. You are unready and surprised, and, thus, much less likely to make the shot.

When you have a visual on a buffalo that has been shot, whether you think it's dead or not, you should be as ready as when you're flushing a pointed bird. The problem is you often don't have a visual before a charge is launched, and not all charges come from wounded buffaloes. Ideally, then, you should be just as ready at all times when hunting buffaloes. This is not possible, but you should strive to stay fully ready throughout the follow-up, regardless of how long it goes on. A little thing I usually do after the shot and before starting to follow a hit buffalo is to remove the sling on my rifle. Depending on cover and circumstance, I may do the same while tracking and stalking. Obviously, the sling is just one more thing that might catch on brush, and even its slight swinging motion adds unnecessary and unnatural movement to an environment you are trying to control. This is a not so obvious suggestion: Take off the sling and stow it in pack or pocket. That will remove the temptation to use it. When following a hit buffalo, the rifle must be ready . . . and you must be mentally ready to use it.

The last time I visited with Mark Sullivan we were at the big Harrisburg sports show, and he told me he'd recently had one of his closest calls, a buffalo that came out of nowhere and from fairly close. Still worse, Mark was down a steep bank, with gravity on the side of the buffalo. Sullivan, when casually hunting, may or may not be constantly readier than most of us, but at that time he was taken by surprise and was not fully prepared. He had no chance to choose his ground and make sure his feet were planted. He got the buffalo stopped, but he said that it was a very near thing.

This is the reality of a charge for most of us. It can come at any time, your footing may be bad, trees might be in the way, and trackers might be in front. Although we must strive to be ready, we are almost always surprised. We must overcome this and, just like a flushing pheasant, take the half-second to adjust position and set our feet correctly to meet the danger. There is no way to avoid this initial surprise; the only way to mitigate it is to understand it can come at any moment and *pay attention*.

The crack just below the door is where the buffalo's boss hit when it attacked our BV and seriously rocked the heavy vehicle. We were minding our business, driving through sawgrass, when we came upon the bull unintentionally. I've seen this happen more than once! That's PH Craigh Hamman (left) and Bill Hober.

For many years my premise has been that not all charges can be stopped. This comes under the heading of "bad things can happen to good people." Fortunately, actual charges are uncommon, and most of them can be (and are) stopped. The actual incidence of a genuine buffalo charge is rare enough that, at the time I wrote my previous volume on buffalo hunting, I had never seen one. To some extent this is a matter of luck, whether good or bad, but since then I've done a lot more buffalo hunting and I've seen a half-dozen charges.

I haven't yet seen one that couldn't be stopped, and I hope I never do! Distance, angles, and cover—or one of those seemingly bulletproof buffalo—can cause unsolvable problems with serious consequences. When a charge occurs, the only real solution is to shoot straight. The stopping shot must be fast, but it must also be certain, so *too fast* can be deadly. That said, the buffalo is a very large animal and does not accelerate like a sports car or a leopard. I've followed several buffaloes that had been wounded and I managed to hit them as they turned, thus possibly preempting full-out charges.

Power matters. Most PHs I've known with longtime experience believe that a .375 with a good bullet is adequate for stopping any charge. I believe it, too, but there is a reason why most professional hunters carry more powerful rifles for backup work. Bigger is undoubtedly better in *extremis*, but it's crucial that you are able to handle the rifle easily and shoot well with it.

When it comes to actually *stopping* a buffalo, the only two options are to hit the brain or spine, and both are difficult shots. However, whether either shot should be employed depends on the circumstance. Not all charges come from close range, and there is that matter of acceleration. In thick cover you probably won't see the buffalo launch, but sometimes you do. Depending on your angle, and if you have some standoff distance, you may be able to take a much easier frontal chest shot. This will not normally *stop* a buffalo, and additional shots will probably be required, but it may not be necessary to wait until the last moment.

If the bull is close, then go for the brain or spine. With the head up, a shot between the eyes should work, whether with solid or a good, tough modern expanding bullet. Your angle can vary, and not all ground is level. As we've seen, the buffalo, not you, chooses the ground. As the buffalo comes toward you with its head up, the gleaming black muzzle (nose) becomes a perfectly suitable target . . . this is where those rarely used solids you carry "just in case" pay their way. Depending on the angle, such a shot may penetrate to the brain or the solid should pass through the nasal cavities and disrupt the spine.

My old friend and mentor Geoff Broom taught me that an alternative, and easier target, is to fade to one side if you can and, as the buffalo comes with its head up, shoot just under the curve of the horn. This will catch the spine at the base of the neck, as it curves down into the shoulder. I have done this shot a couple of times and it's an amazing shot; typically the buffalo folds in midstride and slides forward, completely dead.

How many chances you get to do it right depends on time and distance. This is not the time to short-stroke a bolt-action, but a practiced hand can often, certainly not always, work a bolt fast enough to get at least a second chance during a charge. The charge, however, is one situation where a double is absolutely superior to anything else. *But* you only have two chances, so best save the second barrel for a few heartbeats! At the very last the buffalo will drop its head to smash or hook. Any head shot other than high in the forehead just in front of the bosses is now just a facial wound and unlikely to kill the buffalo. The brain is still available, but now it's a small, fast-moving target.

The goal is to kill the buffalo before it drops its head. When it does, it's probably too late to stop the buffalo, but it's far better to be plowed into by a dead buffalo than one still able to use its horns and hoofs. At the last instant before impact, when the head goes down, there is now a huge and vulnerable target—that broad neck to the top of the shoulders, the spine right in the center the whole way. The Marine Corps uses a "fitness report" to report on those in one's command. I used this for thirty-one years, and there is a line in it that asks the commanding officer to judge the person for "presence of mind." This meant, essentially, the ability to think fast under pressure.

My old friend Mike Payne, Zimbabwe PH, caught a charge out of nowhere at very close quarters from a buffalo cow. He knew it was too late to stop her, but somehow, as the head came down at knee level, he had the "presence of mind" to snick the Krieghoff cocking lever and, using the first two fingers of his right hand, fire both barrels of his .470 down into the base of her neck. He rode the instantly dead buffalo for frantic milliseconds and he survived. This is one of those rare instances where a hunter was hit full-on by a buffalo and sustained only minor injuries. Mike's presence of mind saved the day.

The Bullet Does the Work

Chapter 20

Back when I was a lot younger, we expected our bullets to kill game. Most of the time they did, but I guess that wasn't enough. Today we expect our expanding bullets to penetrate, hold together, retain most of their weight, and look catalog-picture-perfect so that we can compare them and endlessly debate their attributes and nuances.

Bullet performance was, and is, a subtle combination of construction, caliber, weight, and velocity. Construction is incredibly important. Today we have a wide selection of wonderfully engineered bullets that perform extremely well. I'm one of the guys who believes that caliber—frontal area—remains important. This is fairly simple to understand. A bullet of .458-inch diameter is larger in caliber and frontal area than a .375-inch bullet. In the most elementary terms it makes a bigger hole. I believe the frontal area aids in energy transfer, thus it hits harder.

Weight is also important. All things being equal—which they are not!—it makes sense that heavier bullets hit harder, which is true to a point. However, weight-for-caliber, which is expressed as sectional density (SD), is perhaps more important than raw weight because again, all things being equal—which they are not!—SD has much to do with a bullet's ability to overcome resistance and penetrate.

Understanding the importance of velocity is a bit more confusing. On the one hand, velocity overcomes resistance. However, the formula that derives kinetic energy, expressed in foot-pounds (ft-lbs), uses the square of velocity, but takes the weight "as is" and does not consider

This Zambezi Valley bull was the first buffalo to fall to Hornady's new .450/.400-3" load. The bullets are a 400-grain DGX and a 400-grain solid fired for insurance; both were recovered from this buffalo and both exhibited perfect performance.

frontal area or SD. So lighter, faster projectiles win the kinetic energy race, but do we believe that, say, a 300-grain projectile from a very fast .375 (like the .378 Weatherby Magnum), which can develop over 6,000 ft-lbs of energy, will stop a buffalo charge more effectively than a 500-grain bullet from a .470 developing about 5,000 ft-lbs? I think not!

John Taylor's "Knock-Out Values," which are mathematical but not especially scientific, were one attempt to characterize and compare the "hitting power" or energy transfer of bullets. Many of us, including me, still sometimes use Taylor's "KO Values," but it's important to understand that Taylor was concerned *only* with nonexpanding "solid" bullets, whose sole job is to provide straight-line penetration with (essentially) a caliber-size wound channel. His term "knock-out" comes from the ability of a solid of certain caliber, weight, and velocity to stun an elephant with a near-miss to the brain. In other words, to knock it out. This is tricky. In my experience, which is nothing compared to Taylor's, near misses to the brain may or may not stun or "knock-out" an elephant. My advice is: Don't count on it!

Anyway, in this discussion we are not concerned with bullet performance on elephants. We do need to talk about whether or not, with our wonderful modern expanding bullets, there remains a role for nonexpanding solid bullets in today's buffalo hunting. We'll get to that, but let's continue for a bit with this business of *energy transfer*. This is one of the least understood concepts in terminal bullet performance, and one that to my knowledge has defied attempts to be properly quantified and compared. We can measure velocity and derive kinetic energy, but exactly how is that energy transferred to the animal?

As hunters, some of us are overjoyed to find our spent and expanded bullets against the hide on the far side. Others want both entrance and exit wounds. A bullet that exits clearly has retained energy. This is irrefutable because I've seen bullets exit and flatten another unseen animal—including a buffalo—on the far side. This is not a good thing, but it can happen. So, did that bullet expend all its energy within the first animal? Obviously, it did not.

The bullet that comes to rest within an animal expended all its energy. Did this happen on impact? Not if it continued to penetrate; it expended energy as resistance overcame velocity. As velocity dropped, so did energy, but did it expend most of its energy in the first few inches of penetration or more gradually? Moreover, doesn't it matter exactly what resistance the bullet encounters—bone, muscle, soft tissue? We don't know exactly how a bullet transmits energy during its passage, and we also don't know precisely how much energy is required for game of various sizes.

Col. Townsend Whelen theorized that 1,000 ft-lbs of energy *on impact* was desirable for deer-size game. I've suggested that 2,000 ft-lbs is a pretty good rule for elk. Conventional wisdom suggests that the .375 H&H's or the .450/.400's roundabout 4,000 ft-lbs is about right for buffalo. Maybe, but these are just theories. If the .375 H&H or .450/.400 bullets stayed inside the buffalo then 4,000 ft-lbs were expended . . . but is the buffalo less dead if the bullet exited and expended some of its energy on the far side? And what about the unknown thousands of buffaloes taken over the years with cartridges producing less than 4,000 ft-lbs of energy? Rules of thumb are good, and so is conventional wisdom, but absolutes are elusive.

We do know that bullet performance is critical. First, the bullet must penetrate and disrupt the vital organs. Nonexpanding solids do this, at least more or less, by pure penetration. Expanding bullets must also penetrate to the vitals from any sane angle. However, they do more disruption by upsetting or expanding, increasing frontal area and creating larger wound channels. Expansion depends on bullet design and construction . . . as well as caliber, weight, and velocity. The larger diameter the bullet is able to expand to, the larger the wound channel.

Expansion is thus good, but only to a point. The more frontal area a bullet has, the more resistance it encounters, causing it to slow more rapidly and eventually come to rest. So, expansion is the enemy of penetration. Velocity helps overcome resistance, but now we must add in SD. Fast bullets that are light for caliber shed velocity more quickly (in both air and flesh) and are less stable than long, heavy-for-caliber bullets. So why not push them faster? You might be able to, but recoil will increase and, depending on the cartridge, you may encounter case capacity or pressure issues or both.

It shouldn't matter for this discussion that a sharp-pointed (spitzer) bullet holds its velocity better and has a flatter trajectory than a blunt-nose bullet of the same weight and diameter. The SD is the same regardless of bullet shape. The index of a bullet's ability to overcome resistance in flight, the ballistic coefficient (BC), varies widely with bullet shape. Bullet aerodynamics aren't important in buffalo hunting, however, because nobody takes long shots. Even though this business of energy transfer is poorly understood, it is generally accepted, including by me, that blunt-nose bullets transfer more energy upon impact, and thus deal a heavier initial blow, than sharp-pointed bullets. Construction does matter, but it's also widely accepted and generally true that blunt-nose, expanding bullets commence expansion more rapidly than sharp-pointed bullets. This also aids in initial energy transfer, and, with its blunt-nose bullets intended for tubular magazines, perhaps this has much to do with the .30-30's legend as a deer cartridge, despite very mild paper ballistics.

When I started hunting, we didn't know bullet construction was so important because we had so few choices. Into the 1980s most of our bullets were simple "cup and core" bullets: A lead core is placed inside a copper jacket. For many years the primary exception was the Nosler Partition, introduced in 1948. The Nosler is a dual-core bullet with a wall of jacket material between the front and rear core. So is the German H-Mantel, with a softer lead front core followed by a harder lead-alloy rear core. The front portion expands rapidly, but the rear portion holds together and continues to penetrate. Like all modern bullets, some swore by Partitions and others swore at them, but it was and is a good design. Unfortunately, Nosler quit making large-caliber Partitions before I came along and didn't resume until the late 1990s. Some of the old-timers I knew hoarded 300-grain .375 Partitions and swore by them for buffalo. I never got a chance to use any of the originals, but I've used "new" Partitions in both .375 and .416. John Nosler's bullet is still a reliable performer!

During the early years of my buffalo hunting, our primary choices were cup-and-core bullets from Barnes (original), Federal, Hornady, Remington, Sierra, Speer, and Winchester. Not all were the same simple jacketed bullets developed in the 1890s. Bullet designers quickly learned

Top row: recovered homogenous alloy bullets; bottom: recovered bonded bullets. The homogenous alloy bullets may lose petals but will reliably penetrate; bonded-core bullets will expand more and retain great weight, but cannot penetrate as deeply because expansion eventually limits penetration.

that expansion could be speeded or slowed by the amount of lead core exposed at the tip as well as the thickness of the copper jacket. Some bullets have mechanical features to help bind core to jacket, such as Remington's Core-Lokt and Hornady's Interlock. Polymer for sexy tips did not exist, but it was known that a tip of harder material protected the point *and*, upon impact, drove down into the bullet to initiate expansion. The two best historical examples are the Remington Bronze Point and the original Winchester Silvertip. The Bronze Point expanded fast, but it was and is a pretty good deer bullet. (O'Connor liked it!) To my knowledge, it was never made in large calibers for buffalo-size game, but the Silvertip was. Some folks loved it, but the 300-grain .375 Silvertip was thought by many to be erratic.

However, in those innocent days before the arrival of today's super bullets, in general the cup-and-core bullets with exposed lead tips worked pretty well . . . and still do. Especially when two important principles are understood and followed. First, velocity is the arch-enemy of bullet performance. High velocity causes more rapid expansion, and at extreme velocities, the older bullets became unreliable, sometimes breaking up on impact and failing to penetrate. In the limited world of cartridges and bullets for buffalo, this was rarely a problem. However, bullets that performed well at Nitro Express velocities of around 2,150 feet per second (fps) didn't always perform as well when several hundred additional fps were added. Existing bullets performed pretty well at the .375 H&H's 2,530 fps, but there weren't many bullets that would hold up at .375 and .378 Weatherby velocities. Back in the 1950s and clear into the 1980s lack of bullets tough enough to withstand the higher speeds gave Weatherby cartridges a bad rap among many hunters. Modern bullet designs have long since cured the problem, but with faster cartridges—especially *much faster* cartridges—it's still wise to use tougher bullets, which we now have.

With our modern bullet designs, the other principle also has less application today, but it's still worth a passing thought: Bullet weight covers a lot of sins in bullet design. The biggest problem with the old cup-and-core bullets was weight retention: During the processes of impact, expansion, and penetration, a lot of bullet material was lost. On this type of bullet, retention of 60 percent of original weight isn't abnormal. Many modern bullets retain over 90 percent of original weight and look pretty. So long as the bullet does the job and performs as designed to do, so what? It stands to reason that a bullet can afford to lose more of its mass if it has more to start with.

This isn't extremely important for bullets for buffalo because few people use the lightest, fastest bullets. Traditional "buffalo bullets" are at least "medium" or heavy-for-caliber. However, some of our modern bullets are *so* good that it really is true that you can sacrifice some bullet weight, increase velocity, flatten trajectory, and reduce recoil without reducing the bullet's effect on game. As examples, the gold standard for large game in caliber .375 is the 300-grain bullet, 400-grain in .416, and 500-grain in .458. With bonded core or homogenous-alloy bullets, you could drop down to 250 grains in .375, 350 grains in .416, and 450 grains in .458. I doubt a buffalo would notice the difference.

Even so, I generally stick with the traditional bullet weights. There is another trend, and that's toward "extra-heavy" bullets: 350 grains in .375, 450 grains in .416, and up to 600 grains in .458. The heavier bullets can penetrate better, but the price is reduced velocity and increased recoil. I would buy into this *if* additional penetration was needed, but in my opinion it is not. The traditional weights—300-

Groups from a Dakota in .400 H&H using Barnes TSXs and Barnes Banded Solids, both 400 grains. Even with bullets of the same make, a slight difference in point of impact is normal between solids and softs. This difference, about an inch at 100 yards, is not enough to matter on really large game.

grain .375, 400-grain .416, 500-grain .458—have provided adequate penetration on buffalo for more than a century. The extra, and to my thinking unnecessary, bullet weight has serious disadvantages. Velocity is so reduced that the trajectory curve is much steeper. This probably doesn't matter on buffaloes, but differences in points of impact are so extreme that it would be impractical to carry one load for plains game and the extra-heavy one for buffalo. And bullet drop at distance is increased so much that the versatility of the .375s and .416s—and similar cartridges—is compromised. Finally, accuracy may also be reduced because standard rifling twists may not be fast enough to stabilize the extra-long and extra-heavy bullets.

So, I prefer to stick with the long-established "medium" bullet weights. As to which bullet I like best, well, I've used many and have seen many in use. I don't believe there are *any* 300-grain .375, 400-grain .416, or 500-grain .458 bullets that are inadequate for buffalo. I've used 300-grain Sierra GameKing bullets with no issues. In the old days, when they were a primary supplier, I used Barnes (original) round-nose bullets. I've also used a lot of Hornady Interlock and the Australian Woodleigh bullets. These are all "cup-and-core" bullets. Federal's Fusion, with the core added by a different process, is another good modern bullet, and the current Nosler Partition is still a fine bullet. All will lose weight during expansion and penetration and are not always "pretty" when recovered. So what? If of adequate weight and caliber, they work just fine, especially when velocities are normal and not extreme.

Today we are in a world of "designer bullets," and with so many choices from so many manufacturers both large and small, no one can claim significant experience with all of them. I certainly do not! In expanding bullets, the two biggest advancements have been core-bonding and homogenous-alloy bullets. In bonded-core bullets the lead core is chemically attached to the jacket. The core and jacket will not separate and little lead is wiped away. Depending on make, bonded-core bullets tend to expand dramatically, but lose little weight. Homogenous-alloy bullets are made of copper or a copper alloy, with no lead core at all. Expansion is caused by a hollow nose cavity with skived edges, causing the nose to peel back in petals. Weight retention is very high, often in the high 90 percent. Typically, homogenous-alloy bullets cannot expand as much as bonded-core bullets. However, since expansion creates more resistance, homogenous-alloy bullets tend to provide deeper penetration than bonded-core bullets.

Nonexpanding solid bullets haven't changed as much. Today the two primary types are the much newer homogenous-alloy solids, essentially copper (copper alloy) or turned brass and the more traditional steel-jacketed solid, which is a lead core covered with a thin sheet of steel and overlaid with traditional jacket material.

One change is nose shape. The original Kynoch steel-jacketed solid was always a round-nose bullet. Hornady's traditional solid and newer Dangerous Game Solid (DGS) are steel-jacketed solids. More recent research suggests that a flat meplat (bullet nose) tends to provide greater straight-line penetration than a round-nose, and for sure a very blunt-nose bullet seems to deliver a heavier initial blow, which seems to make sense. There is a further theory that a flat nose creates sort of a "bubble effect" ahead of the bullet during

The .375 H&H is the most commonly loaded of all potential buffalo cartridges. The choice in bullets is wide as shown by the selection above, and some are better than others, but any and all 300-grain .375 bullets are absolutely "buffalo-capable."

penetration. Swift's "Breakaway" solid with discarding plastic tip and Woodleigh's "Hydro Shock" solid actually have concave tips, dealing a heavy initial blow and, theoretically, enhancing this bubble effect. (Not all bullet manufacturers accept theory.)

I've used the Swift Breakaway and it works well, but I'm convinced all current solids are good at what they do, which is to provide deep, straight-line penetration with no expansion. Several that I've used—Hornady's DGS, Barnes' Super Solid, and the Breakaway—could be reloaded and fired again after I recovered them from game. Nonexpanding solids are essential for hunting elephants and remain the best choices for hippos and rhinos. The question is: With the great expanding bullets we have available today, do solids still have a role in buffalo hunting?

The African buffalo is a big animal, and deep penetration is required. Prior to our modern "super" expanding bullets, most professional hunters recommended "solids only" for buffaloes. Expanding bullets were distrusted for larger game, and there were reasons for this. In the early days of my career in the 1970s, this was still the status quo. Old ways die hard, and this thinking seemed to persist into 1990s. When I did my "professional hunters' survey" for *Safari Rifles* in 1990, the split between "solids and softs" for buffalo was about even. Extensive experience takes time, but in the 1990s, both homogenous-alloy and bonded-core expanding bullets were available and things were changing.

When I did my second survey for *Safari Rifles II* in 2007, most respondents—over one hundred in each survey—were using expanding bullets for buffalo. A significant number, however, added *caveats*, recommending solids for bachelor bulls or for following up a wounded buffalo. Why? Well, solids absolutely ensure penetration, but on broadside shots are almost certain to exit. This is a real problem in herds, but on smaller groups of bachelor bulls, which range from singles to perhaps, rarely, a dozen, it's much easier to be absolutely certain the targeted bull doesn't have another buffalo behind it. When following up a wounded buffalo, you must be prepared for a charge, of course, but when the buffalo is tracked, and especially if it runs away again, which is more likely than a charge, additional shots will be taken. Solids are better than any expanding bullets for "going-away" shots on a wounded buffalo.

Solids are comforting when you face a charge, but I'm pretty sure any charge can be stopped with today's great expanding bullets . . . if you have a shot! Being a bit old-fashioned, I usually still carry a couple of solids and may load them for a follow-up, but I no longer believe they are essential. I'm writing this chapter while hunting with Mark Haldane in Mozambique's Coutada 11, and it's October 2018. Mark's Zambeze Delta Safaris annual buffalo quota has exceeded one hundred bulls for a number of years, so he and his PHs have huge recent experience on buffaloes.

I asked Mark if he thought solids still had a role in buffalo hunting. He thought for a minute and said, "No." He's perfectly comfortable hunting buffaloes loaded only with good softpoints, his favorites being Barnes X (or TSX), Hornady DGX, and Swift A-Frame. However, I checked his cartridge belt, and there was a tidy section of solids along with expanding bullets! On the other hand,

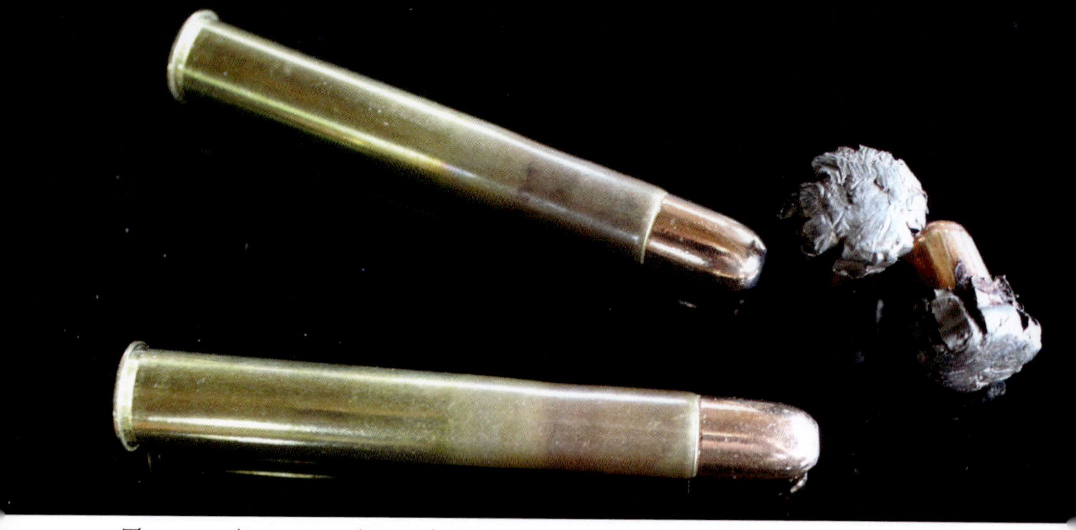

These two 480-grain, .458-inch Hornady DGX-Bonded bullets were recovered from my 2018 Caprivi buffalo. These were the first DGX-Bonded I had used on buffalo, and performance was obviously perfect. These were fired from my Sabatti .450-3¼" Nitro Express double.

while running around in the swamps, there's always the possibility of running afoul of an elephant or hippo at close range. That is why I still carry a few solids . . . just in case.

So, for buffalo hunting, expanding bullets win. As to which are best, most of us have our favorites. Let's be honest, however: None of us have equal experience with all of today's great bullets. It is, thus, not a fair discussion. Without question, the Swift A-Frame is an awesome buffalo bullet. The A-Frame is unique. Like the Partition, it's a dual-core bullet, front and rear core separated by a wall of jacket material. However, the front core is bonded. Hallmarks of the A-Frame are radical expansion and extreme weight retention, generally into the upper ninetieth percentile. Recovered bullets consistently look like catalog photos . . . almost always with that distinctive Swift "bulge" in the bullet shank.

The Barnes X (or TSX) is also a great buffalo bullet. Back in the 1970s and well into the 1980s, when the great British Nitro Express cartridges were unavailable, Barnes kept us in bullets and RCBS-made dies. The old Barnes cup-and-core bullets were fairly soft, but with plenty of weight-for-caliber and not too much velocity, they worked fine. Randy and Coni Brooks acquired Barnes and almost starved, but in the 1990s, Randy developed an expanding copper bullet with a hollow nose cavity that worked extremely well . . . and still does.

About 1991 he and Coni came to visit us at Petersen Publishing with daughters Chandra and Jessica, toddlers then—all still working with Barnes today. Randy already had his homogenous alloy "Super Solid," which is a super-penetrating solid. Randy had prototypes for this weird homogenous alloy, expanding bullet. With nose cavity and sharp, skived meplat, the nose portion peeled back in petals that he swore were consistent. Since he had his Super Solid, he wanted to call it the "Barnes Super Soft." Instinctively I pushed back, telling him that was the wrong message: "Super Soft" meant rapid expansion, and the expansion of this bullet was totally controlled by the nose cavity. As we examined recovered bullets, he said that, from a frontal view, the petals always formed a cross. We turned them this way and that, and realized that the cross could also be an "X." Honest, in my office at the Petersen Publishing Company in Los Angeles, 8490 Sunset Boulevard, the Barnes X was so named.

Today there are other homogenous alloy bullets: Hornady GMX, North Fork, Nosler E-Tip. All are good, deep-penetrating bullets. As with all bullets, some rifles shoot them better than others, and not all are available in calibers large enough for buffalo. If they are, homogenous alloy bullets are buffalo bullets! Expansion is consistent but limited, so penetration is deep. Also, there is a theory that whatever expansion the skived nose and hollow cavity allows, it happens very quickly. My old friend, the late Bob Penfold, famous Australian outfitter, was a huge Barnes X fan because he thought this rapid initial expansion dealt a dramatic and noticeable initial blow.

I can neither confirm nor deny, but the homogenous alloy bullets are effective and penetrate well. In the genuine reality of buffalo hunting, the only issue is that these bullets sometimes penetrate *too well.* They will consistently exit on behind-the-shoulder shots, and often exit on shoulder shots. This depends on the exact placement and angle on the shoulder, and of course caliber and weight. In coastal Mozambique, where I've done so much of my buffalo hunting in the last decade, we are often working in big herds. In this situation, we avoid homogenous alloy bullets because we don't want through-and-through penetration, and for sure we don't use solids. There is too much risk of a bullet passing through and unintentionally hitting another buffalo on the far side.

Here's my full disclosure on my relationship with bullet manufacturers: I am not "on the take" from any bullet manufacturer and never have been. Some of my colleagues are, which is their business and none of mine. My business is writing about this stuff as honestly as I can. You don't have to agree with my opinions or conclusions, but they are not rendered for a motive to make a profit. On the other hand, it is not possible to be unbiased. The Brooks family of Barnes Bullets have been friends since the 1980s. I knew Lee Reid, who invented the Swift A-Frame in the tiny hamlet of Quinter, Kansas, also in the 1980s. Swift's current and long-time owner, Bill Hober, has been a friend since he acquired Swift Bullets in the 1990s.

I knew and greatly respected the late Jack Carter. His Trophy Bonded Bearclaw was not the first bonded-core bullet. That honor goes to Bill Steiger and his Bitterroot Bullet. Those who used Bitterroots raved about them, but they were scarce and hard to come by. The Trophy Bonded Bearclaw was, thus, the first "available" bonded-core bullet. Before his death, Jack Carter licensed his "TBBC" to Federal. Federal still manufactures it, and it's still a fine bullet. Unfortunately, it is not available in a wide caliber selection, especially in the big bores. This also applies to Norma's Oryx, another good bonded-core bullet.

Then there's Hornady Manufacturing. Steve Hornady and I hunted together in Zambia back in 1983, when we were both very young. Steve's dad and Hornady's founder, Joyce Hornady, was killed in a tragic plane crash en route to the SHOT Show in 1981. So, in 1983, Steve had just taken over the reins at Hornady, and I was a new editor at *Petersen's HUNTING* magazine. We go back a long way! In 2004, largely out of long friendship, Steve Hornady agreed to sponsor the *Tracks across Africa* TV program I was hosting.

At that time Hornady made .375, .416, and .458 bullets: Their classic Interlock; and their old steel-jacketed solid were standards. Their Dangerous Game line followed, including the Dangerous Game Expanding (DGX) and Dangerous Game Solid (DGS), soon including some of the old Nitro Express cartridges and their bullet diameters: .409 (.450/.400-3"); .423 (.404 Jeffery); .475 (.470 Nitro Express); and .510 (.500 Nitro Express).

David Porter, PH Debbie Visser, and I with two nasty old swamp bulls from Mozambique's Coutada 14, both taken with David's Dakota .375 firing 300-grain Barnes TSX. His was a shoulder shot; mine was in the neck at the base of the ear, both bulls down.

Thanks to the availability in both bullets and loaded ammo and because Hornady has sponsored multiple TV shows I've been involved with, I have used mostly Hornady bullets, both solids and expanding bullets, for the last fifteen years. I've had excellent results, good enough that I've offered Hornady photos of game and recovered bullets for use in advertisements and such. Although certainly offered, I've refused payment; that's just not the business I'm in. This has left me free to use other great buffalo bullets from Barnes, Federal, North Fork, Swift, and others when circumstances allow.

Now, the original DGX was not bonded. So what? Recovered DGX weren't always pretty and some weight was lost, but in more than a decade and Lord knows how many buffaloes, I never saw a clear example of failure. Was it the "best" buffalo bullet? Perhaps not, but it was readily available, inexpensive, and it worked. It irked me immensely that some of my colleagues were knocking the DGX, especially when I learned that some were being paid by competing bullet companies. I seriously doubt anyone had had as much experience with DGX as I did. The primary complaint wasn't whether the DGX worked or not, but simply that, when recovered, it wasn't as picture-perfect "pretty" as bonded-core or homogenous-alloy bullets. If I was irked, imagine discussions in Grand Island, Nebraska, between Steve Hornady and his management team?

I had this discussion with Steve and his son, Jason Hornady, and with Neil Davies and others of my friends in Grand Island. Having never seen a genuine problem with DGX, my advice was not to bother with going to core-bonding on the DGX bullet. Obviously, the technology was there since Hornady's Interbond is a bonded-core bullet. In any case, quietly at first and now across the line and consistently stated on all packaging and literature, the DGX bullet no longer exists, replaced by the DGX Bonded. My experience is now limited with DGX Bonded and probably will remain so for some time . . . it may take years before I use up all my DGX bullets in some of my favorite arcane calibers and cartridges. I'm certainly not going to throw them out! However, understanding only recent and limited use, I can say that the DGX Bonded expands a bit more consistently, definitely retains more weight, and is "prettier" when recovered. It is a "better bullet."

As to "best," I'm not able to say nor is anyone else. The drum I keep beating is nobody can possibly have equal and extensive experience with all the great bullets we have available today. The good news is there are many fine choices. Remembering, always, that expansion does damage but limits penetration, bonded-core bullets probably deliver the greatest expansion. But, since expansion always limits penetration, lead-core bullets cannot penetrate as deeply as homogenous-alloy bullets. Accuracy will vary from rifle to rifle, but pinpoint accuracy is not critical in hunting buffalo. Confidence is, so, with many good choices, my recommendation is to use one of the great modern bullets that gives you confidence. Put the bullet in the right place and it will work. Put it in the wrong place, as I've learned to my shame and horror, and neither bullet choice, caliber, nor kinetic energy will save you from disaster.

Buffalo Cartridges

Chapter 21

Discussions about buffalo cartridges are the stuff campfire arguments are made of! We hunters often sound like gossipy old ladies, nitpicking endlessly over the slightest minutia. It's silly, but it's also fun . . . and completely harmless as long as we realize how silly we are! Again, it's the bullet that does the work. The rifle, which we'll discuss in the next chapter and avoid as much as possible in this chapter, is just the launching platform for the bullet.

Note, however, that we often confuse *caliber* and *cartridge*. Not to insult anyone, but not all of us have long backgrounds in this stuff, and this volume may be read by some for whom English is not a first language. So, forgive me while I give some basic definitions. *Caliber* refers purely to bullet diameter, typically expressed in thousandths of an inch, as in .375, or .416; or millimeters, as in 9.3mm. *Cartridge* refers to a unique set of case dimensions, which limit the amount of propellant the case can hold, thus controlling velocity. Case dimensions can also be sized for specific rifle actions, thus can also restrict bullet weight. For instance, cartridges designed for shorter repeating actions may not allow feeding with the heaviest and thus longest bullets.

There is, of course, much more. Actual bullet diameters are fairly standard, but American and English cartridge nomenclature often round up or down. So, the .376 Steyr and .375 H&H both use the standard .375-inch bullet diameter; and the .450 Nitro Express, .458 Winchester Magnum, and .460 Weatherby all use .458-inch bullets. Appended at the end of the numbers are often, but not consistently,

The old 9.3x62mm Mauser is a good, sensible, and low-recoiling "minimum" for buffalo. This CZ 550 in 9.3x62 was sweet-shooting and very accurate.

the name of the person or company who developed the cartridge. This often serves to differentiate the specific case dimensions of cartridges that use the same bullet diameters common with other cartridges, such as: .416 Remington, .416 Rigby, and .416 Weatherby Magnum.

Europeans typically use a metric system that, although incomprehensible to we simpleminded Americans, makes lots of sense. The European system expresses bullet diameter in millimeters or fractions of millimeters, followed by case length, followed by the originator; the three together very much define a cartridge with unique case dimension. Examples include 9.3x62 Mauser: 9.3mm (.366-inch), with 62mm case, developed by Peter Paul Mauser; and 9.3x64 Brenneke, also a 9.3mm bullet but with a case length of 64mm, developed by Wilhelm Brenneke. Some cartridges have differing English and metric designations. The European 10.75x73mm and English .404 Jeffery cartridges are exactly the same, both using a .423-inch bullet.

So, how can a .404 be, in reality, a .423? Crazy, but simple. Americans tend to use the actual rifling *groove* or bullet diameter (sometimes rounded one way or the other), while the British, even less consistent, often use the smaller *land* diameter, meaning the distance between the raised portions of a rifled barrel between the grooves. So, a land diameter of .404 equates to a groove diameter of .423. On the other hand, the naming of cartridges can be ridiculously inconsistent. The .370 Sako Magnum is not a .375; it uses a .366-inch bullet . . . with a sensible European designation of 9.3x66mm. OK, enough of this. If caliber and cartridge nomenclature is Greek to you, check references before making assumptions. At least, in this discussion, all examples used are within the limited spectrum of buffalo cartridges!

Often stated is "the .375 is the legal minimum for African dangerous game." If true, this would surely include the buffalo, but it is not true. In the 1950s the old East African Professional Hunters' Association enacted a .40-caliber (.400-inch) minimum for hunting thick-skin dangerous game, which included buffalo. This became part of the game laws in British East Africa, to my knowledge Africa's most rigid caliber requirement. To this day numerous countries do not have minimums. Of those that do, the European 9.3mm (.366-inch), is actually a more common stated minimum than the .375. The 9.3mm is essentially the European equivalent of the .375, with several cartridges to choose from that use that bullet diameter.

It's debatable whether the 9.3mm is *really* the minimum choice for buffalo. Older accounts testify that hunters had a lot of trouble taking buffalo down with slow blackpowder projectiles, which averaged about 1,400 feet per second (fps) and topped out at 1,800 fps. In the 1890s, smokeless propellant and jacketed bullets made a quantum leap forward, increasing velocities beyond 2,000 fps and providing unprecedented penetration. Across the continent, most early settlers, hunters, and explorers used what they could easily obtain, which was often the military cartridge of their parent country. So, in the French sphere, the 8mm Lebel was common. In German East and South-West Africa the 8x57mm Mauser was prevalent, and throughout the British colonies untold numbers of buffaloes were taken—many cleanly, undoubtedly others not—with the .303 British. Some notable early hunters such as C. H. Stigand and W. D. M. Bell were outspoken in their preference for early 6.5mm and 7mm cartridges for *all* game. Others switched to large, powerful cartridges as they became available, but some took the middle ground. Fairly mild medium-bore cartridges such as the .318 Westley Richards (actual bullet diameter .330-inch), .333 Jeffery, and .350 Rigby had followings. Many considered these cartridges adequate to bring down a buffalo, and by using heavy bullets at moderate velocity, power levels were similar to our .35 Whelen with 250-grain bullets.

I could theorize that our .338 Winchester Magnum—and faster .33s—should be adequate, especially with our great modern bullets. The 250-grain .338 actually has slightly higher sectional density (SD) than the 300-grain .375 bullet. The smaller diameter bullet meets less resistance, so, if velocity were equal and bullet construction similar, the .338 should consistently penetrate better than the .375. I've taken just one African buffalo with a .338 and had no problem. CZ's Jason Morton and I used the big .338 Lapua to take several Australian water buffaloes, and, again, no problem.

There remain places in Africa where this would be perfectly legal. However, with buffalo one must always be cognizant of what's going to happen if things go wrong. So, I'm going to side with majority opinion and a century of conventional wisdom and say that the sensible minimum for buffalo is the .375 or its European equivalent, the 9.3mm.

Always it depends on which *cartridge* we're talking about. The gold standard is the .375 H&H, which propels a 300-grain bullet at 2,530 fps and yields a bit over 4,000 ft-lbs of energy. The .375 Ruger is a bit faster and develops more energy. The .375 Weatherby and .375 Remington Ultra Magnum (RUM) are significantly faster, with energy yields of about 5,000 ft-lbs, thus similar in energy to the .416 Remington and Rigby. The .378 Weatherby Magnum is *much* faster and produces even more bullet energy. However, recoil energy also goes up sharply as velocity increases.

There are also slower .375s. The .375 Flanged Magnum is a rimmed version of the .375 H&H intended for double rifles. It is still loaded and chambered to some modern doubles, though mostly seen in older rifles. The .375 Flanged is loaded to lower pressure and is slightly slower than the belted .375 H&H, but it's fast enough that

Left to right: 9.3x74R, 9.3x62, .370 Sako Magnum. In most African jurisdictions, the actual legal "minimum" for dangerous game is usually 9.3mm (.366-inch) rather than the oft-stated .375. Firing a heavy-for-caliber 286-grain bullet, the 9.3s are very adequate for buffalo.

no buffalo is likely to know the difference. Historically there were several small-case .375 cartridges, now obsolete, that were *not* buffalo-capable. Relatively new, the .376 Steyr is on the edge. It was developed by Hornady and Steyr around gun guru Jeff Cooper's concept of a "big bore Scout rifle." It has less case capacity than the .375 H&H and is slower, but its biggest problem is that it was designed for maximum use with 270-grain bullets to reduce cartridge length. We have one, a light MGA rifle. Although intended for North American use, with tough modern bullets like the Barnes X or Hornady GMX, it would be buffalo-capable, but I doubt it will ever see Africa.

There was a time when I questioned the adequacy of the .375 H&H for buffalo. I was wrong. The proliferation and popularity of "lower .40-caliber" cartridges has caused a whole new generation to question the adequacy of the .375. This, too, is wrong. The .375 H&H was adequate for buffalo when introduced in 1912. It remains adequate today, and with modern bullets, it should be considered "more adequate." Recoil is moderate and tolerable, and the .375s remain among our most versatile cartridges, especially in the African context where size of game runs up and down the scale.

I used a light scoped Sabatti double in 9.3x74R to take this buffalo in Mozambique's miombo *forest. I shot the bull on the shoulder, quartering slightly to, and one 286-grain Hornady Interlock did the job perfectly. The bull went less than a hundred yards and was down and completely dead.*

The faster .375s are also "more adequate" than the .375 H&H. With much higher energy, they often seem to hit more like the .416s, but recoil is fast as well as hard. I used a couple of .375 Weatherby Magnums on several safaris, and I used a .375 RUM in Tanzania in 2000. Their effectiveness was fantastic! However, when I carry a .375, it is usually for versatility as well as effect, for it can be employed on a variety of plains game as well as on buffalo.

In the isolated context of buffalo hunting, the faster .375s are marvelous, but for use on plains game, where one might shoot daily, I found the recoil objectionable. Call me a wimp, but I have retreated to the .375 H&H and .375 Ruger. Take your pick. Both are fine, and both are perfectly adequate for and effective on buffalo. These are good base lines, but suggesting them as a sound "minimum" suggests they might be on the margin of effectiveness. This is simply not true. Altogether, I've taken more buffaloes with .375s than anything else. Since I've used the .375 H&H a lot more—and a lot longer—than other .375s, I think I've experienced more one-shot kills with the .375 H&H than anything else. Mild recoil simplifies shot placement; put a good, modern 300-grain bullet where it needs to be, and the .375 H&H will do the job just fine.

I don't have nearly as much experience with the 9.3mms as I do with the .375s; in fact, I actually have very little. However, for a genuine base-line minimum for buffalo, I think the old 9.3x62mm Mauser offers a sound, low-recoil option. Typically loaded with heavy-for-caliber 286-grain bullets, the 9.3mms offer excellent penetration . . . with velocity and thus recoil dependent on case dimensions. The 9.3x62 is often encountered in Africa, and has made a significant comeback in America, both in new rifles and ammunition availability. The 9.3x62 runs about a hundred fps slower than the .375 H&H and so is less powerful, but it also has less recoil and can be housed in a standard .30-06-length bolt-action. I just got a Montana Rifles 9.3x62 on their Mauser-clone action. It hasn't seen action yet, but I look forward to taking it buffalo hunting.

Introduced in 1905, the 9.3x62 was designed to duplicate ballistics of the older 9.3x74R cartridge, a rimmed cartridge popular in European double rifles and single shots. Although Europeans often use the 9.3x74R for buffalo and, with solids, sometimes for elephant, I questioned its suitability. I had long wanted a light double, so a couple years ago I got a very light, inexpensive Sabatti boxlock in 9.3x74R. The regulation was excellent, so I mounted a low-power scope and took a Mozambique buffalo bull with it. The shot was quartering very slightly to from about eighty yards. The bullet, a 286-grain Hornady Interlock, hit in the center of the on-shoulder and was found against the hide on the far side just behind the off-shoulder. The bull went about sixty yards and gave its death bellow before we approached.

Clearly one buffalo proves nothing, but I was extremely impressed. One of our trackers commented, "I didn't think he could kill a buffalo with that little rifle." That double is very light and trim, but recoil is substantial. Admitting limited experience, I'd rate the 9.3x62 and/or 9.3x74R as sensible minimums for buffalo.

Two other 9.3mm cartridges are more powerful. The 9.3x64mm Brenneke has a slightly fatter case and is also loaded to higher pressure.

With a 286-grain bullet at 2,500 fps, it should be considered the equal of the .375 H&H. The same can be said of the .370 Sako Magnum (European designation 9.3x66mm), which has almost identical ballistics. Introduced by Federal and Sako, the .370 Sako Magnum is based on the .30-06 case with a fairly short neck for maximum powder capacity.

In Zimbabwe in 2010 with a Federal group, we shot a number of buffaloes and (using Barnes solids) a couple of tuskless elephants with the .370. Its performance was perfect. With its compact case and ability to fit into a .30-06-length action, I thought the .370 Sako would become more popular. It has not caught on well, but certainly offers a sound alternative to the .375. Unlike smaller calibers and cartridges that, theoretically, may or may not be adequate for buffalo, I believe the 9.3mms are adequate; moreover, they are "street legal" for buffalo all across Africa.

Before we jump into larger cartridges for buffalo hunting, I'd like to discuss one matter. It's difficult to completely isolate cartridges from rifles, so let's briefly digress. Break-open actions, which apply to most double rifles and some single-shots, are not as strong as bolt-actions. They also do not have the bolt-action's camming power to extract cases after firing. Cartridges designed for double rifles have always been loaded to lower pressure than cartridges designed for bolt-actions. With modern steel, the strength issue isn't so critical, but this is: Traditionally, double-rifle cartridges have an exposed rim that the extractors and/or ejectors can easily grab. Doubles can certainly be made for rimless and belted rimless cartridges, but the extractors must have spring-loaded plungers that snap into the extractor groove ahead of the rim. There are various arrangements, and most work well . . . most of the time. Since there are perfectly good rimmed cartridges available, a double in a rimless or belted rimless cartridge offers one more point of failure, daring the resurrection of Murphy's Law, and failures to extract or eject are known issues with doubles chambered to anything other than a rimmed cartridge.

Both the 9.3x74R and .375 Flanged Magnum, the former common, the latter less so, are good examples of rimmed double-rifle cartridges loaded to fairly low pressure. As we move up the caliber scale, rimmed cartridges include the .450/.400 in two case lengths and Krieghoff's

This is a "cull" Australian water buffalo that I took with a CZ .338 Lapua Magnum firing 250-grain bullets. The fast .33s are extremely powerful and penetrate well with heavy bullets. Where legal to use, they are definitely "buffalo-capable."

.500/.416. That's about it until we get to true big bores. Starting at .450 (using .458-inch bullets), there are about a dozen British flanged (rimmed) Nitro Express cartridges intended for double rifles. Some, like the .470 Nitro Express, are common. Others are rare, but ammunition, if not currently loaded, can be obtained for all of them.

Double rifles are still manufactured in some belted cartridges, primarily .375 H&H and occasionally .416 Rigby and .458 Winchester Magnum, but with today's ammunition availability, most modern double rifle manufacturers have returned to tried-and-true rimmed cartridges. In *African Rifles and Cartridges*, John Taylor wrote about two rifles, one a bolt, the other a double, chambered to the same cartridge, and he described his mismatched pair as "the best of all worlds." The idea is seductive enough that it persists. My friend Tony Lombardo has a .416 Rigby bolt-action. He has a thirty-day safari booked for 2020, when he intends to take multiple buffaloes and other big game. To simplify ammo, he's looking for a double in .416 Rigby, which a couple of current manufacturers still catalog. Several folks, including me and purveyors of these rifles, are trying to talk him out of it. If he persists, I'll let you know how it worked out!

Most of the "lower .40-caliber" cartridges were older British cartridges, and most were almost obsolete by the 1980s. Today

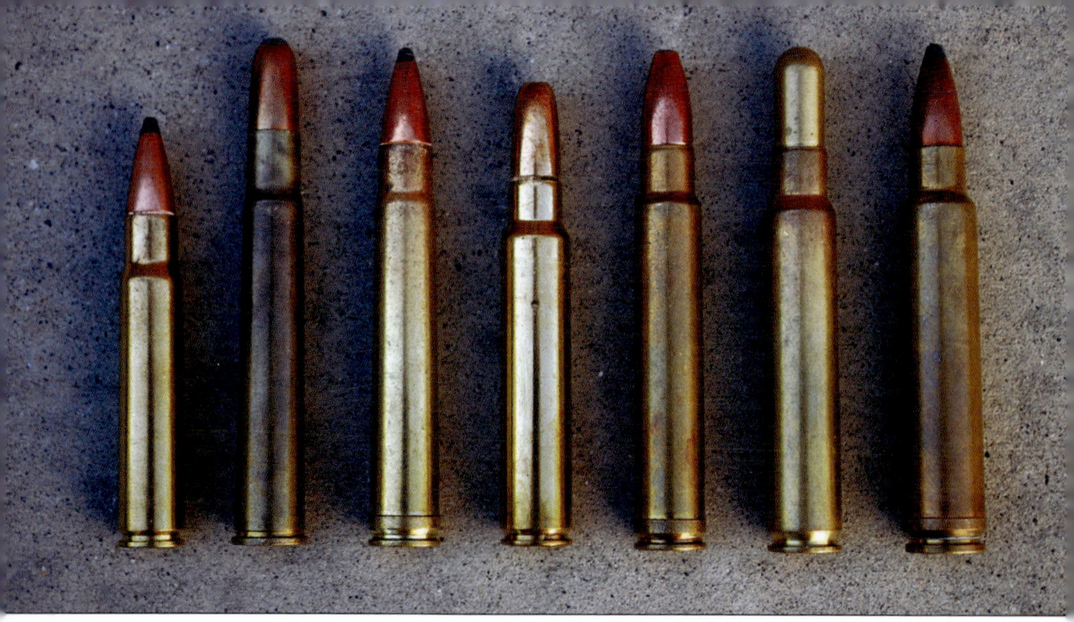

Left to right: .376 Steyr, .375 Flanged, .375 H&H, .375 Ruger, .375 Weatherby Magnum, .375 Remington Ultra Magnum, and .378 Weatherby Magnum. All of the .375s are fully adequate for buffalo, especially with today's great bullets, but the .375 H&H and .375 Ruger are the most likely and most popular choices.

several older cartridges have resurged and there are several new ones. This entire category has become really popular. So much so that, as I said, the efficacy of the .375 is called into question. The .375-caliber cartridges are adequate for buffalo, but there's such a thing as "more adequate." The lower .40s are *more adequate* for buffalo. Given identical shot placement, they usually offer more dramatic effect, and are more capable of getting you out of trouble if things go badly. They are thus "better" for buffalo, but have two disadvantages. First is more recoil. All the power in the world does you no good unless you can consistently apply it in the right places.

Second, although not applicable to a strict discussion of buffalo hunting, they are not as versatile as the .375s. Daughter Brittany and her fiancé, Brad Jannenga, were just with me in Mozambique. Using a "camp rifle," a Blaser R8 in .416 Remington, Brad shot a gorgeous buffalo with 42-inch spread. On the way out of the swamps we spotted the biggest waterbuck I've ever seen. The closest we could get was just this side of three hundred yards. That's a long poke with a .416 but very "do-able"—except it was so unexpected that the precise holdover was unknown. He had one opportunity and the shot hit just under the animal. Such a shot would have been a lot easier with a more versatile and flatter-shooting .375.

The granddaddy of the lower-.40 crowd is the .450/.400-3¼" Nitro Express. Based on an existing blackpowder cartridge, the nomenclature means a .450 case necked down to .400 (.40-caliber), with a 3.25-inch case. A few years later the firm of W. J. Jeffery developed a true smokeless powder version dubbed .450/.400-3" (or .400 Jeffery), with a shorter three-inch case and thicker rim. The two are not interchangeable but nearly identical in ballistics, both using a 400-grain bullet (actual bullet diameter about .410-inch) at 2,100 fps, producing about 4,000 ft-lbs of energy. Both versions were popular and are often encountered in older rifles. I convinced Steve Hornady to bring back the .450/.400-3". Ruger has made several runs of Number 1 single shots, and all modern double-rifle makers now chamber to this cartridge.

With such moderate velocity, recoil is mild and performance on buffaloes is marvelous. We've had multiple Ruger Number 1s and double rifles in .450/.400-3". Both Donna and I have taken buffaloes and elephants with it. Donna is not especially sensitive to recoil, but she's very comfortable with a .450/.400, and shoots it well, which is really the most important thing.

In 1909 W. J. Jeffery introduced the .404 Jeffery, originally duplicating .450/.400 performance, but in a rimless cartridge designed for the bolt-action. Using a .423-inch 400-grain bullet, the European designation is 10.75x73mm. The .404 Jeffery was probably the most popular of the British "large-medium bores," adopted by several African game departments for control work. Unlike most British cartridges of .40-caliber or greater, the .404 never quite died away, with RWS continuing to load factory ammunition in Germany. Today it has made a significant comeback, with ammo available from multiple sources. Modern loads have been upgraded to about 2,350 fps with a 400-grain bullet, developing about 4,500 ft-lbs.

The .425 Westley Richards was also introduced in 1909. Faster than the .404, it uses a unique .435-inch bullet, developing 235 fps with a 410-grain bullet. The .425 is an odd-looking cartridge with rebated rim and a long neck. Westley Richards made a lot of them, and their .425 was adopted by the Uganda game department. Like the .404 it can be housed in a .375-length bolt action. After a hiatus of some years, Westley Richards continues to chamber their .425 today, and offers ammunition as well.

John Rigby's .416 Rigby, introduced in 1911, was probably the least common British large-medium "in the day," but certainly the most famous today. The .416 Rigby uses an extra-large case that requires a magnum action. To this day that remains a drawback, as actions large enough to house the Rigby case are uncommon and more expensive. Still, it's a marvelous cartridge. Original ballistics were a 410-grain bullet at 2,370 fps, although a 400-grain bullet at 2,400 is more common today. Either way it produces 5,000 fps of energy. Because of the scarcity of loaded ammunition, magnum actions, and .416 bullets, it became increasingly scarce after World War II but got a new lease on life in 1988 when Federal introduced a modern factory load and Ruger brought out a magnum version of their Model 77 to house it.

In the same year Remington brought out its .416 Remington Magnum, roughly based on the .375 H&H case necked up. (In actual fact the .416 Remington is based on that firm's 8mm Remington Magnum case.) Within a year Weatherby introduced its .416 Weatherby Magnum, based on the .460 Weatherby Magnum with the case necked down. The big Weatherby case is essentially the .416 Rigby case with a belt; prior to Federal's .416 Rigby load in 1988, the easiest way to obtain new .416 Rigby brass was to turn the belts off of .378 or .460 Weatherby cases.

In the late 1990s, Krieghoff introduced the .500/.416-3 ¼" Nitro Express, pretty much the only "modern" rimmed double-rifle cartridge. About 2010 Hornady necked up its .375 Ruger case to create the .416 Ruger, sized for .30-06-length actions. That should be enough "lower .40s" to choose from, but apparently not. Holland & Holland necked up its own .375 H&H case to create the .400 H&H, which Dakota Arms has marketed very well in the United States. The .400 H&H uses a .411-inch bullet and has an attractive, gently-tapered case. There are other wildcat and proprietary cartridges, but these are enough to deal with.

OK, all of these lower .40s are eminently and perfectly buffalo-capable, so let's quickly sort through them. Honestly, I don't think

Left to right: .450/.400-3", .404 Jeffery, .416 Ruger, .416 Remington, .416 Rigby. These are the most popular of the numerous "over-.40" cartridges available today. This group probably comprises the very best choices for hunting buffalo . . . but only for those who can shoot them well.

it matters too much. The old .450/.400 is my favorite for double rifles and single-shots. It is a short-range cartridge with more limited versatility, but it's plenty of gun for any buffalo that walks; it's also pleasant to shoot.

All the rest vary somewhat in velocity, power, and recoil. The .404 Jeffery, .416 Ruger, and .400 H&H all propel a 400-grain bullet at about 2,350 fps. The .416 Rigby and .416 Remington are identical with a 400-grain bullet at 2,400 fps. They have a bit more recoil, but velocity and energy differences aren't enough that any buffalo will know the difference. The .416 Weatherby Magnum is much faster and delivers a lot more energy, but recoil is ferocious. For handloaders, the .416 Rigby has the same case capacity as the .416 Weatherby. Factory loads have always been mild, so, through careful loading, you can increase the .416 Rigby by a couple hundred feet per second, but why would you want to? A 400-grain bullet at 2,400 fps is plenty of gun for any buffalo ever calved!

We think of cartridges from .45-caliber and above as "large bores." Rifle nuts have long been interested in big bores far beyond their actual need or use. Combining factory cartridges, wildcats, and proprietaries, there are dozens . . . and all are effective on buffalo. This may surprise you, but in this discussion of cartridges specifically for buffalo, I'm not going to waste your time or mine—or paper and ink—on detailed discussion of the big bores. The 9.3mms and .375s are adequate. I'm convinced, specifically for buffalo, the lower .40s are slightly better. The big bores work, you bet, and if you have one you wish to use, by all means go forth. However, cartridges of .45-caliber and above are not necessary for buffalo, so they are beyond the scope of this discussion.

There is one exception: Because of its continued popularity in this country and our long tradition of lever-actions, I'm often asked about the .45-70. I wouldn't try it with the traditional trapdoor Springfield load at very low velocity; however, in stronger actions, including the 1886 Winchester and 1895 Marlin, hard-cast bullets pushed faster are absolutely buffalo-capable. I haven't used the .45-70 for African buffalo, but I might with the right loads, such as Garrett's "super hard-cast" flat-points. I did use a Turnbull '86 in .475 Turnbull to take a big Mozambique bull. It worked just fine but, as we'll discuss in the next chapter, the open sights made an easy shot difficult!

So, let's get to the bottom line: What do I really recommend for buffalo? As I think I said once before, the .375 is the base line. Recoil is survivable and shot placement is simple. Take your pick between a .375 H&H and a .375 Ruger, load it up with good bullets, practice a lot, and you can take your buffalo and everything else on license. If you want more, then look to the lower .40s. There are too many and they are too similar to pick among or make sensible arguments for one or another. The .416 Remington and .416 Ruger will generally be the most affordable in both rifles and ammo. If nostalgia and tradition beckon, then the .416 Rigby may have the most appeal. Over the past thirty-five years I've had a half-dozen .416 rifles in various case dimensions. I don't have one now, but I've decided I need one more. It will be a .416 Rigby, based largely on nostalgia and tradition . . . but I have a serious soft spot for the .404 Jeffery. Take your pick but, whatever you choose, make sure you can place your shot!

Buffalo Rifles and Buffalo Sights

Chapter 22

To some extent the choice of cartridge dictates the rifle. Doubles are at their best with rimmed cartridges that develop relatively low pressure compared to modern, high-intensity cartridges. Bolt-actions are stronger and have much greater camming power for primary extraction, and certainly are available in the largest selection of cartridges. Bolt-actions are probably at their best with rimless and belted rimless cartridges. Rimmed cartridges are possible, but the magazine needs to be angled so the rims are stacked against each other top to bottom to prevent jamming.

Recently I got an email from a reader who had read about the .450/.400 cartridge and wondered if anyone offered a .450/.400 bolt-action. Not today, and not for many years, but such rifles did exist. Back in 1973 Dad and I hunted in northern British Columbia with outfitter Frank Cook, only recently deceased. Cook had a very old British bolt-action—I think it was a Cogswell and Harrison—in .450/.400. I wish I'd taken some photos; that was the only bolt-action I've ever seen that was chambered to a rimmed Nitro Express cartridge.

Like doubles, most single-shots also have relatively weak extraction systems, but actual action strength varies. Break-open single-shots aren't particularly strong, but falling-block single-shots like the old British Farquharson, Ruger Number 1, and Winchester 1885 are among the strongest of all actions. Single-shots have been made in a wide array of buffalo-capable cartridges. The obvious limitation is that one shot, which does tend to make you very careful, but there's a bit more.

This is the only buffalo I ever took with a lever-action, a Winchester 1886 by Doug Turnbull in .475 Turnbull. The cartridge is very powerful, but the traditional buckhorn iron sights made a simple shot more difficult than necessary.

Most single-shots are "extractor guns," meaning the extractor starts the case out of the chamber, but there is no ejection mechanism, so you must manually pluck out the cartridge case. Bill Ruger borrowed heavily from the Farquharson when he designed his Number 1, but he broke the code with his extraction/ejection system. The Ruger Number 1 is unique among single-shots in having a strong and almost infallible ejector. I suppose it's not a critical point because, on buffalo, you typically either have lots of time for a follow-up shot, or you need it immediately. In the latter case, *nobody* is fast enough to reload a single shot. However, because of that magic ejector, the Ruger Number 1 is a very fast single-shot.

Because of availability in appropriate chamberings, the double-rifle, bolt-action, and single-shot are the most likely choices for a buffalo rifle. Other options are limited, but they do exist. Krieghoff's unique Semprio is chambered to 9.3x62mm Mauser, so it is certainly buffalo-capable. Krieghoff describes the Semprio as "in-line." I would call it a slide-action, except operation is opposite. Instead of pulling the fore-end back to open the action and then forward to carry a round into the chamber, the Semprio operates by pushing the fore-end forward and then back. The action is very fast, accuracy is excellent, and, like all Krieghoff firearms, the Semprio is extremely well-made . . . so, there you have it, a slide-action buffalo rifle!

The problem with a semiautomatic is twofold. First, a number of African countries don't allow semiautomatic rifles. Second, no semiautomatic sporters are chambered to adequate cartridges. Browning's BAR is offered in .338 Winchester Magnum, which means it could theoretically house the .375 Ruger and certainly the 9.3x62, but the .338 is the largest and most powerful cartridge it has ever been chambered to. Back in the 1970s Jack Lott (of .458 Lott fame) rebarreled a BAR to .458 Winchester Magnum and, after a lot of work, got it to function reliably. So, it's possible, but you still have to get past the gun permit issue.

Last but not least, there's the good old all-American lever action. Choices are limited, but they do exist. The .405 Winchester, Theodore Roosevelt's "lion medicine," was essentially created for the 1895 Winchester and "maxes" out the action. It was always hampered by a light-for-caliber 300-grain bullet; the 1895 action won't allow heavier bullets without eating too deeply into powder space. In my humble opinion President Roosevelt got it right; the .405 should be fine for lions, but in a lever action very marginal for buffaloes because of the light-for-caliber bullet. Our bullets today, however, are a whole lot better than what Roosevelt had in 1909, so it could certainly be used.

A better bet, and certainly much more available, is the great old .45-70. The original "blackpowder equivalent" 405-grain bullet at 1,300 fps just isn't enough, and faster modern loads with light bullets aren't intended for really large game, but there are solutions. Garrett Cartridges of Texas specializes in .45-70 loads, offering several "grades" intended for use in strong modern actions. In a Browning/Winchester 1886 reissue or a Marlin 1895, Garrett offers a 420-grain "super-hard-cast flat-point at 1,850 fps, yielding over 3,000 fps of energy. I would have no hesitation in tackling a buffalo with a .45-70 with that load or a similar handload, and quite a few hunters have. The .450 Marlin is also a player. It's a bit of an oddity, essentially a .45-70 cartridge but with a belt ahead of the rim, thus preventing "hot" loads from being chambered in weak older actions such as the trapdoor Springfield. It offers no real advantage over the .45-70, but can be loaded to the same levels in strong modern actions.

There are also some big-bore wildcats and proprietary cartridges. The last iteration of the Winchester Model 1886 was the Model 71 in .348 Winchester. The Model 71 was made from 1935 until 1958; the .348 was its only chambering, and no other factory rifle was ever chambered to the .348. In 1952 Harold Johnson of Cooper Landing, Alaska, wildcatted the .450 Alaskan, rebarreling a Model 71 and necking the .348 case up to take a .458-inch bullet. The .450 Alaskan was actually a fairly popular wildcat and quite a few are still around. It propels a 400-grain bullet at over 2,000 fps, so is definitely buffalo-capable. There were other versions; I had a Model 71 .450 Alaskan Ackley Improved. It was even faster; with a light barrel and the Model 71's narrow butt, it was probably the hardest-kicking rifle I ever owned!

Doug Turnbull, famous for restoration work on vintage firearms, created the .475 Turnbull for the Model 1886 action, essentially using the old .50-110 Winchester blackpowder case necked down to take a .475-inch bullet. Although a proprietary cartridge, Turnbull jumped through all the necessary hoops to get the .475 Turnbull standardized by the Sporting Arms and Ammunition Manufacturers Institute (SAAMI). I have one of his .475 Turnbull rifles, and it's absolutely gorgeous. With a long octagon barrel and full magazine, it has plenty of weight and is actually a joy to shoot. Using a 400-grain Barnes bullet at 2,150 fps, I had no problem taking a really good Mozambique buffalo with it. The .475 Turnbull is sized perfectly for the Winchester 1886 action, but it's a bit too long for the 1895 Marlin action. Turnbull's solution is the .470 Turnbull, simply a shortened version sized for the Marlin action. Also using a .475-inch bullet, the .470 Turnbull doesn't have as much powder capacity, so it runs a bit slower, but no buffalo is likely to notice the difference. The .470 Turnbull has not been standardized by SAAMI, but reamers, dies, and loading data are readily available.

That one Mozambique bull with a .475 Turnbull is the only African buffalo I've ever taken with a lever action. Over the years I've taken several buffaloes with Ruger Number 1 single-shots and a couple with Dakota Model 10 single-shots. I've taken a fair number

This Zimbabwe bull fell to an open-sight Heym double in .450/.400-3", and at a hundred yards, it is pretty much the maximum for open sights. Regardless of the platform, the problem with hunting buffaloes with open sights is you invariably give up a lot of potential shots.

with a variety of double rifles, but the majority of my buffaloes have been taken with bolt-action rifles.

So, does that mean I think the bolt-action is best? It's certainly the most available and the most common choice, but I don't have any issues with a lever-action with the right loads. I am *not* convinced that a lever-action is *faster* than a bolt-action. Although I guess this is true of everything, the real secret to a bolt-action is practice. The idea is to learn how to work the bolt with the rifle shouldered, maintaining sight picture. Too many of us take the rifle halfway down to work the bolt . . . and then, yes, the bolt-action is slow. Practice both offhand and off sticks with a full magazine. Obviously, you must do this a fair amount with your buffalo rifle, but you can do a lot of practicing with a lighter rifle. At the SAAM shooting school, they got Ruger to make up some Hawkeyes with iron sights in .223. It was Brilliant!

I like single-shots, but they're not for everyone. Again, having just that one shot is almost a subconscious thing; it makes you extra

Saso Ivanov took this "forest" water buffalo in the Philippines with a semiautomatic M14 in 7.62x51 (.308 Winchester). That's what we had, so that's what we used! Aside from legality in many jurisdictions, the biggest problem with semiautos is availability of suitable cartridges.

careful, and that's not a bad thing at all. Also, we are generally not hunting buffaloes by ourselves. I think a single-shot is a terrible idea for a PH, yet it's not a big deal for you and me. Just understand that, no matter how much you practice, you cannot have a second shot ready as quickly as you would with a double or repeating action, and, remember, sometimes additional shots with buffalo are needed. So, with a single-shot, there is a greater likelihood that your PH might have to fire. This has not come to pass with the buffaloes I've taken with single-shots, but the concept doesn't concern me.

What about the old "double versus magazine" question? As I've said before, *nothing* offers a faster or more reliable second shot than a double rifle. I am absolutely convinced that a double rifle is superior for elephant hunting. It is probably better when hunting buffaloes, too, given the chance of a charge, but, as we've seen, this is a fairly rare event. I am not convinced that a double rifle is better than a bolt-action for all-round buffalo hunting. It depends a lot on the person. You've read about double rifles your whole life and always wanted one. Your sainted aunt left you an unexpected bundle or your lottery ticket paid off, so you take the plunge and you now have the double rifle you've dreamed of. Most hunters don't suddenly awaken in their middle years and find themselves proficient with double rifles. I'm in a slightly different position; I got my first double-trigger, side-by-side shotgun when I was fifteen, so transitioning to a double rifle felt natural.

Absent that shotgunning background, learning to shoot a double well may not be so easy. It takes a lot of shooting for the two-trigger arrangement to become familiar. Also, compared to the average bolt-action, double rifles typically have awful triggers. Re-read Hemingway's *Green Hills of Africa*. He took a double .470 on that safari but hated its heavy trigger pull, shot it poorly, and knew he shot it poorly. Most of the time he relied on his Griffin & Howe Springfield .30-06.

One attribute double rifles have, shared by single-shots: Absent a repeating action, doubles are very compact. A double or single-shot will be several inches shorter than a repeater with an identical barrel length. This is not a major big deal in buffalo hunting, but shorter is definitely handier. Of course, stock fit is everything, but that applies evenly regardless of action: Your buffalo rifle must fit you and must come up naturally and on target.

Raw accuracy is also not a big deal. Bolt-actions and single-shots tend to be very accurate. Lever-actions can be accurate, but often are fairly pedestrian. Compared to the rest, double rifles are usually not very accurate at all. I've seen some that were amazing, but a double that will consistently print both barrels within four inches at a hundred yards is pretty darned good . . . and that's plenty good enough for any sensible shot at a buffalo.

To shoot buffalo effectively has little to do with your rifle's ability to shoot teeny little groups. If you—and your rifle—have the capability to hit a twenty-inch circle, you shouldn't have to track your buffalo very far. It is not, however, quite that simple. You must be able to visualize the shot and make sure the twenty-inch circle you're aiming at is in the right place on your buffalo!

There are dozens of cartridges suitable for buffalo, and many dozens of suitable rifles. So long as you are comfortable with and confident in your choice, I don't think the rifle action matters all that much. However, sighting equipment matters a great deal. I've said this before, but you will take more buffaloes and bigger buffaloes—and do less tracking—with a scoped rifle.

Going back to my story about suddenly becoming the proud owner of a double rifle, we do not wake up one day in our middle years and instantly acquire proficiency with iron sights. Most of us who were born after World War II are children of the riflescope era. Many of us have this weird, romantic concept that we should hunt our buffalo with an iron-sighted big bore. You can, and sometimes you can get close enough, but sometimes you can't, and you will give up a lot of shots. I am still convinced that iron sights are superior for elephant hunting, but buffalo hunting is not the same game. Forty yards is an extremely long shot on an elephant, and most shots will be at half that distance . . . or less.

Areas vary and buffalo vary. I'm no expert on buffalo hunting in the Caprivi since I've shot just two buffaloes there. Two years ago, hunting with Dawid Muller, we got a really fine bull, taken at twenty yards with my iron-sighted Krieghoff double .500. *Cool.* This past year, in 2018, I took a Caprivi bull at, maybe, fifteen yards. I had an Aimpoint on a double .450, but for that shot, sighting equipment wasn't of critical importance. In recent years I've done most of my buffalo hunting in coastal Mozambique. It happens, but I don't think I've ever gotten a shot closer than about sixty yards. The "normal" shot there seems to be about eighty to one hundred yards. Usually we're working in herds. The more buffaloes you're dealing with, the more difficult it is to isolate a bull and get close, and eighty yards is already past the capability of most shooters to be certain and consistent with iron sights.

Let's go back to my friend Mark Sullivan of the "Black Death" DVD fame. I hunted buffalo almost annually for more than thirty years before I ever saw a charge, so naturally I long wondered how he managed to get so many charges on camera. Yes, there are rumors about wounding buffalo on purpose. To this I give no credence. Yes,

This excellent Mozambique buffalo was Donna Boddington's first use of the Aimpoint red-dot sight, mounted on her Blaser R8 in .375 H&H. The shot was a bit past a hundred yards, a long shot on buffalo. Her first shot was perfect, as was her second; this buffalo went nowhere.

he approaches a downed buffalo frontally, making eye contact and, thus, inciting confrontation. That's not the real secret, however. He strongly discourages use of optical sights and doesn't use shooting sticks. Buffaloes won't always let you get as close as you'd like, especially if your goal is to take the best mature bull you can find. Whale away while standing, unsupported, with iron sights, and you'll end up tracking a lot of buffaloes. Eventually the law of averages kicks in and there will be charges!

I practice shooting standing, unsupported a lot, and although I am definitely a child of the scope era, I've done a lot of shooting with iron sights and became quite proficient with them. Mind you, I also practice a lot with sticks, and I will always use a rest when one is available. There was a time when, especially off sticks, I could confidently take a buffalo with iron sights at a hundred yards and maybe a bit more. That .475 Turnbull '86 Winchester has the classic "buckhorn" rear sight with a bold ivory bead front. The herd was bedded a bit over a hundred yards out when we ran out of cover. The bull was big

Gordon Marsh, center, mounted a low-power scope on his Sabatti .450/.400 for his 2017 Mozambique safari. Although nontraditional, doubles can be mounted with scopes and red-dot sights . . . and, for buffalo hunting, should be!

and obvious, so we waited him out. When he finally got up, I was very steady on sticks, but the front bead seemed to cover most of the buffalo. Keeping steady, I moved the rifle up, down, and sideways, making sure I had the bead centered and in the right place.

The shot was perfect, but that was then and now is now. Those days are over. I can no longer resolve iron sights well enough to be certain with them. Sure, if the shot is very close—but you can't bank on a close shot. So, I'm starting to practice what I've preached for years. I simply hate the "look" of an optical sight on a double rifle, but it's all about shot placement, and if you can see better, you can place your shot better.

I have a Leupold VXR 1–4X scope on a Sabatti 9.3x74R double, and I put an Aimpoint on a .450 double of the same make. There is something about black animals that confounds the eye, so, while a lot of magnification isn't needed, a little bit helps a lot, and an illuminated reticle is marvelous. The Aimpoint is, of course, a red-dot or "reflex" sight with no magnification, but that bold red dot is fantastic. I hate to admit it, but my days of hunting buffalo with iron sights are probably over . . . and definitely *should* be over!

One of the problems with Winchester's classic top-eject lever-actions, which I admire greatly, is it's the Devil to put an optical sight on them, and they look even worse than a scope on a fine double. I'd like to use my .475 Turnbull a lot more, but putting an optical sight on it would ruin it, so it needs to stay "as is." Marlin fans will be quick to point out that the side-ejecting, flat-topped Marlin lever-action is perfect for a scope or reflex sight.

Let's get to the bottom line: What do I really think is best? If you have a double, by all means use it, but sight it so you can get the best utility from it. In this discussion we're trying to put our buffalo in a vacuum and ignore everything else. When you are hunting in Africa, you are not hunting in a vacuum chamber. Your shot(s) at your buffalo may be the most important of your safari, but probably not the only shots you will take. Because of accuracy, heavy triggers, and just perhaps your familiarity, a double rifle is probably not the only rifle you will take on your safari. If you had a scoped .375, it could be!

Again, we're trying to stick with buffalo. The target is huge, and although you may not get the forty-yard shot you dreamed of, a hundred and fifty yards is a very long shot on a buffalo. Magnification isn't essential, although a bit of magnification will make resolving your bull a lot easier. Absent magnification, with dust, mirage, and shifting black bodies, you may find even a hundred-yard frontal shot almost impossible. A compact 1–4X scope changes the game, and a lighted reticle is even better. Although not essential for buffalo, the accurate, versatile bolt-action in a buffalo-capable caliber deserves a bit more scope. These days I tend to put something like a 2–7X on my .375s, and a 3–9X isn't out of the question.

So, is that the final answer, a scoped .375? Almost. I'm very comfortable with a .375 H&H for buffalo, but I also have .375 Rugers in both bolt-action and single-shot. I also have a .404 Jeffery, an awesome cartridge. Regrettably, mine is set up for use with an aperture sight. An aperture sight is always a sound option, much better than an open rear sight, but my problem remains the same: I can no longer resolve the front sight, and while new eyeglasses have this mostly corrected, the reality is that it will never again be perfect.

Missing from my eclectic (and often redundant) array of hunting rifles right now is a .416. I've had several, going clear back to the mid-1980s, before the revival of the .416. I've watched this revival, and I think I've used *all* of our several .416-caliber cartridges. I don't have one now, so I've decided I probably need one more buffalo rifle. It will have to be a .416, probably a Rigby just for nostalgia. Left-hand bolt, of course, and it will wear a scope, probably Leupold's bright little VXR 2–7x33. Across the spectrum, the "over .40s" are not as versatile as the .375s, but, always provided the ability to shoot them well, they are slightly better for buffalo. In this discussion that's what we care about most . . . and, for the African hunting that remains to me, that's what I care about most!

Looking Ahead

Chapter 23

The syndrome I call "gloom-and-doom-itis" seems part and parcel to African hunting. In 1910 Roosevelt lamented how fast the game was going. In 1935, Hemingway commented on how rapidly the opportunities were shrinking. Ruark did the same in 1953, as did a much younger Boddington in the late 1970s. For some reason we African hunters, especially those of us with limited experience, are compelled to describe our own experiences as the best Africa can be and pitying those who will follow because their adventures can never match our own. It is true that hunting, in general, has problems today, and African hunting has serious challenges.

The furor over the lion called Cecil was a watershed event. Unfortunately, the net result was not good for the African lion. Our First World nations, ensconced in our ivory towers, simply cannot put ourselves in the place of rural Africans who must deal with lions—and the rest of the Big Nasties—on a daily basis. Depending on which animal we're talking about, rural Africans must contend with having their crops raided and trampled, losing livestock, and occasionally losing their lives. Whether one approves of the concept or not, regulated and sustainable sport hunting places value on animals. Absent that value, to the rural African dangerous animals become dangerous nuisances. Realistically, the inability of Americans and citizens of other First World nations to import legally taken lions and elephant ivory has removed the value. Absent the ability to market safaris that might include lions and elephants, hunting blocks comprising *millions* of wild acres in Tanzania alone have been returned to the government. The wildlife doesn't win because much of this habitat will be converted to subsistence farming and pastoral grazing.

A young colleague of mine who has a fair amount of African experience recently asked me if I thought the recent bans on importation of lions and elephant tusks signaled the beginning of the end of African hunting. Such thinking is a clear symptom of "gloom-and-doom-itis." Unfortunately, this time he might be right. However, we have seen good times and bad, and wildlife is more resilient than we sometimes credit. Let's hope hunting and we hunters are equally resilient.

In the 1970s, when organized ivory poaching swept the continent, we thought elephant hunting—and the African elephant—was doomed. The northern herds were, in fact, almost eradicated in many areas, but the southern herds were spared the worst, have expanded, and in many areas have exceeded carrying capacity. As a practical necessity, elephants are hunted in Namibia, South Africa, and Zimbabwe. After a five-year suspension, at this writing in early 2019, it seems almost certain that Botswana will reopen hunting, including elephant hunting. By last aerial survey, Botswana's elephants, still increasing, exceed 250,000 individuals,

Buffaloes still occupy a huge range across most of sub-Saharan Africa except for the great deserts. Overall numbers in Central and West Africa are generally not known, but there are concentrations in certain areas such as eastern Burkina Faso and northern Benin. (Photo courtesy of Christophe Morio)

possibly half the entire continent's total. Botswana's elephants have grossly overpopulated the country and are destroying their habitat. Hunting is almost essential, and Botswana's officials are making no bones about it.

We also forget that, in the 1970s when leopard coats were high fashion, Americans were not allowed to import legally taken leopards. The permit process for importing sport-hunted leopards has been in place for thirty-five years. This process continues, and leopards have increased—dramatically in some areas—across much of their range.

Like everyone in my business, I get occasional grief from antihunters. Not long ago, however, I got an email from a gent who claimed to be a hunter. He was wondering exactly how I could support the hunting of "endangered" lions, leopards, elephants, rhinos, and buffaloes. In the lexicon of wildlife science there is a huge difference between the word "endangered" and the word "threatened." Endangered means imminent danger of extinction. This brings to mind the very best (of many) damning missives I've received from an antihunter. Amidst other colorful invective, this person wrote: "Real men don't hunt extinct species." *Uh,* no, we don't, and we don't hunt endangered species, either. According to the international body, CITES, none of Africa's Big Five are considered endangered, not even the black rhino. However, all, even the buffalo, can be considered threatened in some areas. Come to think of it, in certain circumstances, every living creature on this planet can be considered threatened, even us.

The Cape buffalo is far from endangered in any way, and none of his several races and subspecies is endangered. However, the African buffalo is extinct in some portions of his original range, and numerous populations are threatened. Some of this is natural. The buffalo must have grass and water, so the desertification of Africa and the advancement of her great deserts have removed much of the buffalo's former habitat. Also, at times man has purposefully eradicated whole swathes of buffaloes because they carry bovine diseases deadly to cattle.

Most of South Africa was once buffalo country, but in the course of her settlement, buffaloes were nearly wiped out. When the great Kruger Park was created in 1898, it was wild buffalo country. It is still wild, and still buffalo country, but these are not disease-free buffaloes. Far to the south, in the almost impenetrable Addo thornbush, a small population of buffaloes persisted. Oddly, perhaps because of cold winters, Addo buffaloes are disease-free, and these formed a nucleus for South Africa's incredibly successful breeding programs for disease-free buffaloes.

In addition to disease, the African buffaloes and the pesky tsetse fly go together like peas and carrots, as Forrest Gump would say. Although the buffalo is immune, the tsetse fly carries sleeping sickness fatal to many domestic animals, including cattle, horses, and dogs. In Rhodesia a "fly barrier" was created on the borders and on the escarpment above the Zambezi Valley. Untold thousands of animals were shot on "tsetse control" in an effort to control the fly by killing its hosts. Much money and effort were expended and incredible carnage wreaked, but results were questionable; today the tsetse fly has moved back into a lot of farming areas.

Despite man's best—and worst—efforts, there are still lots of buffaloes in Africa, and they occupy a huge range. Even so, the population has ebbed and flowed. By 1890 and before the great rinderpest, buffaloes were already gone from most of South Africa. It's impossible to guess how many millions of buffaloes might have roamed between the Limpopo and the Sahara. When the Roosevelt safari took to the field in 1909, the rinderpest had mostly run its course, but there were probably far fewer buffaloes then than exist today.

Fast-forward a half-century, and there was probably another peak in buffalo populations in the years following World War II. Franz Coupé was born in the Belgian Congo; his father was a riverboat captain. As a boy, Franz remembers seeing vast herds of buffaloes along the banks of the rivers in the now-southern Democratic Republic of the Congo. This was in country that, today, we don't really think of as "buffalo country." He recalls them as "black buffaloes," but neither he nor I are certain which subspecies his young eyes observed.

Since my time in the 1970s, it's probably fair to say that, overall, Africa's buffalo population has slowly deteriorated, mostly due to loss of habitat from Africa's burgeoning human population. This is a tide that seems unstoppable, but where land has been set aside and wildlife allowed to thrive, there are still plenty of buffaloes. Exact populations are rarely known, but we could make a conservative guess that there are at least a million buffaloes roaming in today's Africa . . . and perhaps even twice that. Concentrations are known to be in the Selous Reserve, Kruger, Serengeti, Luangwa Valley, Zambezi Valley, and more.

Buffaloes are slow breeders, much slower than their cousins, domestic cattle. However, given habitat and protection (primarily against meat poaching), the buffalo can thrive. When Mozambique's civil war ended in 1990, there were thought to be about twelve hundred buffaloes in the Marromeu Reserve. In 2016 the aerial survey hit 25,000. This miracle occurred only because pioneer outfitters moved back in, placed value on buffaloes, and protected them.

Although frightfully expensive, know-how now exists to live-trap and translocate buffalo on a fairly large scale. Several hundred Marromeu buffaloes have been live-captured and moved to repopulate Coutada 9 off to the west. In Zimbabwe, buffaloes have been reintroduced into the large conservancies—first in Save Valley, then in Bubye, and most recently in Nuanetsi. These are all now good buffalo areas and good buffalo hunting areas.

The successful breeding of disease-free buffalo in South Africa is another miracle. Progress was slow for many years, but today growth is exponential. As we've discussed, the availability of South African buffalo is a game-changer in modern buffalo hunting.

In neighboring Namibia game ranchers and breeders are just as advanced as their South African colleagues, but their hands are tied. Namibia has a "red line" in the far north, south of which no buffaloes are allowed. In cattle country this is understandable, but there must be a way,

To me this is the most exciting part, creeping and crawling and trying to sort out a bull.

I love getting into the big herds in coastal Mozambique where most herds contain mature bulls.

and someday there will be. In the meantime, arid Namibia has relatively little natural buffalo habitat, so overall numbers are small and available off-take limited. Even so, Namibia's buffaloes have changed the game. Quality is excellent, and most of Namibia's buffaloes are free-range. Namibia offers a viable alternative to South Africa, where most buffaloes hunted today are not free-range; Namibia also offers an alternative to traditional buffalo countries such as Mozambique, Tanzania, Zambia, and Zimbabwe.

The days are long since over when it was common to have several buffaloes on license. Today most operators do the math as "one buffalo on quota equals one safari," and prices for buffalo safaris have gone up. South Africa is the exception, for there prices have come way down. This is an anomaly; with exponential growth in privatized buffalo, supply suddenly exceeded demand and prices dropped below the competition, which, for a basic buffalo safari, is primarily Mozambique and Zimbabwe.

Don't expect this to be a trend! Prices will continue to go up . . . but so do most things in our world. That said, a buffalo safari remains an extremely affordable adventure. A ten-day safari with a buffalo as a primary goal remains available at cost similar to a medium-level outfitted elk hunt in the American West, and it's considerably less than an outfitted Dall sheep, grizzly, or moose hunt in Alaska or Yukon.

Again, good options include Mozambique, South Africa, and Zimbabwe. Of course, costs vary among the countries and outfitters. As with many game animals, there are "premium areas" known for better horn quality, and also premium outfitters who command higher prices because of their reputations. However, because of its variety and species diversity, Africa is a bit different from most places. Safari costs are heavily influenced by trophy fees, so the bottom line can be somewhat controlled by focusing on a buffalo and not taking other game. In this context, a primary buffalo safari can be affordable in Namibia, Tanzania, and Zambia as well.

Obviously, the number of hunting days also greatly influences the cost. In areas that have high concentrations of buffaloes, seven days really is enough, but even in great areas, I much prefer a ten-day hunt for buffalo. Success might come on the first day, but the last day is always just as good as the first. Sometimes in especially wet or dry years, game movement can change and you need the extra time. That said, hunting is hunting. There are no guarantees, but if you set as your goal a good, mature buffalo, you should be successful. Just do your homework. Your job is to find a good outfitter and area, and then prepare yourself well by spending lots of time on the range and getting in the best shape your age and overall health will allow.

Nobody has an effective crystal ball, yet I don't expect any of this to change much in the time I have left, and probably not until long after I'm gone. The best areas will shift around, and new options will open up. Because of its elephant overpopulation, Botswana's buffalo numbers aren't what they were in the 1980s, but Botswana still has plenty of buffaloes. At this writing I'm confident Botswana will reopen and will include opportunities for buffalo.

Although southeastern Angola has a large buffalo population, I'm much less sanguine about Angola reopening. Much effort has been expended—and wasted—but it seems just too politically complicated. I think South Sudan will open, and just in case, I still have a Sudan safari on my bucket list. Important will be her long-unhunted antelopes,

That's an awesome dwarf forest buffalo bull on the left, shown with a red female. The dwarf forest buffalo has been high on my shrinking bucket list for years; I was finally successful in Cameroon in March 2019. (Photo courtesy of Christophe Morio)

This represents a nice herd of buffaloes in Botswana's open grasslands. Botswana is plagued by an overpopulation of elephants, but when she reopens safari hunting, there will almost certainly be opportunities to again hunt buffaloes there.

especially Nile lechwe. Sudan still holds a lot of Nile buffaloes. Traditionally, Gabon was one of the best places to hunt dwarf forest buffalo. Always an on-again, off-again safari destination, Gabon had a "soft" reopening in 2018, but only for small game. If Gabon reopened for forest buffalo—and it might—I'd like to hunt there.

These options lie in the unknown future, but the primary countries where we're hunting buffalo today all seem solid, so I'm confident there will be a lot of great buffalo hunting in years to come. Then, I am simply not a gloom-and-doom guy! As discussed, we have serious issues with public perceptions and the West's environmental imperialism in restricting importation of legally taken animals, neither of which is good for wildlife. However, I believe that, on an increasingly limited basis and at higher cost, Africa's entire Big Five will continue to be "huntable."

I hope so, because I hate the thought of an Africa where younger hunters cannot dream of tracking an elephant or facing a lion. I also believe that the buffalo will continue to be, by far, the most available and most affordable of Africa's dangerous game. This is a good thing because Africa's great black buffalo remains a favorite pursuit for not just me but many hunters. I've been extremely fortunate to have done as much of it as I have, and I suppose by any sane and sensible standards, I've done enough, certainly more than my share in this lifetime. Even so, I love getting in the middle of them, smelling the cattle smell, hearing their grunts and bellows, watching the oxpeckers and egrets . . . and all the time wondering what might happen next. I'm not in the least ashamed to say that, God willing and health allowing, I'm not done yet!